A Practical Guide to

Earned Value Project Management

Second Edition

A Practical Guide to

Earned Value Project Management

Second Edition

Charles I. Budd, MDv, PMP
Charlene S. Budd, PhD, CPA, CMA, CFM, PMP

MANAGEMENTCONCEPTS

MANAGEMENTCONCEPTS

8230 Leesburg Pike, Suite 800
Vienna, VA 22182
(703) 790-9595
Fax: (703) 790-1371
www.managementconcepts.com

Printed in the United States of America

Library of Congress Cataloging-in-Publication Data

Budd, Charles I., 1936–
A practical guide to earned value project management / Charles I. Budd, Charlene S. Budd. — 2nd ed.
    p. cm.
ISBN 978-1-56726-256-8
1. Project management.   I. Budd, Charlene S., 1938–   II. Title.
HD69.P75B83 2009
658.4'04—dc22

2009028831

10   9   8   7   6   5   4   3   2   1

About the Authors

Charles I. Budd (Chuck) is a principal of Budd Management Systems in Atlanta, Georgia. His career began in computer programming and grew into executive management. He has been CEO of Financial Information Trust in Des Moines, president of International Computer Systems, Inc., in Akron, president of Technology Connections, Inc., in Atlanta, senior project manager for Softlab Enabling Technologies, also in Atlanta, and operations vice president for Intercontinental Computing, Inc., in Kansas City.

He is a Project Management Professional and currently is developing project management automation tools, consulting on information systems projects, conducting seminars, and writing with his coauthor, Charlene Budd. He has taught webinar classes and conducted workshops and presentations around the world. Some of his international consulting engagements included major Y2K remediation projects in the United States, Germany, and South Africa, where he began using earned value management concepts.

Chuck is active in several civic volunteer organizations, the Project Management Institute, and information systems organizations. He is a graduate of Baldwin-Wallace College, has been certified as a systems analyst by the Foundation for Administrative Research, attended MBA classes at Drake University, and has a graduate degree from Baylor University.

Charlene Spoede Budd (Charli), PhD, is professor emeritus of accounting at Baylor University, where she has taught graduate management accounting and graduate project management classes. She has a PhD in business administration and holds certifications as a CPA, CMA, CFM, and PMP, and in all six professional categories of the Theory of Constraints International Certification Organization (TOCICO).

Her research has been published primarily in practitioner journals, and she has been awarded three Certificates of Merit for articles (one of which explained why multiproject management is an essential skill for management accountants) published in *Strategic Finance*. She also has published in *Today's CPA, The Counselor,* other journals, and many conference proceedings. She has written two accounting textbooks, and currently she and coauthor Charles Budd are working on two other books.

Charli is active in several professional organizations, including the American Institute of CPAs (AICPA), the American Accounting Association, the Financial Executives Institute, and the Project Management Institute. She also is an active member of the Finance and Metrics Committee of the TOCICO and assisted the AICPA in developing questions and simulations for the Business Environment component of the new computerized CPA examinations.

To all project managers and especially to Hal Budd, one of the best. Thanks for everything. Special thanks also to Steve Holt at Boeing and all the others who shared their comments on the first edition.

Contents

Preface to the Second Edition xix

PART I: Introduction 1

CHAPTER 1: Background and Motivation 3
Our Basic Premise 4
The Three Basic Parameters of Project Management 4
Business Changes 5
The Need for a Cost and Schedule Control System 6
Project Management Maturity 8
Looking for Value in All the Wrong Places 9
Our Example Project 10
Discussion Questions 11

CHAPTER 2: Project Management 13
A Project 14
The Project Charter 15
Project Life Cycles 18
    The Basic Approach 19
    A More Comprehensive Approach 20
    Minimum Life Cycle Requirements 23

EVMS Projects   23
The Project Management Office   25
Evolving Project Management Maturity   27
The Project Manager   29
    A Personal Observation of Authority   30
The Project Team   30
Discussion Questions   32

PART II: The Basics of Earned Value **35**

CHAPTER 3: Earned Value Metrics **37**
Primary Metrics   37
    Total Value (TV) or Budget at Completion (BAC)   38
    Planned Value (PV) or Budgeted Cost of Work
        Scheduled (BCWS)   38
    Earned Value or Budgeted Cost of Work
        Performed (BCWP)   39
    Actual Cost (AC) or Actual Cost of Work
        Performed (ACWP)   39
    Reporting and Comparison Metrics   39
Analogy to the Standard Cost System   40
Calculation of Ratios   40
    Forecasting Metrics   42
    Calculations Example   43
Using the Measurements   45
    The Challenge of Meeting All Targets   45
    Information and Motivation   47
Discussion Questions and Practice Calculations   51
    Questions   51
    Practice Calculations   51

CHAPTER 4: The Earned Value Management System **53**
Evolution of the Earned Value Management System   53
    Concepts of Earned Value Management   54
    Earned Value Defined   55
    Criteria and Metrics   56

Requiring the Use of EVMS.   57
Driving Force for Using EVMS   58
Why All the Interest in EVMS?   59
    Support for the Value of EVMS   60
    Discussion of the Evidence   61
The Dark Side   65
    Some Missing Information   65
    Dollars, Time, and the Schedule.   67
    Dysfunctional Behavior   68
A High-Level View of the 32 EVMS Criteria   68
    Organization   69
    Planning and Budgeting   69
    Accounting Considerations   69
    Analysis and Management Reports   70
    Revisions and Data Maintenance   70
Discussion Questions   71

PART III: It's All in the Plan **73**

CHAPTER 5: The Project Plan (Criterion 1) **75**
EVMS Criterion 1   75
The Work Breakdown Structure   76
    WBS Definitions and Standards   77
    Two Possible WBS Structures   78
    Steps in Constructing a WBS   79
Defining the Project   81
The Mechanics of a WBS   83
    WBS Charts   84
    WBS Levels   86
    A WBS Dictionary   87
Control Accounts   88
Work Packages   90
Discussion Questions   94

CHAPTER 6: The Organization (Criteria 2–5) **95**
Organizational Configurations 95
    Functional Style 96
    Matrix Style 97
    Project-Oriented Style 98
EVMS Criterion 2 99
    Organizational Breakdown Structure 99
    Project Staffing 100
    OBS Limitations 101
EVMS Criterion 3 102
    Linear Responsibility Chart 103
    Control Account Plan 105
EVMS Criterion 4 107
EVMS Criterion 5 109
Discussion Questions 111

CHAPTER 7: The Schedule (Criteria 6–8) **113**
Schedule Uncertainty 114
    Challenges in Constructing a Realistic Schedule 114
    Overcoming Schedule Problems 117
    A Bit of Statistics and Probability 118
EVMS Criterion 6 121
    Sequence of Work 121
    Task Dependencies 123
Schedule Representation and Evaluation 125
    Lists 125
    Bar Charts 125
    Networks 126
    Critical Path Method 130
EVMS Criterion 7 131
EVMS Criterion 8 132
    The Target Baseline 133
    Summary-Level Planning Packages 134
    Controls and Reporting 135
    Over-Target Baseline 135
Discussion Questions 137

CHAPTER 8: The Budget (Criteria 9–15) **139**
EVMS Criterion 9 140
EVMS Criterion 10 142
    Work Packages and Planning Packages 144
    Special Packages 144
EVMS Criterion 11 145
EVMS Criterion 12 145
EVMS Criterion 13 147
EVMS Criterion 14 148
EVMS Criterion 15 150
Project Cost Estimation 151
    Cost Data 152
    Project Controls 152
    Estimating Methods 153
Discussion Questions 157

PART IV: Project Status **159**

CHAPTER 9: Tracking Performance (Criteria 16–21) **161**
EVMS Accounting 162
EVMS Criterion 16 163
    Direct Costs 163
    Special Circumstances 165
EVMS Criterion 17 166
EVMS Criterion 18 166
EVMS Criterion 19 167
    Cost Pools 169
    Cost Pool Drivers 169
Cost Allocation Methods 170
    Direct Allocation Method 171
    Step-Down Allocation Method 172
    Reciprocal Allocation Method 173
    Activity-Based Costing Method 174
EVMS Criterion 20 176
EVMS Criterion 21 178
Accounting and Earned Value Software 180
Discussion Questions 181

Appendix 9-A. Reciprocal Allocation of
  Overhead Costs 183

CHAPTER 10: Reporting Variances (Criteria 22–27) **187**
EVMS Criterion 22 188
EVMS Criterion 23 191
  Schedule Variance 192
  Cost Variance 192
  Explaining Variances 193
EVMS Criterion 24 194
EVMS Criterion 25 195
EVMS Criterion 26 196
EVMS Criterion 27 197
  Performance to Date 197
  Interpreting the Variances 200
  Technical Performance 200
  Updated Values for Materials 202
  Estimates of Future Conditions 203
  Performance Reporting 203
Practice Calculations 209
  Exercise 1 209
  Exercise 2 210

PART V: Handling a Project's Changes and Termination.... **211**

CHAPTER 11: Time for a Change (Criteria 28–32) **213**
Uncertainty May Be the Only Certainty 213
Understanding the Elements of Risk 215
Risk Management 216
  Risk Assessment 217
  Risk Disposition 222
  Risk Monitoring 223
  Continuous Risk Management 224
  Risk Management Tools 225
When Change Becomes Necessary 226
EVMS Criterion 28 227
  Authorized Changes 228
  Directed Effort 231

EVMS Criterion 29 232
EVMS Criterion 30 232
EVMS Criterion 31 233
EVMS Criterion 32 233
Discussion Questions 235

CHAPTER 12: Are We There Yet? 237
Project Termination 238
    Completing the Project 239
    Post-Project Activities 244
Discussion Questions 248

PART VI: Earned Value Implementations 251

CHAPTER 13: Implementing EVMS 253
Reasons to Implement EVMS 254
The Implementation Plan 255
Details of Implementation 255
    Organizational Support 256
    Education and Training 257
    Eliciting Desired Behavior 258
Do Your Own Thing, But Carefully 261
Software Assistance 262
Implementation Cost 263
Discussion Questions 265

CHAPTER 14: Government Contracts 267
Information Sources 268
    DoD Websites 268
    Federal Acquisition Regulation System 269
    DoD Reference Material 271
    Councils and Agencies 273
Compliance, Validation, and Surveillance 278
    Initial Compliance Review 279
    Integrated Baseline Review 279
    Surveillance 280

CHAPTER 15: Partial EV Implementations 287
Earned Value for Project Control 288

Abridged EV Implementations............................ 289
    First Alternative: An Informal EVMS Implementation... 289
    Second Alternative: High-Level Control Accounts 290
    Third Alternative: Follow Basic EVMS Principles 291
    Fourth Alternative: The Very Least EV
        Implementation.................................... 295
Discussion Questions...................................... 296

PART VII: Emerging Practices 299
Performance-Based Earned Value 299
Schedule Margin 300
Emerging Practices to Be Treated in Greater Detail......... 301

CHAPTER 16: Earned Schedule 303
Rationale for the Development of Earned Schedule 304
Earned Schedule Concepts................................ 305
    Calculating Earned Schedule 306
    Definitions 307
Example of Earned Schedule Computations 307
Other Earned Schedule Metrics 314
    Time-Based Metrics For Forecasting 314
    Performance Factor (Time) 315
Reconciling Schedule Variance in Time with
    Schedule Variance in Dollars........................ 316
Validation of Usefulness of Earned Schedule 319
Practice Calculations and Discussion Questions 320

CHAPTER 17: Critical Chain Project Management 323
Background 323
Development of Critical Chain 324
    Traditional Project Management Problems............ 326
    The Critical Chain Solution 330
A Single Project Environment 331
    Traditional Scheduling 331
    A Simulated Result from Traditional Scheduling....... 332
    Critical Chain Scheduling........................... 333
    Critical Chain Results 338
    Using Buffer Management To Control Projects 339

Multiproject Environments 341
Use of Critical Chain with EVMS........................... 342
    Critical Chain in Lower Levels of the Performance
        Measurement Baseline 343
    Two Project Plans 344
Practice Calculations 346

APPENDIX A: The 32 EVMS Criteria 349
    Organization 349
    Planning and Budgeting 350
    Accounting Considerations 351
    Analysis and Management Reports 352
    Revisions and Data Maintenance...................... 353

APPENDIX B: Discussion Responses
    and Exercise Solutions 355

Glossary 363

Bibliography... 383

Index 393

Preface to the Second Edition

If a project sponsor has dictated that your project must adhere to the requirements of the Earned Value Management System (EVMS), you need to read this book. If you want to learn the mechanics of a complete project system that is much discussed and well accepted in knowledgeable project management circles, you will want to read this book. If you want to understand a few EVMS concepts, you may find exactly what you need to target in the table of contents or the index.

Many project managers initially are opposed to implementing EVMS. Change in any form is often feared. After all, if project managers are successful to some degree without EVMS, they naturally will wonder how successful they will be in a new environment that uses EVMS. Project managers who are accustomed to and comfortable with their particular system may now feel that their every move will be studied microscopically and that they will be compelled to waste time explaining their every action. But consider this: If you are extremely competent, don't you want top management to recognize your value on the basis of criteria other than your ability to promote yourself (or another manager's ability to promote you)?

This practical guide provides two perspectives on EVMS: an academic perspective to give you insight into the mechanics of the system and a practical perspective to assist you in its everyday implementation and use.

We have heard several complaints that the requirements of EVMS are too complicated, too detailed, and too difficult to understand. It is our intent to walk you through the EVMS criteria in a way that clarifies the requirements and untangles possible complications. This second edition of *A Practical Guide to Earned Value Project Management* not only will bring the EVMS requirements into your world but also will guide you in applying additional successful project management techniques and tools.

We also have heard comments that some of the EVMS requirements overlap, some are too "picky," and some are just not necessary in the commercial and industrial worlds. We believe all the requirements are reasonable ingredients of sound project management. However, initiating and tracking all the EVMS criteria—especially for every project—can require a significant effort. For small, fast-track projects, using a subset of earned valued (EV) measures still may be beneficial. You should not try to shortcut EVMS criteria when they are required, but when they are not, we can show you some effective shortcuts to reduce implementation effort. There is a point, however, when reduction effectively becomes elimination.

Although we use EVMS and tout its strengths, we do not mean to imply it doesn't have some shortcomings. It does, and we point out those weak and sometimes treacherous aspects. But our purpose is to guide you on a practical route through EVMS and to give you some no-nonsense ideas for ways to meet its criteria and complete your projects successfully.

EVMS is a highly effective project management tool, but it is not a standalone project management system. Project managers need much more in their tool bag. So before we begin to discuss the details of EVMS, we review project management in general. We realize that most of our readers already have good project management skills, so some information will seem very basic. For that reason, we only skim the surface; however, it is our hope that these discussions may introduce unfamiliar topics or stimulate your interest in further examining a well-known topic. You might find a nugget or two to engage your mind while you mull over the challenges of your current project.

Most of our readers are accomplished project managers who, for any number of reasons, want to learn about EVMS criteria and how they can conform to the detailed requirements of EVMS while still completing their projects. We do our best to give you this knowledge. This is not a project management how-to book. Many books and classes on the techniques for successful project management are available. While virtually all these books and classes use EV concepts, few discuss the formal EVMS criteria and even fewer offer project managers practical advice on interpreting and using the criteria to manage their projects.

To understand EVMS, you don't need to be an expert in accounting or even to have had any college accounting classes. We guide you step-by-step through everything you need to understand the requirements. Checkpoints throughout the material (*gates* in project management terminology) allow you to review your progress and retrace your steps if necessary. Anticipating that some readers will be involved in EVMS projects that will be audited (internally or by a government agency) for compliance with all 32 criteria, we cover the entire set.

Throughout the book, we try to communicate our perspective in a straightforward manner. Figures and tables are provided to enable readers to grasp concepts readily through visual depictions.

In Part I, Chapter 1 provides the book's purpose and organization, and Chapter 2 sets the stage for a shared understanding of general project management. Part II presents the basics of earned value; Chapter 3 provides the EV metrics that are the basis of any complete or abridged EV project management system, and Chapter 4 introduces the concepts of EVMS and gives a preliminary view of the EVMS criteria. The 32 criteria of EVMS are discussed in detail in Chapters 5 through 11 of Parts III (It's All in the Plan), IV (Project Status), and V (Handling a Project's Changes and Terminations). Part V also includes Chapter 12, which deals with the termination of a project.

In the first edition of this book, published in 2005, we wrote quite specifically for those whose projects were required to meet the full requirements of EVMS as specified primarily by government entities. Now, for even some small projects, we have found that corporate management is requiring a more unbiased project-reporting mechanism. In addition, regulations like the Sarbanes-Oxley Act have reinforced the need for more stringent internal reporting on projects. Auditors of companies required to file financial information with the Securities and Exchange Commission now want detailed information on projects that affect the financial reporting process. In our experience, EV is being used more frequently to satisfy these requirements.

In this second edition, we have added two new parts, Parts VI and VII, to address some common needs not covered in the first edition. In Part VI, Implementations, we present some practical advice to companies that are not required to meet all the formal EVMS criteria but want to obtain the benefits of EVMS. Chapters 13 through 15 deal with various implementation processes and requirements. The new Part VII, Emerging Practices, introduces some developing EV practices: Chapters 16 and 17 present details of two popular emerging practices developed to mitigate some of the recognized shortcomings of EVMS.

Other changes and new items in this second edition include clarification and reorganization of the material, as well as the most recent changes in EVMS regulation, acceptance, and certification. This edition also provides a bibliography, a glossary of key terms, the complete 32 criteria presented in numerical order (Appendix A), and the answers and solutions to problems from some of the chapter reviews (Appendix B).

We hope that you will find our travel together through the Earned Value Management System enlightening, interesting, and beneficial.

Charles I. Budd
Charlene S. Budd
Jackson, Georgia

Introduction

Part I is a condensed introduction to the many facets of project management. If you are an experienced project manager, you may choose to skip portions of this introduction. However, we hope that if you do read these first two chapters, you will find some helpful insights.

The purpose of this book and its organization are discussed in Chapter 1. Background on general project management is presented in Chapter 2. Obviously, project managers need more than knowledge of EVMS to be successful. Although we do not intend to present a comprehensive treatment of project management, we try to broaden your understanding of the project management environment. In addition to discussing what it takes to be a successful project manager and project team, we briefly address project life cycles, the project management office, and the stages of project management maturity.

CHAPTER 1

Background and Motivation

Most project managers are passionate about accomplishing challenging objectives but lack similar passion for doing detailed planning, reporting progress, or explaining their success or failure in meeting baseline targets. Projects often prove difficult because project managers are striving to accomplish their targets while working through previously uncharted territory without dedicated resources. Therefore, a good deal of a project manager's time might be spent in negotiations to acquire the resources needed.

People intimately involved in a project have knowledge that others do not possess. Sometimes we take advantage of this information asymmetry to protect the project or the project team or to buy ourselves more time for solving problems and reaching project goals. Regardless of the project manager's or team's feeling about the project, its continuation depends on communication with owners and other interested parties about the project's status. An earned value management system (EVMS) is a commonly accepted methodology for objectively communicating project progress.

OUR BASIC PREMISE

Although your company may be an exception, most organizations do not have a well-organized and functioning project office that controls the entry of projects into the system and tracks progress on all active projects from charter to close. It is widely accepted that projects are unique and inherently risky. Nevertheless, rather than being subject to controls commensurate with their risk, they are usually not even subject to the same degree of internal control that is applied to repetitive operations with far less risk.

Projects traditionally have populated the twilight area between current reality and desired future position. We usually know where we are; we also know where we would like to be, but sometimes we don't know exactly how to get there. That's where projects enter the picture. Rather than being integrated into a coordinated organizational portfolio, projects typically have been "sold" independently, by clients or by the heads of various organizational divisions. We are not suggesting that projects are promoted for nefarious reasons, but merely that divisional responsibilities drive spirited competition for funding.

Once projects are approved and funded, progress is generally not well tracked by project owners. For the most part, project metrics are rudimentary and primarily involve milestone achievement, budget consumption, and subjective progress reporting by the project manager.

THE THREE BASIC PARAMETERS OF PROJECT MANAGEMENT

Project management revolves around the three basic project characteristics: scope, schedule, and budget. EVMS provides the metrics for comparing what has been planned with what has been completed within these three parameters (Figure 1.1). Although EVMS establishes very precise organizational and reporting requirements, it does not prescribe how the project must be managed. It allows the flexibility to use a variety of project management processes as long as they meet the required criteria. While the critical path method is most common, it is not generally required; newer methods, such as critical chain, are permitted and sometimes encouraged.

Outcomes / Actions	SCOPE	SCHEDULE	BUDGET
PLAN	What are the deliverables?	When are they due?	How much will it cost?
PROGRESS	What tasks have been completed?	How long has it taken to complete the work accomplished?	How much have we spent to complete the tasks reported as finished?
PROJECTION	Will all project specifications be met?	When will the project be completed?	What is the estimated total cost at completion?

FIGURE 1.1   Basic Project Metrics

BUSINESS CHANGES

Several recent events have encouraged organizations to restrain their "everyone-for-themselves" mentality concerning project management. Our increased pace means we don't have time for a major failure. We can't spend months working on a project, bring it to a successful but delayed conclusion, and find that the environment has changed so that the deliverables no longer have value. A project like that should have been sped up, if possible, or killed early enough to transfer its resources to projects with better prospects. Without critical project information, decision makers charged with global project responsibility sometimes operate blindly.

The completion of some projects might determine the life or death of the organization. Other projects have profound influence on the company's future success. Many if not most projects have some effect on the entity's financial reporting. If so, stringent internal controls dictated by the Sarbanes-Oxley Act of 2002 (SOX) (Sarbanes and Oxley 2002) might apply. Even if a project currently is not required to meet the law's financial operations internal control criteria, it might be required to do so in the future. EVMS offers an internal control environment that should meet SOX internal control requirements.

THE NEED FOR A COST AND SCHEDULE CONTROL SYSTEM

Recognizing the problem of poor project performance and having dealt repeatedly with the shock of overruns and underperformances, the federal government more than 40 years ago commissioned the development of a project measurement system based on a standard cost model. This system became known as Cost/Schedule Control Systems Criteria (C/SCSC). Private industry found the requirements cumbersome and suggested a revision in the mid-1990s. The new criteria were formally named the Earned Value Management System, and in 1996 the government formally adopted 32 revised EVMS criteria. The American National Standards Institute Guidelines for EVMS, ANSI/EIA-748-1998, were issued in 1998, and government requirements were adjusted to the 1998 standard. Another minor update occurred in 2006.

For many years, private governmental contractors have been required to use EVMS on large government projects. On operations performed by the U.S. government for itself, such as work at repair depots and other project-oriented work, the government is rapidly implementing earned value metrics that affect total funding. Because EVMS offers enhanced control features, many companies are now interested in employing it for nongovernmental work.

Meanwhile, the accounting profession has had its own problems over the past few years with scandals that have prompted investors to demand more transparency from corporations. SOX established the Public Company Accounting Oversight Board to rein in auditing firms by instituting rigorous control over their activities. One of the board's first pronouncements, formally approved by the SEC (U.S. Securities and Exchange Commission 2003, 96), establishes exactly how public accounting firms must audit internal controls. In 2008, similar rules were established for nonaccelerated filers (U.S. Securities and Exchange Commission 2008). If an external or internal auditor decides to look at your project, you must be prepared to show adequate internal controls.

Part of the reason many corporations are not forthcoming about their plans is that they do not want to provide their competitors with information about their strategies. Nor does top management want to risk embarrassment by public strategic failures resulting from commissioning the wrong projects or having the projects' deliverables not align with the organization's strategic initiatives. However, in light of recent scandals and public attention in the media, corporations are being pressured to be more candid and transparent about the status of their future plans. And if the boss is being pressured, you know it won't be long before the project managers begin to feel the heat!

The biggest impetus to the intense spotlight on project control is the enactment of SOX. While the act itself emphasizes internal control over financial processes, the final rules issued by the SEC introduced a newly defined phrase: "disclosure controls and procedures." This phrase expands the concept of internal controls over financial reporting into the broader area of controls and procedures with regard to disclosure of material financial and nonfinancial information in public reports. Disclosure controls and procedures are likely to encompass project performance.

PROJECT MANAGEMENT MATURITY

The project management profession has recognized the need to improve. Its response to dismal internal control over projects has been to detail the formal steps of organizational maturity in managing and delivering projects. Project management maturity models have been devised to standardize and improve an organization's ability to implement its strategy by consistently delivering successful projects.

Although organizations are aware of the various versions of the project maturity model, most organizations are at the lowest steps of the model's progression. For example, consider a typical five-level model. Those at Level 1 have a project management process, but not a generalized structured process and standards. To achieve Level 2, it is necessary to achieve Level 1 and also to have standard project metrics in place. To reach Level 3, the organization must possess standards and institutionalized processes that involve project metrics and must evaluate performance among projects. An organization must adopt either earned value or comparable metrics to master Levels 2 and 3 of project management maturity.

Only after achieving Level 3 (necessitating that the requirements of Levels 1 and 2 also have been met) can an organization attempt Levels 4 and 5, which tackle continuous improvement efforts. These last levels offer tremendous benefits to organizations—especially those that arrive there before their competitors!

Thus, implementing EVMS is a worthy goal for you and your organization. However, even though EVMS is useful for reporting general progress to persons outside the project team, it does not solve all project management problems and, in certain cases, creates problems of its own. Earned value metrics were developed as an extension of a standard cost system, and attempting to manage a project using EVMS metrics alone can be disastrous. In subsequent chapters, we discuss exactly how to comply with EVMS and still successfully manage your project work. Along the way, we will present additional ideas and project management tools that can be used profitably with EVMS.

LOOKING FOR VALUE IN ALL THE WRONG PLACES

It is especially true in difficult economic times that organizations must be very careful about investments in new initiatives and very hard-nosed about return on those investments. Projects must realize their objectives; however, achieving project success does not have to be a complicated process. Success is not about mastering complicated theories or finding and adopting the latest business fad. Project success is about discipline—being able to stick to a proven process, starting with a well-planned project.

No project plan can be considered complete without having some way of measuring how well the project earns its expected value. One recommended approach is for project plans to explicitly include the deliverables in the project's baseline. The number of additional tasks that fully utilize the deliverables in the manner intended may be surprising.

It's all about value—perceived or real. In the movie *Trading Places*, Dan Aykroyd played a character who lost his job and had to pawn his wristwatch. No matter how hard he tried to convince the pawnbroker that the watch was actually worth thousands of dollars, the pawnbroker's response was, "In Philadelphia, it's worth 50 bucks." More recently, banks holding portfolios of derivative securities, especially residential mortgage-backed securities and collateralized debt obligations, have been forced to write them down drastically to more realistic values. You might not be the one who initially sold your project, but you must continually sell yourself and your work on that project to demonstrate value to your organization. One way to do that compellingly and objectively is with EVMS. Keep in mind that even though EVMS informs others about your work, you must still use good project management judgment and skills.

Today, we face immense pressure to take shortcuts in order to deliver value faster. The result is that we do not take the time to plan our activities fully. Following EVMS requirements will give you the opportunity to overcome most deficiencies in planning and controlling your projects. EVMS helps justify the project's value by requiring careful definition of the program objective, directing continual focus on ongoing project costs, and incorporating very stringent progress measurement processes.

OUR EXAMPLE PROJECT

To maintain continuity and to facilitate understanding of the requirements of EVMS concepts, we have created a common baseline project. We have attempted to keep the example project simple enough for illustration purposes yet realistic enough to enable you to translate the concepts into your own project environment.

Many exciting projects are being managed all over the world. For example, some very intriguing ones are being conducted or considered through a program called the Intelligent Manufacturing Systems, an international research and development program designed to develop the next generation of manufacturing and processing technologies. Other projects are underway to deliver medical miracles or to explore uncharted areas of the earth and the universe. While these projects are exciting, they also are extremely complex. Of necessity, our example project must be both one that is simple to understand and one to which we can all relate. Although we look at several historical projects, some of which are very complex, we use our example project to illustrate important points.

The example project is to install a new information technology (IT) system—specifically, a customer relations management (CRM) system. In this project, CRM is intended to give our example organization complete access to and control over all information about customers and prospects. We expect the system to automate all the day-to-day tasks for our sales and marketing professionals, as well as our office and field customer service; to interface with production; and to integrate with our other back-office systems. Many companies that have attempted to install this system have found the process extremely challenging—a "mission impossible" without a happy ending.

An entire CRM implementation from conception to completion would be too complex for our simple illustration, so we will use a subproject. Our assumptions are that a new CRM software system has been researched, approved, purchased, customized, and tested. A new data store has been defined and created for the required information elements. Our project is called "Project CRM: The Final Step." It is intended to train the users, install the hardware, distribute the workstation software, and provide a support system.

This brief, user-friendly introduction to EVMS for project managers promises to make your study as painless as possible. This chapter establishes the need for EVMS from the perspectives of internal control and return on investment.

Although change is always difficult, it need not be tortuous. There are benefits to be gained from implementing EVMS—and even greater benefits from implementing it correctly! Many of the EVMS concepts are simply good business practices that can easily be employed in other environments. You may love your work now, but at some point you will want to broaden your horizons by moving into another position. Your knowledge of EVMS will serve you well whether you remain a project manager or move to a higher level of management.

DISCUSSION QUESTIONS

1. Discuss with your colleagues some major project management failures of which you have personal knowledge. Try to establish the root cause of the failures.

2. List some factors you believe would create a major project success.

3. At what level of project management maturity is your organization, and where does it aspire to be?

4. Why are you interested in learning about EVMS?

5. What impact do you think the Sarbanes-Oxley Act has on project management?

6. Why do you believe it is difficult to deliver a project on time, within budget, and with full specifications intact?

CHAPTER 2

Project Management

Before we begin to discuss the application of the Earned Value Management System to projects, we will review some basic project management principles to ensure a common starting point. Experienced project managers may elect to skim this chapter. A common understanding of projects and their management provides the basic structure required to support EVMS.

Using project methods has become the recognized way to perform an organization's work. After all, the work of most top executives primarily involves projects. The Project Management Institute, headquartered in the United States, and several comparable organizations in other parts of the world are dedicated to having *project management* achieve professional status through programs and constant updating of materials. In addition, many other professions recognize the desirability of project management knowledge. For example, the new Content and Skill Specification Outline for the Uniform CPA Examination, approved by the Board of Examiners and expected to take effect in future years, for the first time includes a section on project management (American Institute of Certified Public Accountants 2008, 30–31).

A PROJECT

A project is a unique production event in the life of an individual or organization. While similar events may have been accomplished in the past, the type of event, the people working on it, the deliverables, and the environment in which it takes place, or all of these elements, differentiate this event. A project can be as small as trying a new dinner recipe or as complex as constructing a space station—they all take planning, organization, and control. R.E. Westney, an engineer, suggests a definition of a project that we really like: "A project can be defined as the work required to take an opportunity and convert it into an asset" (Westney 2001, 128).

Setting out activities in an orderly way to accomplish a goal is the result of an orderly thought process that has been occurring as long as humankind has been recording history. Thomas P. Hughes wrote about four incredibly complex projects in his book *Rescuing Prometheus* (Hughes 1998). Hughes describes Prometheus as a mythological second creator and uses this reference to describe the transformation of our world from a natural state to a technological one. As these four enormous projects progressed, new ways of managing activities had to be developed. If your project seems overwhelming at times, read in Hughes' book about some of the trials and accomplishments of the SAGE air-defense project, the Atlas missile project, the Boston Central Artery/Tunnel project, and the development of the Internet. From these projects came the inspiration for new technology, new organizational structures, and new management styles.

Most studies show that the majority of projects do not meet at least one criterion for the estimates of their original cost, schedule, or expected result. Indeed, the Boston project described by Hughes was popularly christened the "Big Dig" and later the "Big Leak." It became infamous for its cost overruns and unsatisfactory management. Project goals will not be realized if the efforts to meet them are unrealistic, not approved, underestimated, or not planned, or if the project is not given adequate resources. Managing a project requires extensive planning and careful management using a consistent system.

A tremendous amount of material about project management has been published. The material is becoming fairly well defined as associations such as the Project Management Institute (www.pmi.org), the Association of Project Management (www.apm.org.uk), and the International Project Management Association (www.ipma.ch/intro) publish and continue to update their bodies of knowledge on project management.

A project is a temporary and unique activity. Projects are usually undertaken by extensions of the organization that existed before and will exist after the duration of the project. As we will see in later discussions of project organization, this typical organizational approach means that a project rarely has fully committed resources. Projects are not production-oriented, even though they might have a production component. They begin and end to fulfill a particular need. The features "temporary" and "unique" describe not only the project but also its organizational system. The resources assigned to a project do not usually make up a permanent functional unit; they are linked together in a constantly changing and evolving way.

THE PROJECT CHARTER

Many activities and documents are part of a project. The project charter is one of the first and one of the most important documents. It is the primary agreement between the organization requesting a product or service and the organization providing that product or service. The charter identifies the project stakeholders and the project team's roles, responsibilities, and accountabilities. In other words, a charter establishes who will do what for whom.

The project manager should develop the project charter in cooperation with the project sponsor. It is not uncommon, however, for the project manager to draft the charter for the sponsor's signature. The charter ensures clear communication about what is to be accomplished, the timeframe in which it will be completed, and the resource support that the project team can expect. The charter provides an overview created at the project's initiation—before any detailed planning—and key stakeholders should sign the charter to indicate their approval.

The charter provides a brief description of the scope of the project and its objectives. Detailed specifications will be developed later in the planning process. Because the project charter typically becomes the basic reference document for large and/or complex projects, it also should discuss how the project will be structured, the acceptance criteria, and the processes for mitigating potential risks, resolving issues, and managing project changes. In addition, it is a good idea to specify project deliverables and conditions under which the project will end.

There are some generally accepted components that a project charter should contain. We have compiled an outline of typical items that should be included (Figure 2.1), but the size and complexity of the project will dictate the amount of detail for each entry. Your organization may have a template for constructing a project charter. If not, you may have to create a charter from scratch. Even for a small project, we recommend that you list some information for each of the standard headings shown in Figure 2.1, even if that information only cites a standard procedure.

Charters for large and complex projects undoubtedly will require the use of brief summaries and references to other documents that contain the detailed information. Charters for such projects also may contain information that could be considered part of the project planning that is completed after the initial project is approved. Examples include a Gantt chart, work breakdown structure, organizational breakdown structure, risk analysis and management, project control methodologies (including required progress reporting), quality control activities, plans for project support activities such as training and documentation assistance, project facilities and resource requirements, required interim approvals, and change con-

I. Details of the project sponsor

    A. Name, title, authority

    B. Authorization signature(s)

II. Introduction

    A. Background required to understand why the project is being undertaken

    B. Purpose of charter document (generally provides authority to begin project work)

III. Overview of the project (in smaller projects, this section may be prepared in narrative form in one or a few paragraphs)

    A. Purpose of project

    B. Scope encompassed

    C. Objectives to be achieved and project deliverables

    D. Project manager and project team members

    E. Dependencies outside the project manager's control

    F. Method for determining when project is complete

    G. Unsettled issues

IV. Project timeframe

    A. Expected start date

    B. Expected final deliverable date

V. Expected cost of the project

    A. Materials

    B. Personnel

    C. Subcontract work

FIGURE 2.1   Essential Charter Elements

trol procedures. Although these elements are project requirements, they may be shown in the project charter as planning deliverables.

The term *statement of work* (SOW) is used in many different ways. Many times it is considered interchangeable with *project charter*; at other times it refers to a very detailed description of the activities required to fulfill the objectives of a low-level part of the project plan. We describe some different uses of the term in later chapters.

PROJECT LIFE CYCLES

The term *life cycle* probably became popular because most projects follow a very general pattern of investigation, approval, definition, resource assignment, implementation, and termination. We agree with Wideman (2004) that *life span* might be a more appropriate description. Your organization may have a standardized project pattern (life cycle) or may allow each project team to develop the pattern that its project will follow.

There have been many approaches to defining a generally accepted project life cycle. They all attempt to lend some standardization to the very difficult process of including all necessary elements of a successful project. Sometimes, generally accepted life cycles emerge for a particular industry. For example, several industry groups have established accepted standards that provide a structure for the processes of the software development life cycle from conception through termination.

The International Organization for Standardization (ISO)/International Engineering Consortium (IEC) 12207, created by committees of national representatives, and IEEE/EIA 12207, created by the Institute of Electrical and Electronics Engineers (IEEE) and the Electronics Alliance Industry (EIA), were developed with some of the same leadership and share the same life cycle process. The documents are very similar; IEEE/EIA incorporates ISO/IEC 12207 and adds a foreword, a series of annexes, and much more extensive guidance. The ISO/IEC standard is voluntarily followed by businesses in the United States, whereas the IEEE/EIA standard may be required for companies doing business with the Department of Defense (DoD).

The Basic Approach

We are all familiar with the age-old argument about how we should divide time between planning the project and doing the project. This basic debate is illustrated in Figure 2.2. Part a of the figure follows the thoughts "Do we waste our precious time planning?" and "We need to get started on the necessary work right away." The second illustrates the idea that if your plan is thoughtful and complete, it will take less time to deliver.

a. Typical allocation of time between planning and doing

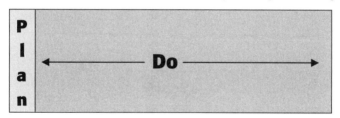

b. Recommended allocation of time between planning and doing

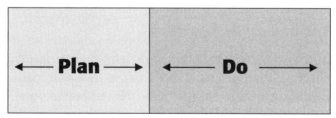

FIGURE 2.2   A Time for Planning, a Time for Doing

We often hear the familiar exhortation, "Plan your work, and work your plan," but how much time do we actually devote to planning? Hoping to reduce the constant variations normally encountered in meeting customer requirements, W. Edwards Deming originated a cycle for business planning and continuous improvement that is relevant for projects. It is described in some detail by Henry Neave (1990, 143). Deming's cycle is commonly called the *PDCA Cycle* because it contains four primary elements: plan, do, check, and act (Figure 2.3). The model is applied in projects through attention to feedback, an essential element for all projects.

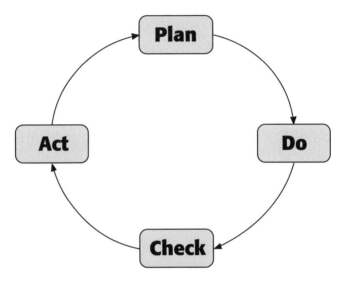

FIGURE 2.3   Deming's Plan, Do, Check, and Act (PDCA) Cycle

A More Comprehensive Approach

One traditional pattern in software development projects is called the waterfall approach. The approach got its name because the activity cascades down a single line. The idea was to construct the software product with the same methodology used for hard products—a serial process (Figure 2.4). One of the major problems with this approach is that most projects require some iterative or review activities between stages and do not proceed continuously down the waterfall process. For many years, the software industry has been evolving the process to move from the waterfall model to a more modern, iterative development model.

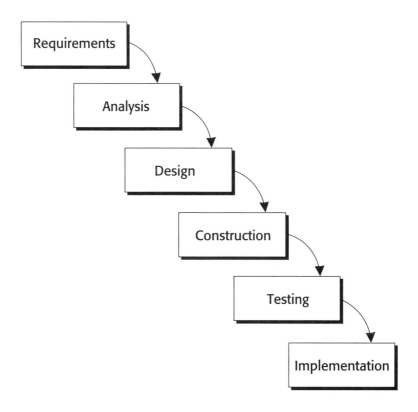

FIGURE 2.4   Waterfall Development Model

An alternative approach that overcomes the lack of iterations in the typical waterfall model is the spiral development model. Barry Boehm (1988, 64) described this concept for a software development project, but it can be applied to any project that requires iterative stages. Each iteration in this model provides increasing capability. This concept is shown in Figure 2.5.

The model is divided into four quadrants representing the major phases of the management process: determine objectives, evalu- ate alternatives, develop/verify, and plan next phases. Beginning at the center of the spiral and moving clockwise, each transverse goes through each of the four management processes (resulting in the four prototypes) with increasing detail added at each loop. One caveat about using a spiral model is that you must limit the number of cycles, or the project will just keep going around in circles. As a project manager, especially if you tend to be a perfectionist, you need to learn the phrase "It's good enough!"

There is often a conflict between those who would like to have a complete and detailed plan before any activity is started and those who prefer an iterative approach, with details only for the beginning of the project. For a large project using EVMS, it is very difficult to plan using the same level of detail over the entire project's duration.

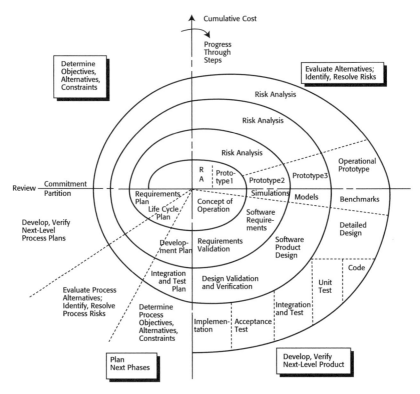

From Boehm, Barry W. "A Spiral Model of Software Development and Enhancement." *Computer* 21 (1988), no. 5: 61–72. © 1988, IEEE. Reprinted with permission.

FIGURE 2.5   Boehm's Spiral Development

Minimum Life Cycle Requirements

Regardless of the model used, it is helpful in the planning stage to divide the project into phases. Along with a controlling function that runs throughout the project, the four commonly accepted phases for the project life cycle are:

1. *Initiation:* the concept and initiation phase
2. *Planning:* the design and development phase
3. *Execution:* the implementation or construction phase
4. *Closeout:* the commissioning or termination phase.

It is important to note that each of these phases can be subphased using the same four phases, and the deconstruction can continue until you reach a desired level of detail.

Almost all discussions on project life cycles insist that there be checkpoints at each phase for evaluation, proposed change, and approval for continuation. For your projects, you may choose one of the models we have discussed or create one of your own; however, as our foray into the world of project life cycles shows, you can't just dive in and do the work—even on a small project. That is where project management tools like EVMS enter the picture.

EVMS PROJECTS

EVMS specifically uses a work breakdown structure to delineate the authorized work elements of a project into identifiable pieces. A *work package* refers to a deliverable at the lowest level of the work breakdown structure and describes a work unit or one element of work in the project. There is an unusual but interesting example of the term *work unit* in the breakdown of the very unusual distributed computing project for the SETI program, which searches for signals of extraterrestrial life. Ksetiwatch is a monitoring tool that logs and manages all the sessions that are assigned to home computers for the project participants. The program appropriately calls these participant sessions work units (SETI@home 2005).

Of course, in a book on earned value that has a great deal to do with metrics, the importance of project measurements must be emphasized early in our discussion. You've certainly heard the expression "What gets measured gets done" or "You can't manage what you can't measure." People always find a way to deal with the way they are being measured, so it is most important to have measurements that will promote desired rather than dysfunctional behavior.

We need measurements to understand how well we are meeting the estimates for all projects. We need to measure—even if it is done informally—progress in time (schedule), cost (budget), scope (requirements), and quality to know where we are and how closely we are following the project plan. It is necessary to rely on metrics to communicate information, from the use of a simple three-color "traffic light" approach to a complete EVMS. We also use measurement information to help develop corrective actions when we are off track and to predict where we will be at the end of the project.

In general, and especially with EVMS, a metric used to communicate progress may not be the best metric for developing corrective action plans. Measurements are designed to provide a basis for decisions and are reported to project owners so they can make priority and resource allocation decisions. The same measures are seldom useful in making corrective-action decisions on project work. Very often a metric tells us where we are but does not give us any indication of what to do.

Metrics cannot replace experience and good judgment. Poor project management generates poor EVMS data. Just as costs cannot be reduced by focusing on the costs instead of focusing on the processes that generate them, EVMS metrics cannot be improved by trying to directly influence the metrics. Instead, you must focus on the project processes that generate the metrics.

THE PROJECT MANAGEMENT OFFICE

The use of project management processes for accomplishing more of the work of an organization is rapidly increasing. This concept has become known by such names as *managing by project* and *enterprise project management*. A slightly different concept, project portfolio management (PPM), is about managing all the projects in the organization; however, that does not mean that the organization is managed by projects. Many organizations have adopted an organizational concept called a *project management office* (PMO) to deal with the growing phenomenon of project portfolio management. The basic functions of the PMO are summarized in Figure 2.6.

Project Management Capability	Business Process Coordination	Project Priorities	Business Metrics
• Project Management Practices • Project Management Maturity	• Strategic View • Goal Alignment • Business Collaboration	• Business Priorities • Resource Application • Leverage Skills	• Progress Reporting • Performance Feedback • Customer Satisfaction

FIGURE 2.6   Project Management Office (PMO) Functions

If you are involved in establishing or operating a PMO, you should be aware that not everyone will appreciate the benefits of such an office. Be sure to publicize the PMO's mission as one that will support the entire organization and will not serve merely as the project police. In trying to address all concerns up front, be aware that you may be required to deal with different and sometimes very personal agendas. To counteract these forces, the PMO must have firm senior management commitment and support.

A team of senior-level representatives from each functional area, with representation by the PMO, is the control behind PPM. This team sets the policies that the PMO will follow. One of the biggest challenges to successful project management is that the project resources most often are owned by various functional departments and not by the project managers. It is easier to apply these resources to the most strategic projects if there is a portfolio management process in place.

An often-unrecognized challenge is managing the number of projects that the organization has active at any given time. The prevailing management thought is the more projects in the pipeline, the busier everyone will be and the more projects will be completed. Whenever an opportunity arises, it is tempting to start a project right away; once it is started, everyone involved will be pressured to keep the project active by reporting its progress.

A great deal of anecdotal evidence strongly indicates that when resources are stretched, efficiency and effectiveness are drastically reduced. In general, the more projects in the pipeline, the longer it will take for any one project to finish because resources are rarely sufficient to complete work on one task or project without interruption.

The selection, prioritization, and termination of projects are very important functions of PPM. Having a balanced view from outside the project management function (including the PMO) can allow you to concentrate on potential overall value and control the number of projects in order to better accomplish resource utilization and quicker returns. An analysis from a PPM team of the strategic value of projects will eliminate most of the parochial interests too often used as selection criteria.

The PPM team may use a risk/benefit grid to be more selective and to ensure a balanced project selection. Figure 2.7 illustrates a simple risk/benefit decision grid with example projects located at various points within the grid. A continuing risk/benefit analysis should be made for each project after every major phase. Early termination can be as valuable as appropriate selection and initiation.

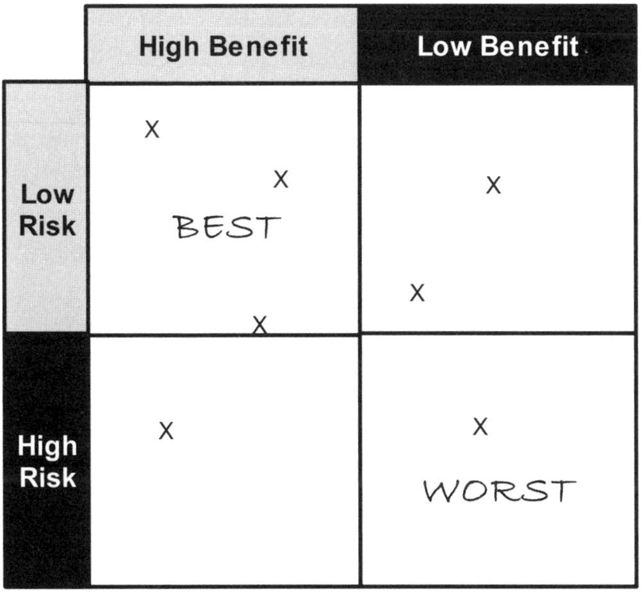

	High Benefit	Low Benefit
Low Risk	X X BEST X	X X
High Risk	X	X WORST

FIGURE 2.7   Simple Risk/Benefit Grid

A great deal of software is available to help with both PPM and enterprise project management. An Internet search on either term will provide voluminous data about these vital components of project management.

EVOLVING PROJECT MANAGEMENT MATURITY

Public literature and the media abound with personal improvement schemes. We all want to be better at something—our appearance, our job performance, our relationships, something. You probably want to be a better project manager, or you wouldn't be reading this book! Organizations, too, should have a plan to continuously improve their ability to gather the right measurements, construct realistic plans, and exploit their constraints.

Several tools and programs offer guidance in improving an organization's project management maturity. They are designed to move an organization's processes from an unpredictable, sometimes chaotic state to a disciplined process of continuous improvement. Most of the models include four basic steps:

1. An early learning phase
2. The integration of lessons learned with processes
3. A reengineering of the business processes
4. Moving to a new phase of maturity.

Maturity models are becoming more sophisticated as they are updated over time. A detailed explanation of improvement programs is beyond the scope of this book, so we have provided the following abbreviated list if you wish to investigate further:

- *Organizational Project Management Maturity Model (OPM3ᴿ)*, second edition (Project Management Institute 2008b). The standard details knowledge, assessment, and improvement elements and probably is the most comprehensive treatment for projects.
- *CMMI-ACQ, V1.2 Capability Maturity Model Integration for Acquisition Software.* This document addresses specific and generic practices for both capability levels and maturity levels. Capability levels include incomplete, performed, managed, defined, quantitatively managed, and optimizing (numbered from Level 0 to Level 5, respectively); maturity levels include initial, managed, defined, quantitatively managed, and optimizing (numbered from Level 1 to Level 5, respectively) (Software Engineering Institute 2007, 22).
- *Project Management Maturity Model,* second edition (Crawford 2006). In addition to covering the usual five levels of maturity, this second edition provides a comprehensive framework for continuously improving project management skills and results.
- *ISO 9001:2008 Quality Management Systems* (International Organization for Standardization 2008). In this family of standards, most of the standards are highly specific, but they are considered generic management system standards because

they can be applied across almost all sectors of business, industry, and technology.

A maturity model—*The Earned Value Management Maturity Model* or EVM³ (Stratton 2006)—also has been developed for EVMS itself. The EVM³ and its key process areas are described fully in Stratton's book.

The objective of all of these models is to continually enhance the project delivery processes of the organization, with the goal of reaching a consistent level of success.

THE PROJECT MANAGER

Successfully managing a project has a set of very demanding requirements, including organizational ability, communication skills, leadership, persistence, consistency, hard work, and a system (think EVMS). Too often, we expect the best technical person in a particular area to be the most capable of managing a project in that area. It is true that technical knowledge may be required for a project, but that knowledge does not necessarily have to be possessed by the project manager, who must exhibit all the skills of a successful salesperson, a disarming negotiator, a clear communicator, and a charismatic leader. A perfect example is the coach of a winning athletic team made up of individual stars.

The most important characteristic for a project manager is goal orientation. All human beings have an innate desire to achieve goals—even our games have goals. Numerous journal articles and books have been written on the subject. One such book is even called *The Goal: A Process of Ongoing Improvement* (Goldratt and Cox 1992).

Establishing a baseline in EVMS has very practical benefits for a project's goals. Beyond the obvious benefits, working toward a goal is a major motivational factor for the project team. Locke and Latham developed this idea in their goal-setting theory (Locke et al. 1990).

One of the project manager's greatest challenges is dealing with many different people both inside and outside the organization. To further complicate matters, some of them will be managers of functional areas who control resources that affect the project. The project manager's degree of power and authority depends to a great extent on the organizational structure.

Organizational structures are generally considered functional, matrixed, project-oriented, or some combination of the three. Of course, the project manager will find the most organizational power in project-oriented structures. (Organizational structures are covered in detail in Part III, where we discuss EVMS Criterion 2.)

A Personal Observation of Authority

We were coming back into port from our short cruise in the Caribbean when the captain invited us to the bridge to watch the docking maneuvers. A local harbor captain had come out to actually dock the ship because he was familiar with the harbor and with the tug operators who would be helping with the many small and careful adjustments that had to be made to bring such a large ship into the dock. At first, the local captain would bark out an order, but the ship's crew would not move until the ship's captain repeated it. After a short time, the crew began responding almost immediately to the local captain even though the ship's captain continued to repeat the orders. It was interesting to observe the nuances of the shift and change in authority.

THE PROJECT TEAM

When you have the authority to choose team members, you must be very careful to resist selection by reputation alone. Sometimes personal reputations are developed at the expense of others. Remember that your project will be evaluated not on the reputation or popularity of its team members but on its results. Herb Brooks, the coach of the U.S. 1980 Olympic gold medal hockey team, often said that he did not want the "best" players—he wanted the "right" players.

A manager once told us that the ideal player has four traits: intelligence, professional skills, a pioneering spirit, and a hint of excellence in innovation and creativity. Having team members with diversity in both their work backgrounds and skills will foster your team's inventiveness and creativity. In today's more competitive marketplace, the old ways of working no longer ensure success.

For all team members to be on the same page, the project manager must communicate with them and not just establish rules. The project's mission statement is a perfect example. The team must understand what it is trying to accomplish; therefore, it is necessary to hold straight-to-the-point discussions of the project's objectives and what will be required to accomplish them. Some questions that need to be asked and answered are:

- Why are they on the team?
- What are they individually expected to accomplish?
- How must they operate differently?

You may find it useful to construct a team charter establishing the team's operating assumptions and rules.

In our efforts to improve team performance, we have spent a substantial amount of time looking at the problems experienced by teams. If you are interested in learning more about teams, we recommend Lencioni's *Five Dysfunctions of a Team*, in which he lists absence of trust, fear of conflict, lack of commitment, avoidance of accountability, and inattention to results as the most significant problems affecting team effectiveness (Lencioni 2002, 240). Kerzner (2005) and Flannes and Levin (2001) have some interesting material in their chapters on resolving conflict for project managers that you will find very helpful. For a more positive approach, try Glickman's *Optimal Thinking* (Glickman 2002).

One more term, *expectation*, must be mentioned. Although you will not usually find this term in project management journals, we think it is one of the most important aspects of team leadership. Our good friend Harry Morgan coached a very successful high school football team for many years. His secret was not hard-driving discipline, expert football strategy, or rigorous conditioning (although these also were part of his philosophy); his teams executed well because that was what he expected.

Joe Batten—author, speaker, trainer, one of the authors' mentors, and the person who created the U.S. Army tagline "Be all you can be"—often said that the finest gift we can give another person is a stretching expectation of excellence. One of his numerous publications that we refer to often is *Expectations and Possibilities* (Batten 2003).

> This chapter is the deliverable of the authors' own "mission impossible": to summarize in one chapter all the basics of projects, project managers, and project teams. Each of these topics has been the subject of entire books. Our primary objective has been to alert you, as a project manager, to the topics you should be aware of and some sources that you might like to consider for future education.

DISCUSSION QUESTIONS

1. Discuss the following statement: "The processes of performing repetitive manufacturing processes and project management are entirely different."

2. In your experience, what is the major reason that a project succeeds in delivering on time, on budget, and with full specifications?

3. Are charters necessary for internal projects?

4. How long and detailed should a charter be?

5. Why is it important to understand project life cycles?

6. Describe your organization's project life cycle template. If none exists, how would you initiate one?

7. In general, what percentage of total project time should be consumed in planning the project?

8. Respond to the following statement: "Earned value is primarily a project management philosophy."

9. What are the major objectives of a project management office (PMO)?

10. What is the major purpose of project maturity models?

11. Discuss the following statement: "Project managers have power only through their position."

12. Describe your ideal project team.

The Basics of Earned Value

Thus far, we have reviewed some general project management information that most of you already knew. Even so, we hope you have picked up a few new ideas to store in your personal portfolio or have been made aware of a few trails to investigate later.

Now, with some common background, we begin our exploration of earned value. Many of you may not be required to use a full-blown earned value management system that adheres to the 32 criteria but want to use earned value's metrics and reporting mechanisms. In this book, we often refer to the required complete system as *EVMS* and to basic parts of earned value and its metrics as *EV*.

Part II presents the basics of EV, along with some rules and guidelines for implementation. Chapter 3 gets to the heart of EV with both the traditional EV metrics and an introduction to those that have been developed for emerging practices (detailed in Part VII). Simple examples illustrate the calculations, and sample problems provide an opportunity for practice. Chapter 4 provides an overview of EVMS—what's good, what's not so good, and a big-picture view of the 32 criteria.

CHAPTER 3

Earned Value Metrics

Our first discussion point is the metrics. Even if you do not plan a full-blown earned value management system implementation, you must understand this most important part of the system.

Earned value metrics play an increasingly important role because project management is now recognized as a desirable professional skill. Many organizations require project management applicants to be certified by a recognized professional organization. To acquire any professional project proficiency designation, such as the Project Management Institute's Project Management Professional certification, you will have to master certain metrics.

PRIMARY METRICS

There are four primary EV metrics. The names given first in the following paragraphs are more popular in industry and are becoming more universally adopted. The second names are those originally used, which are most often the primary references in government documents.

Total Value (TV) or Budget at Completion (BAC)

The first EV measure, *total value* or *budget at completion*, is prepared in the planning stage before the project is begun. Total value more accurately should be called *total cost* or *total budget*, but we'll use the term "value." TV is developed by examining all the work to be accomplished on the project and the estimated cost of each portion of work. The budget and the project schedule then become the baseline against which the project progress is measured. Remember that this metric is established before work is begun. Having all required information prior to beginning work sometimes is referred to as a "full kit" concept.

As work on the project progresses, EVMS requires periodic status reports. At each status point, three periodic measures are used to report the project status and to derive other report metrics. The first two are budgeted costs, and the last one is actual costs. Another distinction is that the first metric represents scheduled work, and the last two are for completed work. They are:

- The budgeted cost (planned value) for the work scheduled to have been completed
- The budgeted cost for the work actually completed (earned)
- The actual cost of the work actually completed (performed).

Planned Value (PV) or Budgeted Cost of Work Scheduled (BCWS)

At each status reporting date, the portion of the project's planned value or BAC corresponding to the elapsed time from the beginning of the project to the status date details both the work that should have been completed and the costs that should have been incurred. The U.S. Department of Defense calls this subset of BAC the *budgeted cost of work scheduled*; others refer to it as *planned value*. BCWS or PV is the dollar value of the work that was scheduled for completion by this point in the project's schedule.

Earned Value or Budgeted Cost of Work Performed (BCWP)

This periodic measurement shows the original estimated costs for work actually completed. This can be the most confusing of the basic measures because it uses both an actual measurement and a budget measurement. It is a measure of the work actually performed during the status period, but at its planned (budgeted) amount—not its actual cost. Both EV and PV typically represent *cumulative-to-date* values, but this additional label is seldom used.

Actual Cost (AC) or Actual Cost of Work Performed (ACWP)

The actual costs incurred from the beginning of the project represent the third periodic measure. Note that costs incurred (direct or indirect costs used on the project) are not necessarily the same as costs paid in cash. Like the other two basic periodic status measures, this is usually a cumulative amount.

Again, the terminology can be confusing. We would prefer to use the term *actual value* to maintain the "value" terminology, but although we might point out occasional inconsistencies in term definitions, in this book we use those that are more generally accepted in industry.

Reporting and Comparison Metrics

We have presented the four basic measurements as TV or BAC, PV or BCWS, EV or BCWP, and AC or ACWP. Other major reporting metrics that are derived from these basic measures are cost and schedule variances, their related ratios, and future performance estimates. The variances are designed to illustrate the difference between planned and actual project performance; the ratios are relative metrics that can be compared across projects.

The *cost variance* (CV) is the difference between the budgeted cost of work actually performed (EV) and the actual cost of that work (AC). The formula for the cost variance is EV – AC or BCWP – ACWP.

The CV's related ratio is the *cost performance index* (CPI). The formula is EV / AC or BCWP / ACWP.

The *schedule variance* (SV) is the difference between the budgeted cost of the work actually completed (EV) and the budgeted cost of work scheduled for completion (PV). The formula for schedule variance is EV – PV or BCWP – BCWS. The SV's related ratio is the *schedule performance index* (SPI). The formula is EV / PV or BCWP / BCWS.

The formulas are designed so that a positive amount represents favorable performance, and a negative amount signals unfavorable performance.

In addition, there are two forecasting metrics: an *estimate to complete* the remainder of the project (ETC) and an *estimate at completion* (EAC). These can be more easily explained after a look at an analogy to the standard cost system and some example calculations of ratios.

An emerging practice in EV uses an additional measurement called *earned schedule* (ES), which is presented in Part VII.

ANALOGY TO THE STANDARD COST SYSTEM

A perfect analogy to EV analysis is found in a standard cost system. If you have ever taken a management accounting class, you probably were exposed to the bar or triangle approach to calculating variances in a standard cost system. This triangle approach also can be applied to compute EV variances, as shown in Figure 3.1.

CALCULATION OF RATIOS

The cost and schedule variances are absolute amounts that are influenced by the size of the project and thus are difficult to compare with performance on other projects. Converting the variances into schedule and cost ratios standardizes them.

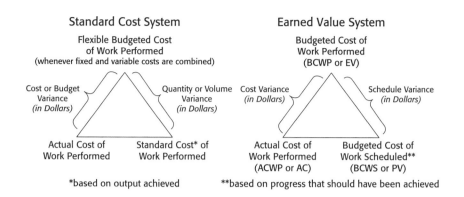

FIGURE 3.1   Standard Cost System and EV Triangle Approaches

The SPI is the result of dividing the EV (at the top of the EV triangle illustrated in Figure 3.1) by the PV (bottom right of the EV portion of Figure 3.1); the CPI is the result of dividing the EV by the AC. The SPI and CPI are relative measures, and they enable comparisons across projects. Further, these two indices, or ratios, are included in formulas used to produce a host of other metrics that provide estimates of total cost at completion. They also are used in an index ratio that measures the additional effort required to complete the project, which can be used to compare performance on many different projects.

The SPI, therefore, shows schedule completion (the EV) on the measurement date relative to planned completion by that date. A ratio of 1 indicates that EV and PV are identical. An amount greater than 1 indicates a favorable performance; an amount less than 1 indicates unfavorable performance.

The CPI indicates the cost performance that should have been achieved for the project portion completed—the EV relative to the costs actually incurred as of the status date. A ratio greater than 1 indicates favorable performance (compared with the baseline budget), while a ratio less than 1 means that actual costs are higher than were expected for the work completed.

In an EV system, we never make any comparisons across the bottom of the triangle—ACWP and BCWS (actual cost and planned value). Although computing this variance makes sense in certain environments, such as in standard cost systems where the standard costs applied during the period are computed for work actually completed, it is uninformative and can be misleading for projects. This total variance merely indicates that actual costs do not equal the amounts budgeted as of the time elapsed since the project started, and it is meaningless without knowing how much of the project's work has been completed.

Forecasting Metrics

So far we have seen from the standard cost triangle how the EV can be compared against the PV and the AC to calculate the project's performance variances and the related performance indices. We can now use the CPI (and the SPI) to predict the project's remaining cost and its total revised cost.

The two predictive metrics are called the *estimate to complete* (ETC) and the *estimate at completion* (EAC). And, as you might have expected, a ratio also can be calculated for the ETC, and it is called the *to-complete performance index* (TCI). Generally, only the CPI is used to calculate the ETC, but a more realistic number could include the SPI by multiplying the two together. The formulas for ETC, EAC, and TCI are:

$$\text{Estimate to Complete (ETC)} = \frac{Total\ Value - Earned\ Value}{Cost\ Performance\ Index}\ or\ \frac{TV - EV}{CPI},$$

sometimes modified to show the impact of SPI as well: $\frac{TV - EV}{CPI * SPI}$. To differentiate this ratio from the more common version shown just above, this ratio is often called the *critical ratio.*

Estimate at Completion (EAC) = Actual Cost + Estimate to Complete,
or *AC + ETC.*

To-Complete Performance Index (TCI) = $\dfrac{Budget\ for\ Remaining\ Work}{Estimated\ Cost\ of\ Remaining\ Work}$

or $\dfrac{TV - EV}{EAC - AC}$

Now let's see how these formulas work, using a simple example.

Calculations Example

A status is taken at the end of week 2 for a 12-week project. The total planned budget for the project is $120,000 for work that is evenly spread over 12 weeks. The project staff has completed work that was scheduled to have been completed by halfway through the middle of week 2. Actual costs incurred to date on this project total $16,000. Figure 3.2 shows the tasks and costs involved.

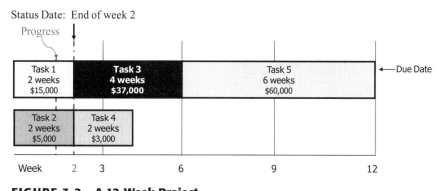

FIGURE 3.2   A 12-Week Project

BAC or TV = $120,000

AC = $16,000

EV = $\dfrac{\$120,000}{12}$ = *(budget per week) * (1½ weeks)* = $15,000

$$PV = \frac{\$120,000}{12} * 2 \text{ weeks} = \$20,000$$

$CV = 15,000 - 16,000 = (\$1,000)$ (unfavorable)

$$CPI = \frac{\$15,000}{\$16,000} = 0.9375 \text{ (Less than 1, so less than planned performance)}$$

$SV = \$15,000 - \$20,000 = (\$5,000)$
(Unfavorable—schedule
is slipping)

$$SPI = \frac{\$15,000}{\$20,000} = 0.75 \text{ (unfavorable)}$$

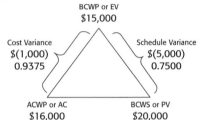

To-Complete: Calculations that consider only the CPI provide the most optimistic estimates:

$$ETC = \frac{\$120,000 - \$15,000}{0.9375} = \$112,000$$

$EAC = \$16,000 + 112,000 = \$128,000$ ($8,000 more than the original estimate)

$$TCI = \frac{\$120,000 - \$15,000}{\$120,000 - \$16,000} = 1.01 \text{ (Great than 1 = unfavorable)}$$

Alternative to Complete: Calculations that take into account both the CPI and the SPI provide more pessimistic estimates:

$$ETC = \frac{\$120,000 - \$15,000}{0.9375 * 0.75} = \$149,333$$

$EAC = \$16,000 + \$149,333 = \$165,333$ ($45,333 more than the original estimate to complete)

USING THE MEASUREMENTS

Calculations and measurements can be used in many different ways and accomplish a variety of objectives. Remember, however, that calculating the metrics is only a small part of managing an EVMS project.

The Challenge of Meeting All Targets

Striving to be successful, project managers want to look good on both cost and schedule metrics simultaneously. Textbooks and EV implementation research usually warn that a cost variance and a schedule variance should never be "netted" together. One source specifically cautions that "[a] poor cost variance combined with a good schedule variance does not mean that everything is all right" (Humphreys 2002, 675).

Because meeting the schedule may be critical to the customer—meaning we must meet SPI targets—project teams may be encouraged to spend as much time as necessary to meet SPI targets. At the same time, meeting cost targets is probably critical to the company responsible for completing the project. Therefore, project teams also are pressured to spend as few hours as necessary to meet CPI targets. Project managers are expected to expend the necessary resources to meet SPI targets while at the same time feeling strong pressure to use as few resources as necessary to meet CPI targets.

This conflict between the two metrics typically leads to alternating compromises, as shown in the abbreviated cause-effect diagram of an EV system (Figure 3.3).

W. Edwards Deming (Deming 1993, 101–103) emphasized the importance of distinguishing between two kinds of variation: *common cause variation* (variation within the capability of a system to repeatedly produce results—a system in control) and *special cause variation* (variation beyond the capability of a system to repeatedly produce results, usually variation with causes outside the system—an out-of-control situation). Attempting to "fix" common cause

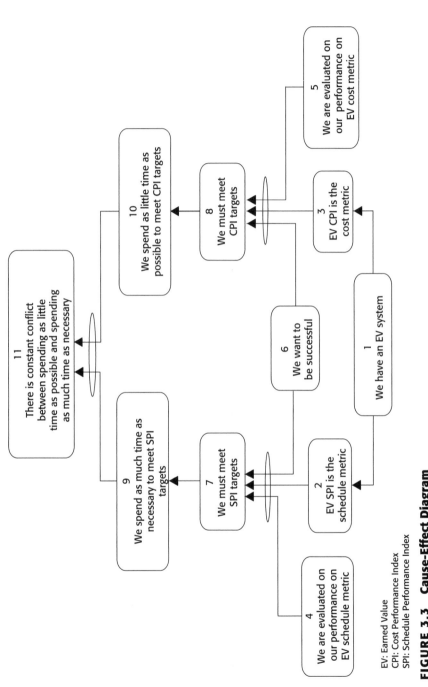

FIGURE 3.3   Cause-Effect Diagram

EV: Earned Value
CPI: Cost Performance Index
SPI: Schedule Performance Index

variation worsens the results by overcorrecting an in-control process to an out-of-control state. The same concept applies to projects. That is, responding to small variances by making frequent project adjustments very likely will result in decreased project performance.

Obviously, there are possible tradeoffs between CPI and SPI. For example, to improve poor schedule performance, additional costs (e.g., overtime, acquisition of additional resources) might be incurred. Another scenario is that the schedule might be put on hold until prior resource commitments have been fulfilled, thereby reducing the need for additional costs but resulting in schedule slippage. The attempt to keep both measures on track instead of making appropriate decisions to complete the project frequently results in conflicted behavior.

Attempting to remain on schedule, as reflected in SPI, and stay within budget, as reflected in CPI, means that project managers will try to make both metrics look better by constantly adjusting behavior to garner better performance on each metric. Because of a tradeoff effect, focus on an unfavorable SPI (or CPI) naturally makes the CPI (or SPI) metric worse. The conflict between spending as few hours as possible and spending as many resources as necessary means that attempting to improve both SPI and CPI simultaneously practically ensures that neither metric will improve.

Neither metric improves because the actions intended to make each metric look better mean that shortcuts and temporary patches may quickly cause other problems. These activities make remaining project tasks even more difficult, and a downward spiral ultimately and inevitably results in failure to meet any of the targets.

Information and Motivation

We must have measurements to communicate progress, but an ideal indicator of performance may be especially difficult to find. Arrow (1971, 278) showed that all measures of performance are not equally easy to measure. Thus, performance metrics adopted by organizations are constrained by practicality and cost. It should not be surprising that not all critical dimensions of project performance are measured and reported.

One Size Does Not Fit All

Robert Austin (1996, 216) partitions measurement into two categories: *motivational measurements,* which are explicitly intended to affect behavior, and *informational measurements,* which are used primarily for the information they convey. He maintains that informational measurements should be used to improve decisions and should not be used to effect behavioral changes.

EV metrics provide information to project owners, but they may inadvertently affect the behavior of project team members attempting to perform to those metrics. In fact, it is as true today as when described by Flamholtz (1979, 71–84) that accounting measurements are simultaneously intended to facilitate multiple functions, including accountability, performance evaluation, and motivation, and to provide information for decision-making. This "one size fits all" objective of internal managerial accounting information must be questioned, just as many analysts recently have questioned the appropriateness of one financial report for external users.

Managers who have made decisions on the basis of their impact on the next quarter's results or annual report rather than the long-term health of the organization for all stakeholders have been severely criticized and punished by the market. Analogously, making project decisions on the basis of an imperfect measurement system that does not measure all critical dimensions of project performance is detrimental to ongoing project process improvement, possibly to project completion, and certainly to project success.

Decision Metrics

In any event, there are some clear implications for any organization that implements EVMS. First, the EV metrics that are a source of information for stakeholders must not be the only information used to make project decisions. That means that the EV metrics must not be used to determine how work should proceed. Project decisions must be based on sound project management practices. Project team members must be motivated to complete a project as quickly as possible and at the lowest cost. Decisions must be made using real-time data, not based on historical data or the impact of the decision on data to be reported in the future.

A 1990 study by Beach illustrated that, as early as 15 percent into a project, EV metrics can predict the ultimate completion date and project cost (Fleming and Koppelman 2000, 39). However, EV measures may not track closely with project performance early in the project. Therefore, management may have to be careful not to be too hasty in demanding corrective action if initial reports show unfavorable EV variances. Management must avoid forcing project people into the destructive spiral of chasing improvement on one EV metric at the expense of another.

At the same time, some projects, for any number of reasons, will not deliver the intended results. These projects should be killed early to release resources for more valuable work. Rarely are such failures the fault of the project teams, and cancellation should not reflect unfavorably on individual performance.

Response to Measurements

Finally, organizations must be very aware of the behavioral responses to measurements and be extremely careful in designing performance evaluation systems. If Austin is correct, motivation and information metrics must be separated to minimize dysfunctional worker behavior. Establishing appropriate organization measurements is hard work, and it may require that management not be allowed access to all the detailed information measures that the project staff needs to do its best work. There are no easy answers where performance evaluation is involved.

Management's not having access to nonaggregate information that workers have might mean that management must place more reliance on the subjective judgment of supervisors and fellow employees.

Now that you have completed this chapter, you are well on your way to understanding the metrics of EVMS. You will have the opportunity to practice your knowledge and ability with the sample problems in the Discussion Questions and Practice Calculations section.

The metrics of EVMS are based on a standard accounting system but have their own nomenclature. The primary measures are:

1. *Total value (TV)* or *budget at completion (BAC)* for the project—the original budget prepared at the initiation of the project.

2. *Planned value (PV) or budgeted cost of work scheduled (BCWS)*—the dollar amount of the work that was planned to be completed by the date of the status report.

3. *Earned value (EV) or budgeted cost of work performed (BCWP)*—the budgeted dollar amount of the work that has been completed by the date of the status report.

4. *Actual cost (AC) or actual cost of work performed (ACWP)*—the dollar amount incurred (charged to the project) by the date of the status report.

From these basic metrics, cost and schedule variances can be calculated to indicate project progress. The variances can be converted to ratios and indices to facilitate comparisons across projects. Further calculations then can be used to predict the final cost of the project. There are many challenges in preparing and using measurements. The project manager must be aware of the informational and motivational aspects of using metrics, as well as the potential consequences.

It can be very difficult for project managers to meet both the schedule and cost requirements of the baseline plan, and this conflict can lead to dysfunctional behavior. Although the measurements can provide valuable information to stakeholders, the dark side is that the metrics can be misleading if other good project management techniques are not employed.

DISCUSSION QUESTIONS AND PRACTICE CALCULATIONS

Questions

1. Name and describe the three points of the EVMS standard cost triangle.

2. Discuss the strengths and weaknesses of using the EVMS metrics.

Practice Calculations

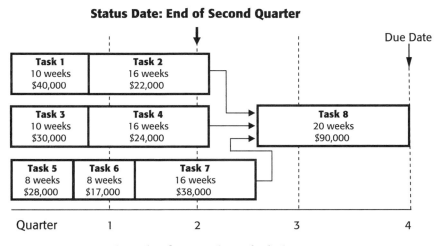

Status Date: End of Second Quarter

FIGURE 3.4   Project Plan for Practice Calculations

Use Figure 3.4 to calculate EVMS metrics for the following test problems:

Plan at end of second quarter: Tasks 1, 3, 5, and 6 should be completed; Tasks 2 and 4 should be 96 percent complete; and Task 7 should be 51 percent complete.

Results at end of second quarter: Tasks 1, 3, 5, and 6 have been completed; Task 2 is 50 percent complete; Task 4 has not been started; and Task 7 is 10 percent complete. $137,500 has been charged to the project.

Calculate the following values (assuming that all tasks incur costs uniformly over time):

1. At project initiation, what was the total projected cost of this project (BAC or TV)?

2. On the status date, what is the budgeted cost of work scheduled (BCWS or PV)?

3. What is the actual cost (AC) of this project on the status date?

4. What is the earned value (BCWP or EV) of this project on the status date?

5. Calculate the cost variance (CV) and the cost performance index (CPI).

6. Calculate the schedule variance (SV) and the schedule performance index (SPI).

7. Compute the "optimistic" and "pessimistic" estimate at completion (EAC).

CHAPTER 4

The Earned Value Management System

Because of the combination of the importance of critical projects, the ever-increasing speed required for completion, and the notorious failures in project management, there is a genuine need for dependable, objective information. Senior management depends on project progress reports and projections of end-of-project results to make vital decisions. The Earned Value Management System arose from these needs and is a valuable, objective process. A later chapter discusses possible implementations of modified earned value systems, but first let's examine the origins, benefits, and deficiencies of EVMS.

EVOLUTION OF THE EARNED VALUE MANAGEMENT SYSTEM

U.S. government entities, such as the Department of Defense (DoD), National Aeronautics and Space Administration (NASA), Department of Energy, and Office of Management and Budget, as well as other international government entities, have set the basic definitions, concepts, and requirements for EVMS through their contract management agencies. In 1999, DoD adopted the 32 criteria of EVMS, as standardized in 1998 by the American National Standards Institute (ANSI) and the Electronic Industries Alliance (EIA). As we present later, the criteria have been revised since that time, and many implementation and intent guides have been published, but the basic requirements have remained very stable.

Concepts of Earned Value Management

EVMS is an integrated project management system that allows for:

- A detailed definition of the work required to complete the project (work breakdown structure, or WBS)
- Assignment of the organizational entities for work performance (organizational breakdown structure)
- A schedule of the work to be performed (project plan)
- Integration of the cost and schedule in a baseline plan (time-phased baseline budget)
- Accumulation of costs
- Measurement of progress (earned value)
- Analysis of variances from the plan
- Reporting to management
- Forecasting of schedule and cost completion data
- Disciplined maintenance of the plan data and proposed revisions (change control plan).

DoD presents an excellent description of EVMS in paragraph 1.1 of the *Earned Value Management Implementation Guide,* stating its concept of the system as follows:

Earned Value Management (EVM) is a program management tool that integrates the technical, cost, and schedule parameters of a contract. During the planning phase, an integrated baseline is developed by time phasing budget resources for defined work. As work is performed and measured against the baseline, the corresponding budget value is "earned." From this earned value metric, cost and schedule variances can be determined and analyzed. From these basic variance measurements, the program manager (PM) can identify significant drivers, forecast future cost and schedule performance, and construct corrective action plans to get the program back on track. EVM therefore encompasses both performance measurement (i.e., what is the program status) and performance management (i.e., what we can do about it). EVM is program management that provides significant benefits to both the Government and the contractor (Department of Defense 2006a).

Earned Value Defined

Earned value refers generally to the primary metrics for progress reporting, as presented in the previous chapter. The term *earned value* has been used and applied in many different ways, but the term *earned value management system* has been universally accepted as signifying a management system that, at a minimum, complies with the 32 criteria set forth in the American National Standards Institute Guidelines, ANSI/EIA-748-1998.

In appendix A of the NASA Procedural Requirements, NPR 7120, NASA defines EVM as:

> a tool for measuring and assessing project performance through the integration of technical scope with schedule and cost objectives during the execution of the project. **EVM** provides quantification of technical progress, enabling management to gain insight into project status and project completion costs and schedules. Two essential characteristics of successful **EVM** are **EVM** system data integrity and carefully targeted monthly **EVM** data analyses (i.e., risky WBS elements). (National Aeronautics and Space Administration 2008b).

The Government Electronics and Information Technology Association's *GEIA Standard for the Earned Value Management Systems* discusses the application of the revised ANSI/EIA 748-98B guidelines, and the foreword of that document states:

> The earned value management system guidelines incorporate best business practices to provide strong benefits for program or enterprise planning and control. The processes include integration of program scope, schedule, and cost objectives, establishment of a

baseline plan for accomplishment of program objectives, and use of earned value techniques for performance measurement during the execution of a program. The system provides a sound basis for problem identification, corrective actions, and management replanning as may be required. (GEIA 2007).

Criteria and Metrics

Of the 32 EVMS criteria, approximately 40 percent establish organizational structure, project planning, and change control requirements; approximately 60 percent involve accounting for costs by way of budgeting, reporting, and forecasting. As presented in the previous chapter, there are four primary measurements: The first launches the expectations of the project's performance, and the other three report periodic progress and forecast end results.

A key component of EVMS is the establishment of control accounts. A *control account* is a portion of the project plan assigned to a specific organizational unit, where costs can be budgeted and actual costs tracked so that performance (EV) can be determined. It requires the cooperation of the accounting department, which must establish appropriate control accounts in the general ledger or a subsidiary ledger with one controlling account in the general ledger.

Facilities that are not required to comply with all the standards of EVMS may still wish to gain the benefits of the objective reporting provided by some of the components of EV. In any case, EV provides objective project progress reporting and furnishes more reliable comparative information across projects.

It is fairly obvious that the traditional metrics in EVMS were developed from "standard cost" system measurements. EV compares cost, budget, and schedule components to produce cost and schedule variances in dollar-denominated metrics. It is a way to express performance measures and variances in comparable financial terms. In contrast to the cost-based metrics of EV, an emerging practice (presented in Chapter 16) is time-based. The basic metric of this proposed extension is called earned schedule (ES), and its use requires some additions to the standard EV metrics.

REQUIRING THE USE OF EVMS

In 2008, DoD issued a defense supplement to the Federal Acquisition Regulation (DFARS), in which subpart 234.2 stated the system requirements for the use of an EVMS as follows (Department of Defense 2008a):

234.201 Policy.
(1) DoD applies the earned value management system requirement as follows:
  (i)   For cost or incentive contracts and subcontracts valued at $20,000,000 or more, the earned value management system shall comply with the guidelines in the American National Standards Institute/Electronic Industries Alliance Standard 748, Earned Value Management Systems (ANSI/EIA-748).
  (ii) For cost or incentive contracts and subcontracts valued at $50,000,000 or more, the contractor shall have an earned value management system that has been determined by the cognizant Federal agency to be in compliance with the guidelines in ANSI/EIA-748.
  (iii) For cost or incentive contracts and subcontracts valued at less than $20,000,000—
    (A) The application of earned value management is optional and is a risk-based decision;
    (B) A decision to apply earned value management shall be documented in the contract file; and
    (C) Follow the procedures at PGI 234.201(1)(iii) for conducting a cost-benefit analysis.
  (iv) For firm-fixed-price contracts and subcontracts of any dollar value—
    (A) The application of earned value management is discouraged; and
    (B) Follow the procedures at PGI 234.201(1)(iv) for obtaining a waiver before applying earned value management.

(2) When an offeror proposes a plan for compliance with the earned value management system guidelines in ANSI/EIA-748, follow the review procedures at PGI 234.201(2).

(3) The Defense Contract Management Agency is responsible for determining earned value management system compliance when DoD is the cognizant Federal agency.

(4) See PGI 234.201(4) for additional guidance on earned value management.

234.203 Solicitation provisions and contract clause.

For cost or incentive contracts valued at $20,000,000 or more, and for other contracts for which EVMS will be applied in accordance with 234.201(1)(iii) and (iv)—

(1) Use the provision at 252.234-7001, Notice of Earned Value Management System, instead of the provisions at FAR 52.234-2, Notice of Earned Value Management System – Pre-Award IBR, and FAR 52.234-3, Notice of Earned Value Management System – Post-Award IBR, in the solicitation; and

(2) Use the clause at 252.234-7002, Earned Value Management System, instead of the clause at FAR 52.234-4, Earned Value Management System, in the solicitation and contract.

Obviously, the U.S. government is a strong proponent of EVMS. One must not infer, however, that EVMS is useful only in a military or government environment. The use of this internal control system has equal merit in the commercial world and is highly valuable in reporting on an entire portfolio of projects.

DRIVING FORCE FOR USING EVMS

To succeed in our current accelerating environment, projects must be completed in record time to take advantage of marketing and other windows of opportunity. However, public reports of project results are not encouraging. Too frequently we read about projects that are dismal failures: They are over their budget by a large amount, the time overrun is measured in months or even years, and the final product of the project (if it emerges at all) lacks some of the planned features or has unexpected performance failures.

In light of these failings, you might ask the same question that Schulte (2006) asked in the title of her presentation, "Is Poor Management a Crime?" Her answer was the same as ours: "Yes, it could be." The Sarbanes-Oxley Act of 2002 (SOX) has some very stringent requirements for internal controls and current reporting of any material changes in the internal control of an organization's financial operations. To fully comply with the intent of SOX, organizations must have detailed cost and schedule measurements, and senior management must have complete, accurate, and timely information on major projects. EVMS can help in providing these controls and fulfilling those reporting requirements (Schulte 2004).

Companies that claim that their projects are never late are probably referring to the latest baseline due date (which may be considerably later than the original date) or are allowing such long task times in their original project plans that the project takes far longer than it should. Thankfully, there are project successes that inspire us to continue examining our processes and searching for better methodologies. EVMS is one methodology that instills confidence that project managers are providing valid information on in-process projects.

As we mentioned earlier, in the 1960s, the U.S. government commissioned a predecessor system composed of 35 requirements that was modified into today's 32 criteria. The objective of the first system, Cost/Schedule Control Systems Criteria (C/SCSC), was to provide a common basis for reporting and decision-making by both the project initiator and the project contractor. The project initiators were seeking current and reliable information on project progress; a valid relationship between cost, schedule, and technical requirements; and information provided in a summarized, but meaningful, format.

WHY ALL THE INTEREST IN EVMS?

You should be getting a general feeling by now for the mechanics of EVMS. At this point, you are probably more interested in learning whether EVMS really helps an organization. The following sections offer some published opinions, along with a detailed illustration that demonstrates the value of EVMS.

Support for the Value of EVMS

Christensen (1998, 380) has published extensively in the area of EV and cites 10 benefits of EVMS:

1. It is a single management control system that provides reliable data.
2. It integrates work, schedule, and cost into a work breakdown structure.
3. The associated database of completed projects is useful for comparative analysis.
4. The cumulative cost performance index (CPI) provides an early warning signal.
5. The schedule performance index (SPI) provides an early warning signal.
6. The CPI is a predictor of the final cost of the project.
7. It uses an index-based method to forecast the final cost of the project.
8. The "to-complete" performance index allows evaluation of the forecasted final cost.
9. The periodic (e.g., weekly or monthly) CPI is a benchmark.
10. The management by exception principle can reduce information overload.

Schulte states, "EVMS is a set of best business practices, processes, and tools for enterprise project planning and control." She adds that "it provides an excellent means to establish and maintain internal processes and controls" (Schulte 2004, 1). Dayal (2008, 59–73) devotes an entire chapter to the benefits of EVM, including how it tracks delays caused by external factors, simplifies project monitoring, improves customer satisfaction, and can forecast needed future efficiency.

With promises like these, is it any wonder that organizations are seriously considering implementing EV even if they aren't required to do so? Let's take a closer look.

Discussion of the Evidence

Companies are adopting EVMS for good reasons. The system requires a work breakdown structure, recognition of task dependencies and organizational responsibilities, a time-phased budget, and other formal planning and reporting procedures that constitute excellent elements of today's best practices in project management. Project status reporting historically has been overly optimistic and very subjective.

Subjective Project Reporting

Without some objective measure of performance, stakeholders (principals who cannot directly monitor the project progress) must rely on the subjective judgment of the project manager, who might be encouraged by optimism to report that everything is progressing as planned (on time, on budget), even if difficulties are requiring more time and money than planned. The manager may truly believe that a time or cost overrun can be made up later and does not want project work to be questioned or stopped. Therefore, it is not uncommon to report after one month of a three-month project that the project is "on time" and "on budget" if one-third of the total budget has been spent, regardless of how much project effort remains. In this way, the bad news may be delayed until it becomes obvious that the project has no possibility of successful completion.

The traditional accounting now used on many projects compares costs incurred to date with expected budgeted expenditures for the period since the project began (sometimes using cash flows without accrual accounting). With no connection to schedule completion, the information content and predictive ability of the resulting variance are extremely low or nonexistent. That is, there are no answers to questions such as "Are we ahead of or behind schedule?" and "Will the project finish on time, within cost, and to specifications?" For example, assuming a $208,000 project for a one-year time period, the cost/funding plan might look something like the one illustrated in Figure 4.1. The project should require $69,000 by the end of the first quarter, $108,000 by the end of the second quarter, $148,000 by the end of the third quarter, and $208,000 by the end of the project.

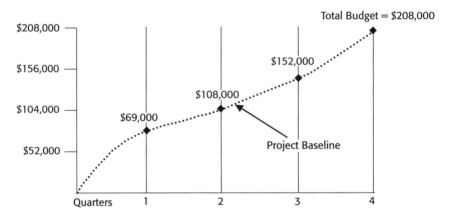

FIGURE 4.1   Project Budget Shown in Phases

The executive management committee fully expects the project manager to stay within the limits of the $208,000 commitment and to continuously monitor performance during the life of the year-long project. At the end of the first quarter, when the plan calls for an expenditure of $69,000, the actual expenditure is only $65,000. When asked if the project is behind schedule, the project manager quickly responds that the project is right on course (meaning that one-quarter of the one-year project has elapsed) and under budget by $4,000.

Another approach sometimes used is to compare actual costs incurred with the project's estimated total completion costs and thereby estimate the percentage completed. This is the standard accounting *percentage of completion* approach. Of course, the estimated cost of the project may change from period to period, but anecdotal evidence suggests that estimated total project cost is sticky and not readily adjusted. Also, a bottom-up approach to estimating the total cost of work yet to be completed is very time-consuming. It should be noted that using this percentage of completion approach and not adjusting the total cost would result in the assumption that the project is over 30 percent complete at the end of the first quarter.

A Better Way

To obtain more relevant information, costs incurred must be tied to schedule completion. EVM requires a time-phased budget baseline against which contract performance can be measured. Thus, EV looks at not only planned and actual spending but also scheduled work. To provide this detail, the project plan must include detailed tasks to be accomplished, estimated durations of the tasks, and a sequencing of the tasks.

A Gantt project network for the previous example is shown in Figure 4.2. The thick line represents the critical path—the longest series of sequential tasks—requiring a total of 52 weeks to complete the project.

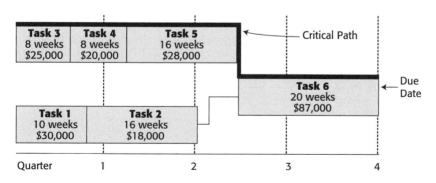

FIGURE 4.2   Gantt Project Network Example

By the end of the first quarter, Tasks 1 and 3 should be completed, Task 2 should be about 14 percent complete, and Task 4 should be about 57 percent complete. Therefore, the anticipated expended budget by this point is approximately $69,000 [$25,000 + $30,000 + (0.14 * $18,000) + (0.57 * $20,000)]. The project manager reports, however, that although Tasks 1 and 3 have been completed, Task 2 has not yet been started, and only 20 percent of Task 4 has been completed. Assuming costs for each task after Tasks 1 and Task 3 are incurred uniformly over time, the project's EV is $59,000 ($30,000 + $25,000 + 0.2 * $20,000). Therefore, the project has earned $59,000, not the $65,000 actually spent. This situation is graphically illustrated in Figure 4.3.

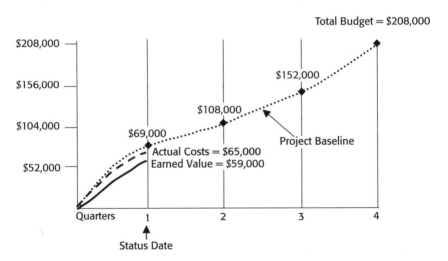

FIGURE 4.3   Earned Value Illustration

It is clear that this project is not on course and not under budget. The schedule variance is $10,000 unfavorable ($59,000 – $69,000); the cost variance is $6,000 unfavorable ($59,000 – $65,000); the SPI is 0.86, meaning this project is running about 14 percent behind schedule; and the CPI is 0.91, showing that the project is almost 10 percent over budget at the end of the first quarter. Further, based on progress to date, the estimate at completion is not $208,000, but somewhere between $228,736 and $255,391.

An EV system provides objective measures of progress and enables some meaningful projections of future costs. Thus, project owners have access to performance data other than the verbal assurances of managers intimately involved with the project. In addition, the planning, reporting, and control requirements of EVMS reflect good project management techniques.

THE DARK SIDE

Like the standard costs from which EV was developed, EV metrics summarize past performance, compare actual results to those planned, and signal developing problems. However, EV metrics do not unambiguously indicate appropriate actions that should be taken. EVMS variances, even more so than standard cost variances, do not report information that is sufficiently timely and transparent to all interested parties.

Some Missing Information

Consider the two projects illustrated in Figure 4.4. They have identical baselines, and the tasks (blocks) require the same time to complete and have the same planned value. The darkened blocks are tasks that have been completed.

Both projects have the same EV, the same SPI, and the same CPI, but which project is likely to be completed first? Other things being equal, the project plans in Figure 4.4 indicate that Project B will be completed before Project A, which has seven incomplete tasks on one path. EV metrics would not signal this situation. EV metrics must be related to a project's time-phased baseline.

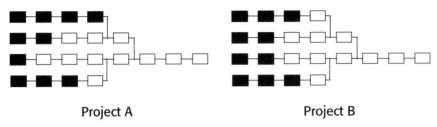

Project A   Project B

Note: Dark boxes show work completed.

FIGURE 4.4   Comparison of Two Projects

The fact that the SPI must be compared with the project schedule to obtain an accurate picture of the project's true schedule position has been well known at least since DoD commissioned an Arthur D. Little Company study in the 1980s (Fleming and Koppelman 2000, 113–120). Stakeholders receiving the EV measures, however, rarely have access to the detailed project plans. Most commonly, comparison of EV measures to the project plan is not a formal part of EV metrics. Even if stakeholders have access to all project plans, they do not have the same information as the project manager, and the proper corrective action is not obvious to either the stakeholders or the project manager.

Resource managers control assignment of resources to projects. Once a project has begun, the resource manager can expect that the project manager will demand his or her share of the resources. A resource manager typically has to show weekly progress on all projects. Because EV metrics are not perfectly linked to the project's plan of work, when managers use EV to manage their projects, priorities between tasks on different paths or between projects are not always clear to the resource manager or the project manager. A project might easily suffer delays due to the assignment of limited resources to noncritical tasks.

Although EV can provide some objective measures of performance, the dollar-aggregated project measurements can point neither to specific areas of good or poor performance nor to their causes. Without knowledge of the area of concern, remedial tactics cannot be undertaken or directed. If corrective action must be taken, other project management tools must be employed to identify problem areas and potential solutions.

Dollars, Time, and the Schedule

None of the EVMS metrics that purport to reflect progress and remaining work actually correlate directly with completion of the project plan itself. While SPI and CPI are designed to measure cost and schedule deviations from the planned baseline, both indices incorporate the EV metrics, and both have components that are denominated in dollars. Therefore, SPI and CPI have the appearance of measuring progress on the project baseline. However, as pointed out by the Arthur D. Little Company's analysis and illustrated in Figure 4.4, the measures are susceptible to manipulation.

One of the most important aspects of project reporting is gauging progress so that predictions can be made about project completion. But as a project progresses, EV always draws closer and closer to planned value. Because EV is the budgeted cost of work completed, when the project is complete, EV will equal the budgeted cost of the project, and the schedule variance will be zero. The total value of the project will be "earned," and this is true regardless of how much was actually spent or how much time was actually consumed. Fortunately, the cost variance does reveal the difference between the amount spent and the amount that should have been spent.

Many project managers and most project staff think of a project schedule only in terms of time. EV metrics, denominated in dollars, can be misleading or confusing. Furthermore, the growing lack of predictability can lead to a false sense of the actual progress. Because of these problems, the emerging practice of using an earned schedule metric has been proposed; it is discussed in Chapter 16.

Dysfunctional Behavior

Because of a basic disconnect between EV metrics and project operations and/or completion, and because project funding often is tied to EVMS performance, some project managers have developed certain EV coping mechanisms. These coping behaviors are an example of the impact of dysfunctional measures that Robert Austin (1996, 10) defines as "consequences of organizational actions that interfere with attainment of the spirit of stated intentions of the organization." He maintains that an incentive system becomes dysfunctional when it encourages people to take actions that reduce value to the customer below what it would have been without the incentive system. Further, Austin maintains that the main problem for most incentive plans is not measurement error but bias intentionally introduced by the people being measured. However, this bias need not be designed to deceive and can result merely from the conscious effort of people doing what they are being asked to do.

A HIGH-LEVEL VIEW OF THE 32 EVMS CRITERIA

The EVMS criteria are usually divided into five sections:

1. Organization
2. Planning and budgeting
3. Accounting considerations
4. Analysis and management reports
5. Revisions and data maintenance.

The 2006 revision of the ANSI/EIA criteria added the word "Scheduling" to the second section (GEIA 2007).

The five-step division shown above was intended to address basic management concepts; however, many management concepts will overlap in this division of the criteria. The criteria are presented fully in Appendix A, but let's take an introductory look at them now by selecting a few keywords from each criterion.

Organization

1. Define the work with a work breakdown structure.
2. Identify organizational structures.
3. Provide for integration of company processes and the program structure.
4. Identify the function for controlling overhead.
5. Provide integration that permits performance measurement from the work breakdown structure and the organizational structure.

Planning and Budgeting

6. Schedule the work with task sequence and interdependence.
7. Identify indicators of measurable progress.
8. Establish and maintain a time-phased budget baseline at the control account level.
9. Establish budgets with identification of significant cost elements.
10. Identify and establish budgets in discrete work packages within control accounts, and identify far-term work in larger planning packages.
11. Ensure that the sum of the work package budgets and planning package budgets within a control account equals the control account budget.
12. Identify and control any work defined as level of effort.
13. Establish overhead budgets.
14. Identify management reserves and undistributed budget.
15. Ensure that the project's target cost equals the sum of all budgets and reserves.

Accounting Considerations

16. Record direct costs in a formal system.
17. Summarize direct costs from control accounts to the work breakdown elements.

18. Summarize direct costs from control accounts into the contractor's organizational elements.
19. Record all indirect costs.
20. Identify unit costs.
21. Provide accountability for a material accounting system.

Analysis and Management Reports

22. Generate management control information at the control account level.
23. Identify and explain differences between actual and planned schedule and cost performance.
24. Identify budgeted and applied indirect costs.
25. Summarize data and variances through program organization or work breakdown structures.
26. Implement managerial actions.
27. Revise estimates of cost at completion based on performance to date.

Revisions and Data Maintenance

28. Incorporate authorized changes.
29. Reconcile current budgets to prior budgets.
30. Control retroactive changes to records.
31. Prevent unauthorized revisions to the program budget.
32. Document changes to the performance measurement baseline.

In the last two chapters, we have covered the metrics and the concepts of EV. This chapter discussed how EVMS started, covering in detail its definition, concepts, and criteria and requirements for its use. Many government agencies are strong proponents of EVMS and have defined the requirements for its use on their contracted projects.

We discussed the benefits of an objective status and reporting system and the interest in and support for using EVMS. Even though there may not be a requirement for implementing a complete EVMS, using some part of the system can have benefits. No discussion of EVMS would be complete, however, without presenting the positives and the negatives. The system has a long list of benefits—notably the integration of work, schedule, and cost into a work breakdown structure and its predictive ability. EVMS "is a set of best business practices, processes, and tools for enterprise project planning and control" (Schulte 2004, 1). The dark side is that the metrics can be misleading without the use of other good project management techniques. The chapter ends with an overview of the 32 EVMS criteria.

DISCUSSION QUESTIONS

1. Name the two structures required for EVMS and discuss their purposes.

2. What would you say is the primary purpose of EVMS, and why you would choose that aspect?

3. What is the key component for cost accounting in an EVMS project?

4. Discuss some other benefits of EVMS.

5. Is EVMS required on all government projects? Why or why not?

6. As a project manager, what would you consider a deficiency of EVMS?

7. Do you think that EVMS reporting can be "gamed"?

PART III

It's All in the Plan

> *"It is better to sleep on what you plan to do than to be kept awake by what you've done."*
>
> —UNKNOWN

The first 15 EVMS criteria are intended to ensure that the project management system is correctly and adequately established. The system must provide the means to:

- Define the project objective
- Assign the major deliverables to functional units (including outside contractors)
- Schedule the work
- Prepare budgets
- Facilitate the collection and reporting of management information
- Provide for accurate estimates of project completion that include both cost and schedule.

To meet these requirements, EVMS relies on the careful construction of a baseline plan. Chapter 5 discusses Criterion 1 and its requirement for detailing the project plan with a work breakdown structure, but it does not deal with the subject of scheduling time. Chapter 6 covers Criteria 2 through 5 and the organizational structure and responsibilities. Then Chapter 7 outlines the requirements of the scheduling process by examining Criteria 6, 7, and 8. Chapter 8 discusses the budgeting requirements of Criteria 9 through 15.

CHAPTER 5

The Project Plan (Criterion 1)

The first EVMS criterion sets the tone for following the entire system. You will need a complete understanding of (1) the work breakdown structure (WBS), which includes work packages (WPs); (2) a WBS dictionary; and (3) additional project input. In this chapter, we recommend some ways to develop the WBS and introduce the concept of the control account and its influence on the construction of the WBS.

EVMS CRITERION 1

Define the authorized work elements for the program. A work breakdown structure (WBS), tailored for effective internal management control, is commonly used in this process.

The first sentence of this EVMS criterion seems quite simple, but it contains two extremely important words: *define* and *authorized*. The EV of any project cannot be measured without having first defined all the deliverables or effort the project requires. Second, an effective project management system must begin with solid management authorization, including all of the organization's functional areas that will contribute to or be affected by the project. We firmly believe that this authorization applies not only to the specific project but also to EVMS itself. Management commitment is extremely important in any organizational endeavor.

Even though you might not know the complete details of the total effort required, EVMS requires a definition and estimation of the entire project scope. Other EVMS criteria will allow for changes and the addition of unauthorized work under specific conditions. You should also note the use of the word *tailored* in this criterion. EVMS is about project control, and it is of special interest to see that the criteria recognize that control is best exercised when it is tailored to the particulars of the organization. The impact of tailoring can be clearly seen throughout our examination of EVMS.

THE WORK BREAKDOWN STRUCTURE

In the 1980s (and occasionally in the present), one of the favorite disparaging phrases about the lack of project planning was "Ready, fire, aim!" Too often a project plan was considered only a quick way to keep management off the project managers' backs so they could get something accomplished. Besides, the thinking went, if project managers told anyone what they were going to do, they would really have to do it. Fortunately, for the most part, especially within the growing ranks of professional project managers, these comments are now used in jest.

There are many serious and compelling reasons to plan carefully, but in implementing EVMS there is one above all others—fulfilling the very first EVMS criterion. Beyond its EVMS requirement, a WBS is a strong foundation for managing any significant project. The EVMS criterion tells us that it is used to "define the authorized work elements" and should be "tailored for effective internal management control." A well-defined project using a WBS is designed to facilitate the collection, analysis, and reporting of the cost and schedule data.

WBS Definitions and Standards

The grandfather of references to a WBS was made by the U.S. defense establishment in Military Standard (MIL-STD) 881 (1 November 1968). That standard was superseded by MIL-STD-881A (25 April 1975) and MIL-STD-881B (25 March 1993). The 1993 revision was developed through the cooperative efforts of the military services with assistance from industrial associations. It talked about the WBS as a product-oriented family tree composed of hardware, software, services, data, and facilities. The WBS, it said, defines the product(s) to be developed and relates the elements of work to be accomplished.

The standard was cancelled about five years later by MIL-STD-881B Notice 1 (2 January 1998), which stated that, "Information . . . for Work Breakdown Structures is now contained in MIL-HDBK-881, 'Work Breakdown Structure.'" Most of the 1993 standard was updated with little material modification and repeated in the new handbook. The WBS has always been considered a primary mechanism for project planning, control, and reporting. The handbook specifically states, "The work breakdown structure forms the basis for reporting structures used for contracts requiring compliance with the Earned Value Management System (EVMS) Criteria" (Department of Defense 2005a, 1.5).

There have been many other definitions and descriptions of the WBS. *A Guide to the Project Management Body of Knowledge* describes the process of creating a WBS as follows: ". . . the process of subdividing project deliverables and project work not in the WBS is outside the scope of the project"(Project Management Institute 2008a, 49). Using the project scope statement, requirements documentation, and organizational process assets results in not only a WBS but a WBS dictionary, a scope baseline, and project documentation updates as well.

Almost all literature on project management devotes significant exposure to the WBS in some form or other. There has been considerable discussion about whether the WBS should be oriented to deliverables or activities, but in any of its many definitions and uses, the WBS offers obvious benefits for all stakeholders in the management of a project. For the implementation of EVMS, the most important aspect of the WBS is that it provides the structure for tracking and reporting on the schedule elements of the project.

Two Possible WBS Structures

In many environments, especially the military environment, the WBS is usually a combination of two structures: a program work breakdown structure (PWBS) and a contract work breakdown structure (CWBS).

The PWBS provides the basic framework on which to hang logical elements of the program. Remember that the WBS definition usually describes a product-oriented set of elements in a hierarchical relationship. It is usually more natural for a project manager to start out thinking about a project in terms of activities and tasks. This could be very acceptable for a small nongovernment program, but the project manager might not be using the EVMS criteria in that situation. When developing the PWBS, the project manager should be oriented to the program deliverables, not to the tasks required to deliver them.

Ideally, the project manager will be involved when the program objective is being defined because this begins the construction of the PWBS and is the initial step in the entire planning process. It is critical that this part of the process be comprehensive and thorough because this first step may characterize the planning for the entire project. If the program deliverables have already been defined when the project manager is appointed, the next best step is for the project manager to develop (rewrite) a PWBS to ensure that all interested participants are in complete agreement prior to further work. Each element in the PWBS is a point at which the EVMS measurements can be evaluated.

The second structure is the CWBS. Your organization may be an outside contractor for a large project (government or commercial), but we can define the project manager as the contractor for any project. The CWBS becomes the mechanism for coordinating all project resources. It includes all the elements of the PWBS but will be further extended to enable the project manager and subcontractors to identify any detail required to meet all the objectives of the program. It is very common and completely acceptable for the CWBS to use more task-oriented language in its extensions.

The purpose of a WBS is to separate a proposed product or objective into its component parts and to clarify the relationship of the parts to each other and to the end product. The WBS is the most important planning tool for assigning management and technical responsibilities. Together, the PWBS and the CWBS are the tools for tracking resource allocations, actual effort, cost estimates, expenditures, and project performance. All project deliverables must be identified in the WBS, and all involved organizational units must work within its parameters.

Steps in Constructing a WBS

Eleven steps are involved in constructing a WBS:

1. The first level of the WBS is the name for the project deliverable, the project objective, or product. This product identification must be one that is widely recognized throughout the organization. This first level is numbered 1.0 or numbered with the assigned project number and .0, such as 242.0.
2. The next level is a list of all the major components. Everything that is a part of the project product must fit somewhere under one of these major components. The components for project 242 would be numbered 242.1, 242.2, etc., out to the number of components at this second level.
3. If at all possible, you should try to construct all the elements of the second level before performing the work breakdown to the next lower level. It is very tempting to begin thinking about

all the products of the first entry in level 2, but doing so can be very distracting. The objective is first to get agreement on all the major components of the project. Some elements may be moved to lower levels as the WBS construction progresses.

4. Next, determine which of the elements require more information, and begin that definition on a subordinate level. Continue breaking down each element at each level into further levels until you reach a level of detail that will provide the organization with the required reporting data and the project manager with sufficient management information without overcontrolling the project team. Each successive level adds another decimal place to the numbering scheme. Level 3 elements in project 242 for element 242.1 are numbered 242.1.1 through 242.1.n. Level 3 elements for element 242.2 are numbered as 242.2.1 through 242.2.n.

5. It may be necessary to vary the defining scope of the products on each level, depending on how many levels the WBS will contain. An element on the second level may be defined very broadly if it is going to be broken down through many levels. Fewer levels may require more elements across each level, but even in very complex projects, 99 elements on a level would be extreme. Group some elements into a more broadly defined element, and then break it down through more levels.

6. Since most reporting is generated from the top levels, the decision about how many elements will reside in upper levels and how many will be delegated to lower levels (or left under the control of team members) will depend greatly on the reporting requirements of the contracting organization. If detailed reporting is not required, you may wish to have fewer elements in each level. Having fewer elements in each level will usually generate additional lower levels, but you will not generate executive reporting at those levels.

7. Break down the WBS elements into only as many subcomponents as you need for the cost/schedule reporting and effective management. You cannot think of everything, nor will a list

of thousands of project elements provide for more effective control. Remember that the project team, not the system, will achieve the project objective! A breakdown into objectives that can be met in periods of one week to eight weeks (depending on project complexity) is a good general rule.

8. The lowest level will be the work package. This is the formal designation to a responsible team member for the delivery of a product of the WBS. The statement of work (SOW) should include enough information to ensure the clarity of the contract between the project manager and the team members.

9. The number of breakdown levels under each element need not be the same. For example, a particular element may be on an upper level for reporting purposes but will not require as many levels of breakdown as others.

10. Do not be overly concerned about the sequence in which the major project objectives will be met. Sequencing can be done later when the time-phased project schedule is completed. Again, the objective in constructing the WBS is to ensure that all the control points for management and reporting are included.

11. Construct a WBS dictionary to describe all components.

DEFINING THE PROJECT

The project's major objective is the global or highest single element of the WBS. The project should have only one objective. If there is more than one project objective, there is almost certainly more than one project. The objective must state not only what the project will include but also what is not expected from the project. Carefully documenting the exclusions will help preclude assumptions that later will lead to possible conflict concerning additions and project changes.

It is not difficult to generate the second level of objectives for the project; often, they are a part of the project charter. What may be difficult is to generate all the intermediate and minor objectives that must be part of the successful project. We were first introduced to a basic process to accomplish this in our study of the theory of constraints. Since then we have expanded our work with this process, used it successfully in several situations, and written software to automate the association and sequencing of its elements.

We call our version *obstacles and required conditions.* The idea is to generate the entire project's intermediate objectives by first imagining all possible obstacles. It is much easier to address the negatives if they are recognized early in the planning stages. Listing obstacles first also overcomes the tendency to jump to what will be partial solutions if potential problems are not identified.

The next step is to visualize the conditions that must exist if the obstacles are to be overcome. These *required conditions* lead to the project's intermediate objectives. Then, "for each intermediate objective, resources and time required are necessary to establish a work breakdown structure that can be entered into project management software, such as Microsoft Project" (Budd 2003, 20–23).

The project's scope encompasses all the objectives and the work required to accomplish them. As a project manager, one of the biggest problems you will encounter is scope creep. An example goes something like this: The project manager has met numerous times with the project sponsor and the implementation staff, and they have carefully documented all the project's requirements—its scope. Now the project is nearing completion, and someone needs just one minor change and then another, and soon the changes have gone from minor to major. Effective project control can be achieved only with careful project planning, a tightly defined deliverable, and a rigorous change control system.

Thus, the initial and most critical activity for a project is to define its scope. The purpose of scope definition is to divide the project's objective into reportable and manageable units. The scope must be defined in just enough detail that the project stakeholders, especially the project team members, understand what must be done. Four important elements of definition during planning are:

1. Technical definition of the product or result
2. Schedule—a clear understanding of available time and required time
3. Cost—an important element of the EVMS
4. Resources required and available to accomplish the objective.

Many project managers believe that the more detail they put into the project plan, the more control they will have. The opposite is more generally true. Breaking the project down into an almost endless series of short tasks makes project tracking much more complicated and difficult to control. It may, in fact, increase the risk of late delivery. When everyone—especially the project manager—has a huge list of tasks, no one will be able to accurately track and report progress, or the project manager may become so busy with minutiae that there is no progress to report. Focusing on a list of individual tasks can cause you to lose sight of the project's objective. Base your project on achieving objectives, not on achieving a multitudinous list of tasks.

THE MECHANICS OF A WBS

The definition of a project includes its being temporary and unique; however, many projects in an organization will have some common features. Project managers should note commonalities that can be used to construct project templates, which can provide a head start in constructing a new project WBS.

There are several ways to represent the data when constructing a WBS for the current project. WBSs are becoming more sophisticated, sometimes adding rationales for why an outcome is required and why it must be accomplished in the sequence portrayed. Software products are available to assist in creating the WBS and converting it from one format to another. An Internet search on "WBS chart" will produce thousands of hits.

WBS Charts

Although one example of a WBS looks similar to an organizational chart, with connected boxes of lower-level detail, the WBS must not be thought of in terms of people, but as a project scope chart. The box at the very top of the chart is the project itself. The next level is a set of boxes connected to the top box (but not to each other) that represents the project's major deliverables. Each major deliverable can then be further described by its subcomponents in a lower level. A partial breakdown of one of the major components of our example project on the customer relations management (CRM) system is illustrated in Figure 5.1.

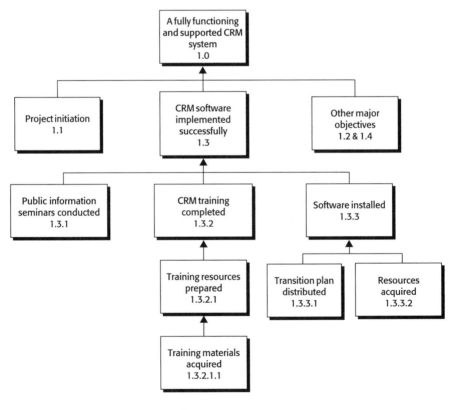

FIGURE 5.1   WBS Project Chart

Those who are familiar with a bill of materials might compare this form of the WBS to what is commonly called a Gozinto chart.[1] That chart describes (from the bottom going up) a breakdown of parts that make up (or go into) more complex parts. The WBS has the same form but not as much detail. In whatever form the WBS is constructed, it represents a hierarchical plan of the project elements.

Another common format, including the one often recommended by the military, is a line-indented format. It is a vertical listing of project elements in which each indentation is an expanded level of detail (a breakdown) of the product at the higher level of indentation. Each line is numbered for easy reference. The first line, representing the entire project, is labeled 1.0. It is quite common for organizations to number their projects, and they often use the project number as the first digits of the line-numbering scheme. For example, the first line in the WBS for project number 242 would be 242.0.

For project number 242, the second level of indentation would be labeled 242.1 to 242.n, depending on the number of major deliverables in the project. It would be quite unusual to have more than seven major deliverables in the project. If there are more than seven, it might be wise to attempt a consolidation to simplify the tracking and reporting function. The indentation continues for each element until a level is reached where the elements of that deliverable are easily understood by all stakeholders in the project and satisfy the reporting requirements. Figure 5.2 illustrates part of our example project in the line-indented format.

---

[1] The fictional mathematician Zepartzat Gozinto was invented around 1956 by Professor Andrew Vazsonyi, professor emeritus at the McLaren School of Business, University of San Francisco. Vazsonyi is a very interesting person, and it's worth a side trip to read about him at http://reallifemath.com/informs_pr.htm.

DESCRIPTION	WBS REF
Customer relationship management system fully functioning and supported	242.0
Project initiation	242.1
Objectives established	242.1.1
Sublevel detail	242.1.1.1
Plans completed	242.2
Training plan completed	242.2.1
Training objectives defined	242.2.1.1
Resources located	242.2.1.2
Training schedule completed	242.2.1.3
Training times estimated	242.2.1.3.1
Facilities arranged	242.2.1.3.2
Training schedule developed	242.2.1.3.3
Set training budget	242.2.1.4

FIGURE 5.2   Line-Indented WBS

WBS Levels

There have been as many disagreements about the required number of levels for a WBS as there have been about its orientation. Many
have advocated a standard number of levels, such as six or seven.
These proponents argue that, with a fixed number of levels, the
project manager would be more inclined to include all the elements
of the project—a forced thinking process. There have also been attempts to name the levels in a fixed hierarchy, but no standard has
emerged. Lewis (and others) call the first six levels (1) Program, (2)
Project, (3) Task, (4) Subtask, (5) Work Package, and (6) Level of Effort or Activity (Lewis 2000, 91).

The military WBS handbook also defines the levels in a WBS. Level
1 is the entire material item, such as an electronic warfare system.
Level 2 elements are the major elements of the material item, such as

an automatic flight control system. Level 3 elements are subordinate elements to level 2 major elements, such as a radar mechanism. The handbook goes on to state:

> A WBS can be expressed down to any level of interest. However the top three levels are as far as any program or contract need go unless the items identified are high cost or high risk. Then, and only then, is it important to take the work breakdown structure to a lower level of definition. (Department of Defense 2005a, 1.6.3).

The preponderance of current project management theory tends to agree that there is no preset number of levels for a properly constructed WBS. A small project may require only a few levels, while a complex one can have 20 or more if all the levels in a CWBS are counted. One leg of the WBS may have a different number of levels than another part. The WBS should be extended only to the number of levels that makes it practical to plan, budget, collect costs, track performance, and satisfy the reporting requirements. Distant deliverables that cannot be planned in detail until earlier work has been completed may be shown only at the highest levels until detailed planning is practical.

A WBS Dictionary

The military WBS handbook requires a WBS dictionary. We (and the Project Management Institute's latest edition of *A Guide to the Project Management Body of Knowledge* [*PMBOK® Guide*]) highly recommend that you prepare one even for projects where it is not required. It is used to describe each WBS element and the resources and processes to produce it. "The work breakdown structure dictionary should be routinely revised to incorporate changes and should reflect the current status of the program throughout the program's life" (Department of Defense 2005a, 2.2.3.1).

A WBS dictionary can be invaluable in cases where the WBS is very large or the elements are not self-explanatory. The dictionary is a more detailed description of each element in the WBS. It clarifies what makes up each element and, in many cases, what is not a part of the element. The description should start with the element's number and its name. The definition should give sufficient information so that all stakeholders understand the nature of the element and how it will be produced. As the dictionary is developed, it may even provide indications of required changes in the WBS. A dictionary entry for an element of our example project is illustrated in Figure 5.3.

WBS # **1.3.3.3** Workstation software downloaded from server. Each organization member who interfaces with the customer relationship management system must download the appropriate software from the CRM file server and send an acknowledgment to the installation team. The installation project team will provide detailed instructions, an online manual, answers to frequently asked questions, and a download schedule. Installation team members will be available for assistance. Training will have been completed through intermediate objective number 1.3.2.

FIGURE 5.3   WBS Dictionary Entry

CONTROL ACCOUNTS

Although the control account or cost account (CA) (synonymous terms) is not mentioned specifically until Criterion 8, there are implicit references in the organization criteria and many explicit references later. The CA has a definite interface with the WBS.

At some point, as the project objective is subdivided into smaller elements at lower WBS levels, the required effort can be allocated to a specific organizational unit. The project manager should have a CA established at the point where the WBS and the organizational structure coincide. A CA is an accounting feature set up to organize and manage the project at juncture points of the WBS and the organizational structure.

The CA is where the schedule and cost numbers for both budgets and actual charges are accumulated and where the earned value comparisons begin. The CAs should be set at the levels where reporting is required. Reporting below the first few levels of the WBS usually does not add significant value; however, it will adversely affect the preparation time and difficulty of accumulating the data. In Chapter 17, we will discuss the use of an effective project management tool in lower levels of the WBS without affecting the CA reporting requirements.

A member of the functional area that is responsible for the delivery of this element of the WBS can manage the CA. The accounting department (with input from the CA manager) will make the actual accounting entries. The CAs are subdivided into WPs and planning packages (PPs). This WBS element may be made up of several WPs as long as all the WPs are assigned within the same organizational area.

There will be much more detail about CAs in discussions of later EVMS criteria. For now, it is sufficient to note that you will need to arrange with the accounting department to establish CAs at certain points in your WBS. As you set up WBS elements, consider the reporting requirements, schedule formats, and potential manager assignments. Figure 5.4 illustrates a CA for our example project WBS and a generic organization.

Control Account ID: WBS # 242.3.2.3

Project Name: Customer Relationship Management: The Final Step

Control Account Title: Customer Relationship Management User Training

Control Account Manager: Training manager, Human Resources department

Planned Duration: February 22 through March 28

Applicable Charges: The control account manager will voucher all expenses for customer relationship management user training, including time, materials, and location rentals and costs for publishing the training schedule, distributing training manuals, and conducting user training.

Notable Exclusions: Preparing trainers, purchasing and preparing training material, and identifying training locations are not charged to this control account.

FIGURE 5.4   Control Account Example

A *planning package* is a part of the CA reserved for work that has not yet been fully defined but might be assigned to an organizational unit. Sometimes there is a portion of the WBS that, during the initial planning stage, cannot be allocated to a CA. One reason may be that a specific organizational unit has not yet been identified. This type of effort is one that is defined and for which a schedule and budget will be prepared. This part of the plan can be allocated to what is called a summary-level planning package (SLPP). WPs, however, are the basic building blocks of the WBS.

WORK PACKAGES

A WP describes a discrete unit of effort assigned, for planning and control, to one organizational unit. WPs can vary in size depending on their WBS level and the complexity of the project. In a moderately sized project, there are often WPs that describe an objective that will take about 10 days to accomplish. Responsible project team members can write the details of the WP for approval by the project manager.

The U.S. Navy WP technical manual defines the WP as follows:

3.2.90 Work packages (WPs). Presentation of information functionally divided into individual task packages in the logical order of work sequence. These WPs should be stand-alone general information, descriptive, theory, operating, maintenance, troubleshooting, parts, and supporting information units containing all information required for directing task performance (Department of the Navy 2001, 12).

A WP is the deliverable unit at the lowest level of a branch of the WBS. This WBS element must have scheduling and accountability because it is assigned to one responsible party, such as an individual team member or a contractor. The WP is the mechanism for passing responsibility for a deliverable to a team member. Even when a product-oriented WBS is used, the language at the level of the WP can usually be stated in measurable *tasks* or *activities*.

"A WP shall consist of an individual unit of information containing all data necessary for a technician to perform a specific task" (Department of the Navy 1997, 10). The WP does not have to be at the same level in every leg of the WBS, and the team member responsible for that WP may further break it down into more detailed activities. In some complex projects, the WP even becomes a subproject of its own; however, the project manager will be concerned only with management down to the WP level. At this level, the project manager can schedule work, measure performance, monitor changes, and collect cost/schedule data.

As we describe more fully later, the WP must be linked to an organizational (functional) CA. A WP is a subdivision of a CA that constitutes the basis for planning, controlling, and reporting on project performance. As stated earlier, it must be assigned to only one specific performing unit of the organization. The WP is the level at which costs are estimated and all reporting data are initiated. For EVMS reporting, it is important that cost data for all elements of the WBS add up through each level to form the total cost for the entire project. In addition to cost information, the WP statement should include a technical description and the standards of the package deliverable, along with reporting and completion requirements.

The Statement of Work (SOW), preferably written as a performance-based statement, describes the effort to produce the specific deliverables of a WP. The SOW outlines what, where, and when (schedule and milestones) required work should be performed. The statement does not usually describe how the work will be accomplished, but it does include standards, requirements, and the acceptance criteria. Figure 5.5 is an example of a simplified SOW (for a WP in our example project).

Work package number and title: Customer Relationship Management (CRM) Information Seminar: WBS Ref# 1.3.1

Type of activity: Conference

Timetable: One day (three two-hour sessions). Start date = 02/21/yyyy.

Preparations: Completed in advance

Objectives: The objective of the package is to inform team members of our organization about the advantages of the CRM system and to introduce the basic concepts.

Description of the contents, the work plan, the steps, the approach, or the methodology: One representative from the software company and one internal trainer will coordinate three two-hour seminars to introduce the advantages and basic concepts of the CRM system. The CRM company representative will introduce another client who has successfully implemented the product. The other client will make a brief presentation about its experience. The CRM company will distribute product brochures. The seminar leader will discuss the decisions and steps already taken, including their rationale, and present the tentative installation schedule. The CRM representative and our company partner will present the basic concepts of the system, its advantages, and the expected benefits.

• Event publicity will be performed upon commencement of this work package.
• Presentations will be made with prepared slides.
• Rooms with necessary equipment will be rented.

Partners involved: Charlene Budd, HR trainer (external: CRM representative).

Deliverables, expected results, milestone for the overall package: We expect to encourage involvement in the new system, elicit suggestions for smooth implementation, answer questions, and overcome possible objections.

FIGURE 5.5   Simplified Statement of Work

Although Figure 5.5 illustrates a simplified SOW, you must consider the items listed below for a complete statement:

• A product description for all required products
• Defined work standards
• Location of work
• Delineation of all necessary interfaces
• Specified dates coordinated with the overall project

- Measurable checkpoints
- List of required logs and reports
- A provision for exception reporting
- A discussion of possible constraints
- Special requirements (such as security clearances, travel, specific training)
- Clearly defined quality criteria
- Formal acceptance requirements.

The SOW differs from a WBS dictionary entry in that the former is written only for the WPs (the lowest level element of the WBS), whereas the dictionary entries describe each WBS element and are not written with nearly as much detail as the SOW. Another form of the SOW is a general one that is sometimes provided by the project sponsor as part of the project charter. It has the same characteristics as those described for the WP but covers the overall project. This general form is often called a *statement of objectives* (SOO), and it provides only the basic top-level objectives of the project. It is similar to a request for proposals (RFP) and specifies the operational and technical requirements of the project. It can be used to develop the WBS, WP, and SOW.

We cannot overemphasize the importance of management support and authorization in project management. Authorization comes up in this chapter as an important part of defining the work of the project. The first EVMS criterion requires that all the work elements of the project be authorized and defined, even if all the future details are not yet known. The extent of the work in a project is known as the project's scope.

A work breakdown structure (WBS) is most commonly used for project definition and can be represented as a diagram, chart, or indented list. The level of detail in the WBS representation will vary depending on the complexity of the project. Each element of the WBS should be described in detail in a WBS dictionary entry.

Control (cost) accounts (CAs) are closely tied with the WBS, primarily through their subparts, the work packages (WPs). CAs are the major element of the accounting system set up at juncture points of the WBS and elements of the organizational breakdown structure. They constitute the basis for performance measurement and should be established at a work level where management reporting is meaningful. A WP describes a discrete unit of work at the lowest level of the WBS and is performed by a specific individual or department of the organization. The statement of work (SOW) describes the full extent of each work package.

DISCUSSION QUESTIONS

1. What are the advantages and disadvantages of constructing a WBS using objectives or deliverables rather than activities?

2. A project is planned to produce some desired result. Should the project planners be concerned with any results that are not to be produced? Why or why not?

3. Define *project scope* and discuss the ramifications of scope creep.

4. What are the four primary elements of consideration in any project plan?

5. Discuss your preference for constructing the WBS in chart or list format.

6. What is an appropriate level of detail in the WBS? Why?

7. What is the primary reason for establishing CAs?

8. Where are WPs depicted, and what do they describe?

9. What would you include in a SOW that describes a WP?

10. Do you think you could use the "Obstacles and Required Conditions" technique to effectively solicit the intermediate and minor objectives of the project? Why or why not?

CHAPTER 6

The Organization (Criteria 2–5)

The breakdown of the project's objectives has been covered and there is still a substantial amount of work to do on the breakdown scheduling, but first we need to look at the structure of the organization. EVMS Criteria 2 through 5 require both an analysis of the organizational structure and integration along several lines of the project's work components and the components of the organization.

In this chapter, we examine how organizations are structured and the challenges you will encounter with each type. The project manager must scrutinize the organization to identify all the processes he or she must understand and with which he or she must work. Then it is possible to isolate all the integration points between the project's components and the organization's structure.

ORGANIZATIONAL CONFIGURATIONS

Every organization has some managerial structure that is expressed in a formal organizational chart or informally followed. These structures are usually classified in three general types by the way the reporting levels of the organization's members are arranged. The three types have many different names, but they are usually referred to as:

- Functional style
- Matrix style
- Project-oriented style.

There are many subdivisions, variations, and combinations of these styles, and organizational style might vary across different segments of the same organization.

Functional Style

Most organizations use the *functional* style, which divides the organization into operational units according to their functions—marketing, sales, operations, research and development, recruiting and training, financial accounting and reporting, and production. All members of each functional area report directly or indirectly through middle managers to the senior management of their respective functional areas. Each member usually has only one direct supervisor. Large projects are often separated into functional pieces, and their management is then maintained within the various departments.

When a project crosses functional boundaries, the functional structure usually gives the project manager little control over the project team members because they are managed and evaluated more directly by their functional managers. In addition, the functional organization is not adept at providing administrative assistance to the project manager because he or she has no functional role.

To be successful in this environment, a project manager must be a skilled negotiator and motivator. The project manager must both convince the functional head that assisting in completion of the project is in the department's best interest and convince the potential team members of the project's challenges and opportunities. Establishing a project management office (PMO) can often help overcome many of the difficulties encountered by the project manager in a functional organization.

Matrix Style

The *matrix* style is typically more responsive than the functional style for the project manager. The word *matrix*, as used for a style of organizational management, is taken from its definition as an array of mathematical elements that can be combined to form sums and products with similar arrays. A member of an organization with a matrix style usually reports to the functional manager but also is expected to have a dotted line to or part-time relationship with other managers. The project team is a new array of members formed from the functional arrays. The strength (weak, balanced, or strong) of the matrix style depends on the amount of supervision that is shared between the managers. Part of a project team formed from an organization's functional areas is illustrated in Figure 6.1.

Project Task / Group Function	Training	Software Distribution	Policies and Procedures
Human Resources	Member of the Project Team		
Technical Writers			Member of the Project Team
Information Systems		Member of the Project Team	

FIGURE 6.1   Project Team Member Matrix

The project manager is given more direct authority in the matrix-style organization because the staff members are usually assigned for part of their time to the project and the project manager. However, the project manager should be aware of potential problems similar to those in the functional organization. Because the team members' time often is divided between the project and the functional area, the project manager must be aware of the amount of time that team members actually spend on the project. In an extreme case, the functional manager may wish to charge as much time to projects as possible to reduce the department's expense; therefore, it is imperative that the project manager be alert to potential problems.

Project-Oriented Style

The project manager has the most authority in the organizational structure with a *project-oriented* style. Some organizations, such as contractors of various types, consulting companies, law firms, and public accounting firms, are particularly suited to the project-oriented style. Others may have instituted a management structure based on a process of treating all work as projects. In a fully project-oriented (project-organized) environment, each project group has its own functional operations, support, and team members reporting to the equivalent of a project manager. This structure is similar to a cell structure design in a manufacturing firm.

Because a project is a temporary construct, the personnel and team relationships are usually temporary as well. Complex projects require effective communication paths between team members of varying technical skills and abilities and with project sponsors and/or owners. Because of these issues, the project manager must use a simple and consistent communication system, such as that required by the EVMS reporting mechanisms.

Even in a project-oriented organizational arrangement, executives with functional expertise in major functional areas typically make up the executive management team.

EVMS CRITERION 2

Identify the program organizational structure, including the major subcontractors responsible for accomplishing the authorized work, and define the organizational elements in which work will be planned and controlled.

This criterion requires identifying and defining two primary elements of the performing organizational structure: those *accomplishing* the work of the project and those *planning and controlling* the project. These two elements almost assuredly will cross the organization's normal functional boundaries and include entities totally outside the organization, as will be the case for subcontracting portions of the project. This will entail creating an organizational breakdown structure (OBS), which will be similar in appearance to the work breakdown structure (WBS).

Organizational Breakdown Structure

The OBS is a graphical representation of the hierarchical management structure of the organization or organizations responsible for completing the project. It designates the areas responsible for the various components of the project. Like the WBS, it is broken down in detail to the lowest levels of management necessary to control the project and identifies the accountability and authority of the functional area.

Like the WBS, the OBS can be graphically displayed in a variety of formats. Figure 6.2 is an illustration of part of an OBS in a chart format.

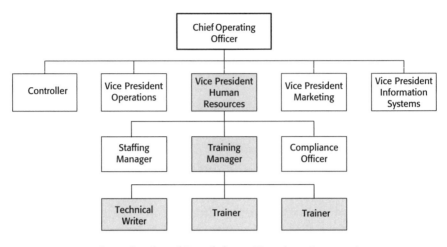

FIGURE 6.2   Organizational Breakdown Structure Segment

A project's OBS can be constructed in the same way as one for the entire organization. The OBS, however, portrays only the organizational units, or individuals, directly responsible for completing some element of the WBS.

Project Staffing

The project manager will need a comprehensive knowledge of the organization to identify and assign project roles. Constructing the OBS is an excellent way for the project manager to gain an understanding of responsibilities, authority, relationships, and staffing opportunities. The first step in getting staff resources is to identify the required skills for the WBS elements and then to determine whether and where the skills exist in the organization. A timing plan is necessary for establishing when and how long resources will be required; however, that requirement falls under the criteria for scheduling and is discussed in Chapter 7. For now, although we are concerned with *who will do what*, we are not necessarily concerned with *when*.

Many interfaces and existing relationships within the organization must be considered as the project plan is developed. Formal reporting relationships should be obvious in the OBS, but the project manager must look at the informal relationships that exist in every organization. Because components of a complex project certainly will cross the technical boundaries within the organization, sensitivity to these technical relationships will increase the probability of project success. Although interpersonal relationships can enhance assignment opportunities, they can also create boundaries similar to technical ones.

The project manager also must be aware of any constraints that may limit the assignment of project elements. The constraints may include legal determinations such as collective bargaining agreements, but the project manager should not overlook possible problems among project team members, who may have preferences and preconceived expectations for certain assignments.

Criterion 2 requires identifying the organizational structures that will be involved in the project. Remember that the requirement extends only a few levels into the WBS. It will be the responsibility of the subcontractors or structural management units to provide resources for the delivery of assigned project objectives. When there is a subcontracted component of the project, a member of the primary organization must be designated to manage the outside effort. This manager should have the same authority and responsibility as other control account managers and have the ability to ensure the proper performance of the subcontractor.

OBS Limitations

Cleland and Ireland list several limitations of the organizational chart:

- It fails to show the nature and limits of the activities required to attain the objectives.

- It does not reflect the myriad reciprocal relationships between peers, associates and many others. . . .
- It is a static, formal portrayal of the organizational structure. . . .
- It . . . neglects the informal, dynamic relationships that are constantly at play in the environment.
- It may confuse organizational position with status and prestige (Cleland and Ireland 2002, 270).

They are absolutely correct when they say that the formal organizational structure does not reveal how individuals work and interact with others.

The OBS is necessary to depict the formal framework and hierarchy of the organization. Of course, more detail is required when work packages (WPs) are described and particularly when the schedule timeline is generated. Also, the project manager must be able to relate the elements of the WBS and the OBS. For that we look to the third criterion.

EVMS CRITERION 3

Provide for the integration of the company's planning, scheduling, budgeting, work authorization, and cost accumulation processes with each other, and as appropriate, the program work breakdown structure and the program organizational structure.

Now the criteria begin to address the issue of integration. The first criterion to do so is a tough one. The first part of the criterion requires tying together the organization's major functions; that can be a very difficult requirement for many organizations, especially those that are functionally organized.

One way to satisfy this criterion is to have a management control system and an integrated data store such as those commonly associated with enterprise resource planning (ERP) systems. A formal ERP system is certainly not the only way, but there must be a mechanism where all project elements can be readily visible to all the planning, scheduling, authorizing, and accounting functions of the organization.

To meet the requirements of this criterion, it is helpful to use at least two organizational constructs: a linear responsibility chart (LRC) and a control account plan (CAP).

Linear Responsibility Chart

Once we have constructed the WBS and the OBS, we can connect the elements of each. The LRC is a matrix view of the intersection of the elements of the WBS and the OBS, and it is known by several names. It is sometimes termed the *responsibility assignment matrix* (Humphreys 2002, 100) and "has been called the *linear organization chart,* the *responsibility interface matrix,* the *matrix responsibility chart,* the *linear chart,* and the *functional chart*" (Cleland and Ireland 2002, 271).

An LRC illustrates which elements of the WBS are performed or managed by the elements of the OBS and to what degree. In other words, it details the responsibility of each category of functional area for its assigned WBS element of the project.

In the matrix view, there are rows, columns, and cells like those you would see in an ordinary spreadsheet showing project data—the WBS elements, the responsible organizational units, and the extent to which the units are responsible for each WBS element. The data may be laid out using the rows, columns, and cells for whichever of the three LRC elements[1] is preferred in each, but the data typically are located in the manner illustrated in Figure 6.3. The innermost cells depict the level of responsibility for the organizational unit that is responsible for the management of a work package. Other

---

[1] That is, who is responsible, in what way, to fulfill accomplishment of a WBS component?

graphical representations of the LRC use the standard symbols of a flow-type diagram, as shown earlier in Figure 6.2.

WBS Elements / OBS Elements			Implementation WBS 1.3					Other 1.n
			CRM Training WBS 1.3.2				Other 1.3.n	
			User Training WBS 1.3.2.3			Other 1.3.2.n		
			Publish WBS 1.3.2.3.1	Distribute WBS 1.3.2.3.2	Conduct WBS 1.3.2.3.3			
Department of Human Resources		V.P.					A	P
		Assistant				N		
		Clerk	N		N			
	Training Area	Manager	S	S	S			
		Technical Writer	P					
		Trainer A			P			
		Trainer B		P				
	Other H.R.				N	C		
Other Departments			N		N	N		

P = Primary Responsibility; S = General Supervision; C = Consultant; N = Notification; A = Approval

FIGURE 6.3   Portion of a Linear Responsibility Chart

Regardless of the type of LRC representation, several components and steps will ensure its accuracy, ease of comprehension, and completeness. Determine the WBS components that will be delivered by each functional area by enlisting the cooperation and assistance of members of the functional areas.

1. Identify organizational units (most often by required category of competency) for different kinds of activity:
2. Primary performance
   • Cross-training
   • Supervising

- Consulting
- Notification
- Review
- Approval.
3. Analyze and review the LRC with all stakeholders to determine where activities should be restructured and to look for other possible improvements.

The LRC provides an excellent point for a review of the planning that went into the construction of the WBS and the OBS. A review at this time presents an opportunity to check for controls in the project plan and the potential for risks to the project. System components to verify include:

- Internal controls, such as verification requirements and segregation of duties
- Compensating factors where traditional internal controls are not feasible
- Cross-training or other types of backup
- Review and approval systems
- Potential risks (legal, financial, technical) and costs to eliminate or minimize
- Corrective action plans.

The LRC can also be a useful place to look for the grouping of work packages that can be summarized to formulate control accounts.

Control Account Plan

To satisfy EVMS criteria, any system—automated or manual—must incorporate a CAP. This plan is the establishment, control, and reporting from control (cost) accounts (CAs). As the WBS product (or deliverable) is subdivided at lower WBS levels, the effort required by each subproduct is assigned to a functional organization unit. CAs must be defined narrowly enough that they do not cross any structural boundaries in the organization so that they can be summarized in the OBS as well as in the WBS. The CA data should be maintained in a common database in order to provide the project information that will be accessed by all of the organization's functional areas.

The concept of the CA was introduced earlier, but Criterion 3 implicitly requires its establishment. Figure 6.4 illustrates the location and makeup of general ledger CAs. They are the heart of EVMS and will be referenced more frequently as we proceed through the discussion of the EVMS criteria.

The CA is the pivotal point for planning, controlling, and reporting the project's activity. These accounts are the focus of budgeting, scheduling, assignments, data collection, progress assessment, and status determination. The difficulty of the activity and the ability of the management at each level should determine the levels at which CAs are established. The CA is the lowest level of planning and control necessary for management reporting. At this level, management should be able to identify any factors that might cause significant cost or schedule variances.

Subdividing the WBS often results in separate elements that are produced by the same functional area of the organization. For example, software development might be a part of different WBS sublevel products. Some care must be exercised so that the WBS is not subdivided so extensively that existing management structures are compromised.

The responsible organizational level is a function of the company's management span of control and upper management's desire to delegate the responsibility for WBS elements to lower management levels. In identifying CAs, the contractor is expected to establish organizational responsibilities at meaningful and appropriate levels. Otherwise, the contractor's existing management control systems and responsibility assignments may be affected adversely (Department of Defense 2005a, 3.1.4).

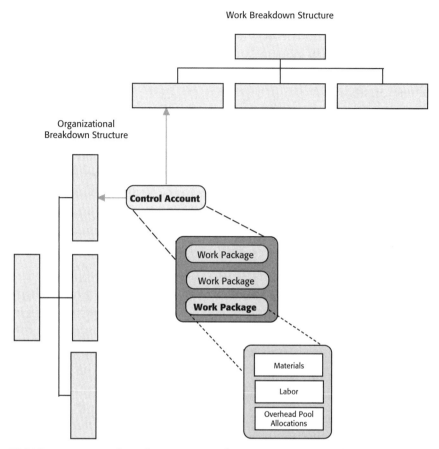

FIGURE 6.4   Work Packages, Control Accounts, WBS, and OBS

EVMS CRITERION 4

Identify the company organization or function responsible for controlling overhead (indirect costs).

One of the elements of providing the OBS is to clearly identify the managerial position responsible for establishing and controlling indirect costs. This position must be clearly identified in the OBS. The management entity should have the authority to approve or to avoid the expenditure of resources.

In addition, EVMS requires a clear definition of the overhead costing system and the policies and procedures set up to control indirect costs. In the policies and procedures, there must be a formal assignment of the required duties and a prescription of the limits of responsibility.

There is usually little argument about the direct costs of a project. The amount of time a team member spends can be tracked to each project on which he or she works, but who decides how much of vacation time and employee benefit programs or the accounting department's time (overhead and indirect costs) is to be allocated to a variety of project and non-project work? Criterion 4 requires the identification of those responsible for overhead allocation and implies that they should be responsible for an equitable and consistent allocation.

Overhead/indirect costs are identified as all costs not originating from direct material purchases and direct labor. They also may include costs that are part of delivering the product, but not usually or historically charged to the product. The key identifier for indirect costs is that they must be allocated on an arbitrary basis; that is, units of production cannot directly measure them. Indirect costs and their allocation are detailed in a later chapter on budgeting. For now, Criterion 4 requires the identification of the functional unit responsible for controlling such expenses.

An interesting point about indirect costs and project costs in general is that the type of contract into which the parties entered for the project can influence their control and reporting. Contract types can vary from cost types, such as *cost plus fixed fee, cost plus incentive,* and *cost plus percentage,* to fixed types, such as *firm fixed, fixed plus incentive,* and *unit price.* In a *cost-type* project, the provider is interested in allocating as much expense to the project as possible, while the recipient is interested in checking expenses very closely. In a *fixed-type* contract, the provider attempts to increase the project profit by minimizing expenses. The EVMS criteria attempt to provide controls that will restrict "gaming" the system.

EVMS CRITERION 5

Provide for integration of the program work breakdown structure and the program organizational structure in a manner that permits cost and schedule performance measurement by elements of either or both structures as needed.

The CA is the key to fulfilling the requirements of this criterion. CAs are established at juncture points of the WBS and the OBS, and therefore they will reflect measurement from elements of either or both structures. When building the OBS, there are natural points where CAs are assigned. Those same points are present in a well-constructed WBS. The organizational elements can report from their CAs, or reporting can be accomplished from the project's breakdown of the deliverables in the WBS. The reporting should be the same from either angle; as a matter of fact, it must be the same to satisfy Criterion 5.

There are many project management reports that are helpful to all project stakeholders. One of the important points of the fifth criterion is that the reporting will be integrated because there is a common point for performance measurement of cost, schedule, and technical perspectives. EVMS also requires that these standard measurements be expressed in a standard measuring unit, usually the dollar. It does not matter how the organization is structured; it can be in any of the styles discussed at the beginning of this chapter. The information available to senior management is the same as the information used by the functional manager when looking at team work assignments and the same as the information seen by the project manager when looking at the project structure.

The contract performance report (CPR) is most often used for EVMS projects; it is covered in detail later, where Criterion 27 requires the generation of management information. The CPR and other reports can vary in format depending on the contracting agency's requirements, but they are used to provide comparisons of EVMS measurements. In general, the reports will contain information about cumulative cost, cost/schedule performance, current budgeted value (cost) of the project, estimates at completion, cost and schedule variances, and narrative descriptions of status and problems.

Keep in mind that reports should be kept to higher levels of the WBS/OBS, almost always at the CA level. That is sufficient for management reporting; however, the project manager may need more detailed information, particularly about the status of specific work packages.

Criteria 2 through 5 separate the first criterion that defines the project's work from the following criteria that begin the planning of that work. This intervening set of criteria ensures that organizational elements are well defined, allowing project work requirements and organizational responses to be integrated prior to detailed planning and execution.

The definition of the organization originates with its organizational style. Organizations are configured in some form of three general classes: functional, matrix, and project-oriented. The functional style, the most common, is organized by groups that provide departmentalized services such as marketing or accounting. A project manager in the functional organization must have special skills because the project team members will have primary responsibilities to their functional departments.

The project manager has more authority in the matrix style because the team members are assigned directly to the project for at least part of their time. However, it is in the project style that the project manager has the most authority. The project teams in organizations such as consulting companies will have at least some of the functional services within the team.

Criterion 2 requires the identification and definition of the elements of the organization(s) that will plan, control, and accomplish the project's work. An organizational breakdown structure (OBS) is best used for satisfying this criterion; like the work breakdown structure (WBS), the OBS can be represented in different formats. The OBS has several limitations in its portrayal of the organizational relationships.

Criterion 3 can be quite difficult to satisfy because many organizations do not have well-integrated functionality. A linear responsibility chart (LRC) is helpful with some aspects of the integration effort, and a control account plan (CAP) is absolutely necessary. The control account (CA) is the pivotal point for planning, controlling, and reporting the project activity.

It is obvious that EVMS considers overhead or indirect costs a vulnerable aspect of project management; Criterion 4 is devoted exclusively to their control. The control of overhead is addressed further in the criteria concerning budgeting, recording, and controlling costs. Criterion 5 requires integration of the project's work breakdown and its organizational structure so that measurements are permitted from either or both structures. The contract performance report is the primary method for reporting these integrated EVMS measurements.

DISCUSSION QUESTIONS

1. Identify the organizational style of your organization. List the advantages and disadvantages of the style for your organization.

2. List your organization's major functional processes.

3. Identify the normal interactions between departments in the organization.

4. Identify the primary staff members and any external influences in each of the functional processes.

5. Identify some informal working relationships or reciprocal arrangements within the organization.

6. Identify any current cross-training practices or other types of personnel backup.

CHAPTER 7

The Schedule (Criteria 6–8)

"The first 90 percent of a project takes 90 percent of the time; the last 10 percent takes the other 90 percent of the time."

—UNKNOWN

A comprehensive project schedule, done properly, is the basic tool for EVMS. It helps determine activity and total project duration, shows the sequence of work, identifies task and resource dependencies, provides the ability to measure progress, and shows time periods when funding is required.

Criteria 6, 7, and 8 deal with project schedules. Criterion 6 requires a sequencing of work that identifies task interdependencies, while Criterion 7 requires schedule indicators for measuring progress. Criterion 8 mandates a time-phased budget baseline, which introduces the criteria on project budgeting.

Two important considerations are associated with preparing a project schedule: schedule uncertainty and management support.

SCHEDULE UNCERTAINTY

The one major project problem that occurs over and over again is that projects overrun their promised completion dates. There are many reasons for project overruns; for example, not working closely with the end user, inadequate planning, incomplete information, and lack of commitment. They usually occur not because of some calamity or a crucial failure but because of the accumulation of day-after-day, small-task-duration overruns.

As you have no doubt experienced, a project's greatest uncertainty is its completion date (which also affects cost). When the project plan is laid out in black and white with activities and times, it becomes a very deterministic view. The project manager must understand the effects of probability and educate the stakeholders concerning the challenges of accurate estimating and its effect on a predetermined schedule.

Challenges in Constructing a Realistic Schedule

One of the major deterrents to achieving a reasonable project schedule is having a completion date forced by some other requirements of the organization. Such a situation is difficult to reconcile, and the best solution is to request and acquire adequate resources. A more prevalent problem is due to the fact that the completion date results from the accumulation of the multitudes of individual task duration estimates.

Estimating Task Times

We believe the most important aspect of duration estimates is to have an open and honest relationship with those who supply the estimates. Very often the people providing the estimates are members of the staff responsible for completing the task. It does not take very long to learn how to play the task estimation game. For example, if estimates are always reduced, the staff quickly learns to make them longer. If they are multitasking on several projects, they will extend completion dates to allow for the uncertainties of moving from one task to another. If the project staff members have regular responsibilities in the organization as well as being assigned to one or more special projects, they must bias the project task estimates to protect their jobs.

Although professional estimators are more often used for cost estimating, they also can be used effectively to determine the expected duration of crucial activities. Whether using outside professionals or project staff, it is vital that they understand which estimating methods are to be used and the reasoning behind the selection.

Even with the best of estimates, individual tasks often take longer than planned. It is easy to see that days of missed task completions easily add up to *months* of delays for the entire project and a missed completion date. This is a mystery to most people, especially when we know that most people give themselves plenty of safety when they estimate a task's duration. Even when management insists on reducing time estimates, the project team members are somewhat assured that they still have a margin of protection. Even new employees quickly learn the rules of the game and make the necessary adjustments. The question remains: What happens to all their protection, and what can be done about it?

Dysfunctional Behaviors

At least four behaviors easily waste the protection built into individual task times. The first is the *student syndrome*—waiting until the last minute to start the task, just as many students delay studying until the night before the big test. A project task originally estimated at three weeks actually may only take two weeks; however, it can still be a week late if it isn't started until the last week of its schedule.

What if we don't fall prey to the student syndrome, and the three-week task (actually two weeks of hands-on activity) is started on time? Won't there be a plus of one week for the project when the task is finished early? Well, not usually! Our second problem—*no early work transfers*—is that little work is transferred to the next phase when a task is finished early. Part of the problem is that there are incentives for not reporting the task's early completion, such as avoiding management's reducing the next task estimate even more stringently. Of course, we are often late in passing work from a task to those dependent on it—resulting in no early passes, only late passes. Therefore, dependent tasks are late getting started, and eventually the project misses its completion date. Besides, if there is some extra time before the task's scheduled delivery date, the task deliverable can be improved—and that leads to the next behavioral pattern.

The third trait is known as *Parkinson's Law*: Work expands to fill the time available. First articulated by C. Northcote Parkinson in his book *Parkinson's Law* (Parkinson 1957), this trait is similar to the *no early work transfers* but has its own rationale. Just as any size closet soon will be filled, the same phenomenon occurs with any task time. We do what we can with the amount of space and time we have.

The final dysfunctional behavior is one that seems a bit counterintuitive. *Polychronicity*, the habit of *multitasking*, would seem to allow more tasks to be completed. Multitasking has been described as "playing a multiplicity of roles with ever more speed and carelessness" (Billet 2009). However, we must distinguish between good multitasking and harmful multitasking. Good multitasking happens when a task must be interrupted because of some outside reason, such as missing information or unavailable material. In that case, it makes perfect sense to work on another task—to multitask. Harmful multitasking occurs when one task is interrupted for no other reason than there are other tasks on which to work. Every time a resource changes tasks, there are switching costs: There is set-down time on the previous task and set-up time on the new task. Even the brain has to set down the old rules and set up the new ones. This type of multitasking is unnecessary and adds extended time to all the tasks involved.

Overcoming Schedule Problems

The EVMS performance measurements are needed in many ways, not the least of which is the very effective early indication if the project is going to be late or over budget. Techniques are needed to prevent schedule problems and minimize them when they occur.

Crashing a Project

Even the best project schedules often encounter difficulties that affect the completion date. There may be resource considerations or a business decision that mandates a shortened project. When the expected duration must be reduced, we refer to the process as *crashing*. A project can be crashed in several ways. One is to devote additional resources to certain activities; another is to reduce the project's complexity by eliminating some of its intermediate objectives or reducing its technical scope. The benefits of crashing must be weighed against the cost of additional resources or the loss of project deliverables.

When determining likely places to crash a project, be sure to select areas that will affect the completion date. There are many project activities whose durations have no immediate effect on the overall project duration. This might be attributed to the adequate availability of the necessary resources and skills, or it might be due to the independence of the activity. If other downstream tasks in the project are not dependent on the completion of a particular task, that first task's duration usually will not affect the overall project completion, and the task is not a good candidate for crashing.

Critical Chain Project Management

Too often, a schedule problem is a result of the behavior patterns described earlier, and changing human behavior is not easy. It is not something that happens by talking about it or even presenting logical proofs. There must be some compelling motivation.

Eli Goldratt (1997, 246) developed a system for project management that he called *critical chain project management* (CCPM). One function of the system operates to remove the protection time built into the individual task duration estimates and to place it strategically to protect critical points in the overall project schedule. Chapter 17 describes CCPM methodology.

Unnecessary Fixes

In Chapter 3, we presented W. Edwards Deming's idea of two kinds of variation that occur in systems. Repeating it here underscores an important point about making adjustments when schedule variances occur. Sometimes a problem is self-inflicted when schedule and resource adjustments are made without regard for differences in variation. *Common cause variation* is the result of expected variety in the normal course of events—the system is still in control. Making adjustments when a system is in control can put it out of control. *Special cause variation* is the result of unexpected events, malfunctioning activities, or both. Special cause variation is the reason for risk management, and that is when the project manager must act.

A Bit of Statistics and Probability

One of the problems of scheduling a project is that the task duration times are estimates. No one knows with certainty how long a specific piece of any schedule will take; it's a future event, and we don't have crystal balls. But even though unpredictable quantities regularly produce unpredictable results, there are ways to address task time uncertainty.

We can use the mathematical concept of subjective probability and some basic knowledge of human behavior to help us improve both our estimates and our control of projects. A barrier to accepting probability concepts is the reality that a task or a project, after the fact, can have only one outcome, while probabilities are based on repetition. The most familiar example is the coin toss and the number of heads that will result from a set of tosses. Because the probability of a head coming up on any one toss is 50 percent, the probability of two heads occurring in only two tosses is 25 percent (0.5 x 0.5), and so on. Unlike objective probabilities associated with coin tosses, task estimates are subjective. Nevertheless, we can use subjective probability theory to examine project estimates.

Look at the very simple set of tasks in Figure 7.1 (illustrating five different resources by shaded tasks). We'll assume that each task has been estimated, with a 90 percent degree of confidence, to be completed in 10 days. Does that mean that there is a 90 percent probability that the project can be completed in 50 days?

No. The probability of completing the project in 50 days is not 90 percent, or even 50 percent, because of task and resource dependencies on each path and the fact that both paths must be completed before the final task can be started. The degree of variation in the project's completion time increases dramatically as the number of tasks and converging paths increase.

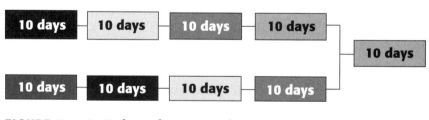

FIGURE 7.1   An Estimated 50-Day Project

In probability statistics, this phenomenon is sometimes referred to as the *multiplication rule*. This rule states that the probabilities of dependent events must be multiplied to produce the probability for all the events. Of course, there is a small probability that the project will be completed in 50 days or less, but there is a greater probability that it will be completed much later. The point is that the degree of variation widens as the number of tasks increases. The project manager must understand and also remind project stakeholders that a point estimate (a single estimated completion time of 10 days, for example) for a task is not precise.

Notice that five different resources are required in Figure 7.1. If the project manager focuses on each task's being completed on time (the estimated date), the resources will do their best to complete work by the due date. However, they may well insist on having sufficient protection built into their estimates.

The probability of 90 percent was used in Figure 7.1 because that is closest to the most common probability estimate that we have experienced. When people are asked how long it will take to complete a task, they will likely quote an estimate in which they have a high degree of confidence. One of the advantages of the program evaluation and review technique (PERT) (discussed in a later section of this chapter) is that it uses three estimates. The method asks for not only the safe or pessimistic estimate (the 90 percent confidence one) but also the most likely and the shortest possible or optimistic estimate.

Figure 7.2 illustrates the elements of a statistical distribution given three estimates, with the earliest possible completion setting the minimum time required, the most likely estimate (which could be the mode, median, or mean) having more weight, and the pessimistic estimate (point "S") having a very high degree of confidence.

Many distributions exhibit the long right-hand tails shown in Figure 7.2, such as the Beta PERT, popularly used in Monte Carlo simulations of task and project completion times, and the lognormal distribution shown in Figure 7.3, which incorporates variability as well as average values.[1]

---

[1]The ability to model spikes or jumps in expected results makes this distribution a favorite for modeling stock prices.

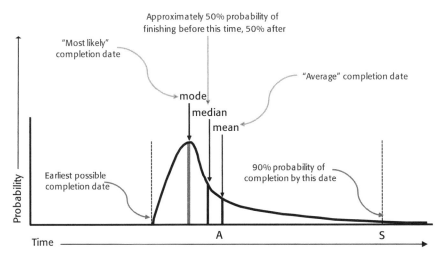

FIGURE 7.2   Statistical Distribution

EVMS CRITERION 6

Schedule the authorized work in a manner that describes the sequence of work and identifies significant task interdependencies required to meet the requirements of the program.

The two important words in this criterion about the project schedule are *sequence* and *interdependencies.* You must use a scheduling system that describes and identifies both the sequence and the interdependencies of the project activities. Criteria 7 and 8 mandate additional basic elements of a good project schedule, but Criterion 6 requires only the identification of sequence and interdependencies.

Sequence of Work

First, of course, the schedule must show all the activities that will make up the project. The work breakdown structure (WBS), created as a requirement of Criterion 1, identified the project objectives or deliverables (sometimes activities), but now those WBS elements must be translated into activities that will accomplish the project

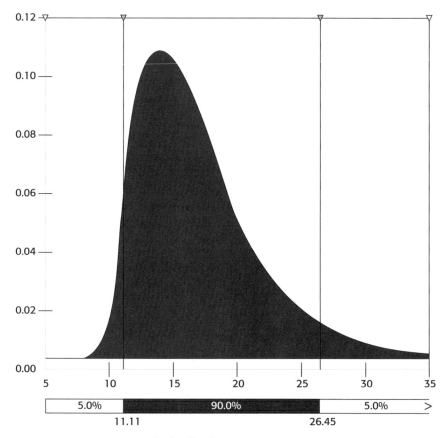

FIGURE 7.3   Lognormal Distribution

objectives. The activities can be decomposed until specific items of work or tasks contain enough detail to ensure adequate management and progress reporting.

Rob Newbold (2008) has estimated that a cross-functional group composed of credible individuals can complete in about four full days a high-level project network of one to two years of work involving about 50 people working on the project.

The schedule should show the sequence in which the tasks must be performed, according to precedence rules resulting from a variety of constraints. The order in which tasks can be performed usually arises from three causes. We refer to the cause as *technical* when a second task, the successor, simply cannot be started until another task, the predecessor, is finished; some element of the first task contributes to the second task. Priorities may also be established when tasks are completed in a *preferred order,* even without any technical or logical dependencies. A third cause for a particular sequencing could be the result of a *resource constraint* under which a specific resource cannot be used on a successor task until that resource has completed the predecessor task. The sequencing of the work should identify any significant task interdependencies.

Task Dependencies

First let's define the various forms of project task dependence. Tasks are *independent* if they have no effect on each other. They are *mutually exclusive* if one cannot occur in the presence of the other. They are *collectively exhaustive* if one of a set must occur, and they are *dependent* (interdependent) if they have some effect on each other.

Task interdependencies can exist in four different ways. (The first part of the relationship is the *predecessor* task and the second part is the *successor.*)

1. The *Finish-to-Start* relationship, the most common, means that a predecessor task (or tasks) must be finished before the successor task can start. To construct a small concrete slab, a frame must be built and concrete must be mixed before the concrete can be poured into the frame. A subroutine of a computer program must be written before testing can begin on the subroutine. Although many tasks must be scheduled as Finish-to-Start, all tasks cannot be scheduled in this way, or the project will take far too long. Many tasks can be overlapped in time.

2. The *Start-to-Start* relationship means that a predecessor task must at least be started before the successor task can be started. Priming the walls of a room must be started before putting

up the wallpaper can be started. The design for a program subroutine must be started before any coding can be started.

3. The *Finish-to-Finish* relationship means that the successor task can start without regard to the start of the predecessor task but cannot finish until its predecessor task is finished. The design of a computer subroutine can begin as soon as some client specifications are received, but the design cannot be completed until all client specifications are complete.

4. The *Start-to-Finish* relationship is rare and can usually be represented in one of the first three relationships. We have even heard the argument that this option is not necessary. When used, it means that the predecessor task must at least be started before the successor task can be completed, or it might be said that the start of the predecessor task causes the finish of the successor task. The terms *predecessor* and *successor* get fuzzy in this relationship. In the coding of computer subroutines, the programmer may continue to tinker with the code until testing starts. The start of testing must end any coding, or the testing will be invalid. A very similar example is expressed in the Finish-to-Start relationship, but in the latter case there is a presumption that the finishing of the predecessor (coding) would not necessarily begin the successor (testing). In this case, the coding might continue indefinitely unless the start of testing ends it.

To schedule the sequence and dependency of project activities, we highly recommend an automated scheduling system that uses techniques similar to the *critical path method* (CPM) of network scheduling. The effect of CPM is to identify the longest path of dependent tasks through the entire project schedule, called the *critical path,* and thereby provide the estimated project duration. Critical chain is a similar method. Most automated project management systems use CPM or a similar network. Manual charting of task sequence and interdependency can be done successfully only on very simple projects.

SCHEDULE REPRESENTATION AND EVALUATION

The many elements of a complete project schedule should be illustrated in a graphical representation. The elements include descriptions of the activities, sequence of events, task durations, start and end times, task interdependencies, milestones, and resources.

There are many ways to represent and articulate the project schedule, and they have been developed for different reasons or because of particular issues. Some of the most common are lists, bar charts, arrow diagrams, and more sophisticated network diagrams. Some of these representations, such as PERT, use statistical formulas to estimate the most likely project schedule.

Lists

The easiest schedule to develop and maintain is a simple list of activities or deliverables. A list can show the grouping of tasks by using indentation similar to the levels of the WBS. A list also can show the sequence of the schedule elements by their order. It cannot, however, convey the required information on interdependency without a great deal of creativity and manipulation; nor can it graphically display any time conditions as a bar chart can.

Bar Charts

The bar chart is more visually oriented. It shows activities in bars, with their length depicting time requirements, and it can indicate some sequence. Again, however, the bar chart is limited in its ability to show interdependency without some further relational mechanism. Several enhancements have been developed for the simple bar chart.

The Gantt chart is a form of bar chart, and there are a host of references to it, starting almost 100 years ago. We'll quote one definition from TechTarget (Rouse 2004):

A Gantt chart is a horizontal bar chart developed as a production control tool in 1917 by Henry L. Gantt, an American engineer and social scientist. . . . Frequently used in project management, a Gantt chart provides a graphical illustration of a schedule that helps to plan, coordinate, and track specific tasks in a project. Gantt charts may be simple versions created on graph paper or more complex automated versions created using applications such as Microsoft Project or Excel.

Figure 7.4 illustrates a portion of a Gantt chart for the CRM example project. In a typical Gantt chart, the activities are listed down the left side and dates are shown across the top. Task start time and duration are indicated by the placement and length of a horizontal bar. Shading a portion of the bar can show work progress. Gantt charts are an excellent way to show planned and actual work progress, but some do not illustrate the necessary information for task dependencies. There is not a good way to determine what effect a late task will have on another task. (Figure 7.4 is an example of a chart that shows task connections.)

There are usually several other optional vertical columns between the list of activities and the date portion of the chart. These columns provide other information about each task, such as duration, staff member assigned, predecessor tasks, and priority information. The time periods can be in any time denomination, such as hours, days, or weeks.

Networks

A well-constructed network has an advantage over the standard bar chart in depicting task interdependencies and independencies. A disadvantage in the early network portrayals was a poor graphical representation of the time scale, but computer-generated networks have generally overcome this problem. There have been several variations of the networks method.

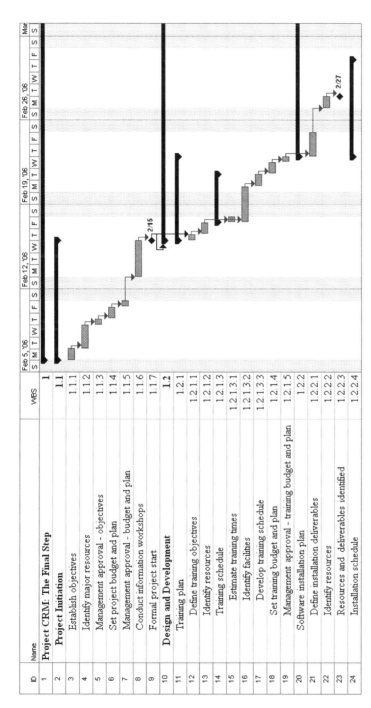

FIGURE 7.4   Portion of a Gantt Chart

Activity on Arrow and Activity on Node

These network designs are excellent for depicting the task sequence or precedence relationships of project activities. They are often called *arrow diagramming* or *precedence diagramming* methods. This type of network is constructed with lines (arrows) that show the flow of activity and are connected at points (nodes). The activities are shown on the arrows themselves (AOA) or on the nodes (AON). The latter is also called *activity in box* (AIB). Historically in AOA, the length of the arrow did not indicate the duration of the activity. In AON, the expected task duration is often listed along with the description of the activity. The PERT diagram shown in Figure 7.5 is a type of AON.

Program Evaluation and Review Technique

PERT was developed in the late 1950s by the U.S. Navy, with the cooperation of Booz-Allen Hamilton and the Lockheed Corporation, for the Polaris submarine missile program (Archibald 1987, 29). It was created as a method to expedite project completion and appears to have descended in some part from the line-of-balance method. PERT uses statistical probabilities to estimate task durations and the project completion date, and it has been closely associated with the CPM.

PERT can be represented as an AOA or AON network. In the AOA style, the tasks are depicted on the arrows (lines), and the nodes represent events or milestones. The network begins with a start node, from which the first task or set of tasks propagates. The first task line (or lines) is then connected to its successor task through a node, and all tasks are thus connected, forming the network. Sometimes a task is not immediately succeeded in time by another task. These tasks are usually connected by a dotted line from the ending node of the predecessor task with the start node of the successor task.

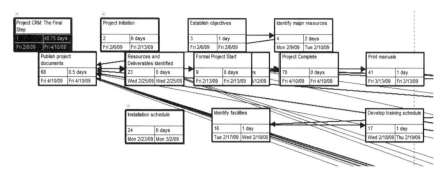

FIGURE 7.5   Portion of a PERT Diagram in AON Format

The task identification, its duration, and assigned resource (re-sources) are stated on the task line, and the length of the line can depict the expected duration. The nodes do not represent any pas-sage of time; therefore, events such as reviews or authorizations that will take time should not be shown as nodes. Instead, they should be shown as tasks with estimates of their duration. In EVMS, some nodes of the PERT chart often represent a measurement control or funding point. A major project can produce a complex PERT chart of many interconnecting lines and nodes, and it is much more con-venient to construct the network in logical pieces of the total project.

PERT is most often used in an attempt to produce a realistic proj-ect schedule. Undertaking that effort requires three duration esti-mates for each activity that represent a *pessimistic time* (p), a *most likely time* (m), and an *optimistic time* (o). The PERT process then calculates:

$$\text{the activity's mean time as } t = (p + 4m + o) \,/\, 6$$
$$\text{and a standard deviation as } s = (o - p) \,/\, 6.$$

Using the estimated mean times, the probability of completing the project in a given time can be calculated.

PERT is sometimes considered a probabilistic model because of the task estimation process. However, its one drawback is that it uses the mean task times to determine a single critical path. (There might be several, and they often change as the project progresses.) This feature tends to reduce the PERT model to a deterministic one. Projects progress more realistically in a stochastic manner and, as a result, the PERT project completion date projections are often short of the projects' actual completion dates. A Monte Carlo simulation can be performed on the network to ameliorate this built-in bias. A. R. Klingel has published calculations for a real network (Klingel 1966, 476–489), but software packages such as @Risk for Project™ (Palisade 2009) can easily perform Monte Carlo simulations.

Graphical Evaluation and Review Technique (GERT)

Pritsker and Happ (1966, 267–274) published their fundamentals of GERT (the first of a series) in the *Journal of Industrial Engineering*. GERT was a modification of PERT that simulated the uncertain nature of project activity by allowing loops through certain parts of the schedule and skipping other parts altogether. In reality, some activities are repeated and some are partially or never performed. This methodology computed activity distributions through Monte Carlo simulation.

Despite the advantages of GERT's probabilistic simulation techniques, very complex projects could result in networks that were difficult, even impossible, to interpret. In response, Pritsker and his associates developed an extension to GERT (Q-GERT) that provided greater flexibility in simulating multiteam and multiproject environments.

Critical Path Method

DuPont, Inc., developed CPM in about the same timeframe as PERT (Peterson 1965, 70). Some representations of a CPM network are similar to PERT charts, and they are often referred to as PERT/

CPM. The critical path in a project is the longest series in time of dependent activities; each task on a particular path of the project network is dependent on its predecessor. As the project progresses, the critical path can change (and very often does) as tasks are completed behind or, rarely, ahead of schedule.

The CPM includes several calculations, and they are easily performed in automated project management software. Basically, the method first determines the dependent relationships and duration for each activity in the project. A network using the relationships and durations is then constructed—usually as an AOA, but automated systems can identify the critical path in most network representations. The next step is to calculate both the earliest start and completion time and the latest start and completion time for each activity and use the results to calculate the slack for each activity. *Slack* is the difference between the early and late start and equals the amount of time an activity may be delayed without delaying the project. The critical path is the line of activities with zero slack.

As mentioned earlier, one variation on CPM is critical chain project management (Goldratt 1997), discussed in Chapter 17. CCPM identifies the critical path of both dependent tasks *and* dependent resources. The CPM usually resolves resource conflicts (resource leveling) after identifying the critical path and based on the resource requirements of the critical path. CCPM first levels the resources and then identifies the critical chain of dependent tasks.

EVMS CRITERION 7

Identify physical products, milestones, technical performance goals, or other indicators that will be used to measure progress.

Now we come to a primary element of EVMS—identifying the indicators on which the earned value will be calculated. We cannot enumerate all the ways to measure project progress, and this criterion does not specify a particular measurement method. It does require identifying *some* measurement techniques. They can be product deliveries, activity completion points, stated performance goals, or other indicators, but they must allow for a measurement of project progress.

In the Gantt chart illustrated in Figure 7.4, you may have noticed some milestone activities (small diamonds). They were placed at convenient measuring points in the schedule at approximately two-week intervals. This is a method of establishing measurement points that coincide with completed deliverables. For example, a contract WBS is often constructed entirely of deliverables, but they are almost always converted to activities for a project schedule. To be effective measurement indicators, milestones must be set frequently enough that their attainment can coincide closely with EVMS status requirements. Completion estimates must be made if a status is taken and there are few coincidental milestone achievements.

Another measurement indicator can be simply the completion of *work packages* (WPs) (activities). WPs should be established with a short duration so that performance measurements for status reporting will be more accurate. It is much easier to make an accurate estimate of the percentage complete when the activity covers only a short time span. This method is one example of realizing technical performance goals as expressed in Criterion 7.

EVMS CRITERION 8

Establish and maintain a time-phased budget baseline at the control account level against which program performance can be measured. Budget for far-term efforts may be held in higher-level accounts until an appropriate time for allocation at the control account level. Initial budgets established for performance measurement will be based on either internal management goals or the external customer-negotiated target cost, including estimates for authorized but undefinitized work. On government contracts, if an over-target baseline is used for performance measurement reporting purposes, prior notification must be provided to the customer.

The control accounts (CAs) in the control account plan—those identified in the discussion of Criterion 5—now come into more direct use as a requirement of Criterion 8. CAs were required at low-level control points during the construction of the WBS. As the work schedule is created from the WBS, the CAs are assigned to specific elements of the schedule. The dollar estimates established for each CA and now related to the project schedule will produce a budget baseline against which performance can be measured as the project progresses.

The Target Baseline

It is very important to understand the need for and use of a project baseline. In sporting events, a *baseline* is usually a boundary line for some part of the field of play so that progress can be measured and out-of-bounds play can be determined. We use a very similar meaning in project management: The project baseline is the boundary marker from which we can measure progress and determine what is included and excluded from our project. It is called the *performance measurement baseline (*PMB).

Most industry sources define the PMB in a manner similar to the definition by the Electronic Industries Alliance:

The total time-phased budget plan against which program performance is measured. It is the schedule for expenditure of the resources allocated to accomplish program scope and schedule objectives, and is formed by the budgets assigned to control accounts and applicable indirect budgets. The Performance Measurement Baseline also includes budget for future effort assigned to higher Work Breakdown Structure levels (summary level planning packages) plus any undistributed budget. Management

Reserve is not included in the baseline as it is not yet designated for specific work scope. (Electronic Industries Alliance 2002, 7).

By this point, you should have expressed the goals for the project in the planning phase, and a method is now required to assess progress toward achieving those goals. The PMB is basically a performance contract. Measurements are needed to judge whether the organization's investments are producing the anticipated benefits. If a project is not performing to its contract, decisions can be made to alter this investment and/or future investments.

Regular performance measurement promotes the effective use of resources and provides valuable information for improving other project efforts. Often the progress measurement is the basis for progress payments and project incentives. Measurement also is an obvious tool for identifying trends in the organization's performance.

All the work authorized for the project, whether performed internally or contracted externally, must be included in the PMB. Some of this work might not yet be defined in detail, but an estimate must be built into the budget. There is no need to construct CAs for an effort that is too far in the future to accurately break down the total budget cost. These estimates can be held at a higher level called *summary-level planning packages* (SLPP).

Summary-Level Planning Packages

Even though some specific work has been authorized, it might not be practical to assign it to CAs. When necessary, this work may be held at a higher level of the WBS or organizational breakdown structure (OBS) in planning packages. The work and its related budget must be time-phased and evaluated periodically. The budget for the SLLP must be tightly controlled to ensure that it is not used for some of the other areas of the project.

The SLPP is not to be used to postpone difficult and more detailed planning. It must be subdivided into the appropriate CAs as soon as possible and always before the actual work begins.

Controls and Reporting

As mentioned, there must be a baseline plan with time-phased budgets that coincide with the work schedules. The schedule must indicate milestones, each of which clearly delineates a specific quantity of work and is related directly to a CA. The quantity of work (it may be a work package) must also have an assigned budget amount. All the assigned budget values should sum to the totals of the CAs.

Funding from the CA plan should coincide with the schedule of the work. If work can begin earlier than the scheduled start date or must start later than that date, the change must be authorized as an exception. Shifting of schedules and budget components can seriously affect the performance measurements of EVMS. It is very important for accurate performance reporting to include any authorized schedule changes.

Over-Target Baseline

For EVMS, the project performance should be measured against the current authorized plan baseline. As a project progresses, it may be discovered that the remaining budget in the target baseline is grossly insufficient and will not produce meaningful progress measurements. To bring the project in line with reasonable control and measurement, it may become necessary to replan the remainder of the project and perhaps even to adjust some past measurements. This new plan is called an *over-target baseline* (OTB). Criterion 8 requires prior notification if the OTB will be used for performance reporting.

This is an unusual procedure, and every alternative must be examined before implementing an OTB. An OTB should be considered only if it is necessary for valid performance management. If the project stakeholders agree that the proposed OTB is reasonable and sufficient, the OTB becomes the approved baseline for the remaining progress measurements. All adjustments, both to the remaining portion of the project and to any existing variances, must be carefully documented and allow for audit procedures. The causes of the unsatisfactory baseline must also be investigated and documented so as to prevent future occurrences. The military has published a 37-page document called the *Over Target Baseline and Over Target Schedule Handbook* to provide guidance on formal rescheduling (Bembers et al. 2003).

This chapter discusses the three EVMS criteria for the project schedule—one of the three basic constraints of project management. The project manager must have an awareness and understanding of the challenges in building a realistic and attainable project schedule. Too often, one of the first challenges is dealing with a compulsory completion date, which is rapidly followed by the difficulties of accurately estimating task duration times and successfully meeting the project schedule. The problem often is a result of the four dysfunctional behavior traits known as the student syndrome, no early work transfers, Parkinson's Law, and polychronicity.

EVMS is a good early warning system for schedule problems, and a management system such as critical chain project management (CCPM) can help address the human behavior encumbrances. (Just don't try to fix a system that is already in control.) Understanding a little bit of statistics and probability can help the project manager in dealing with task time estimates.

Criterion 6 requires a project schedule that describes the sequence and interdependencies of the activities. The sequence of the tasks can be affected by technical or resource constraints or simply be the result of some preferred order. Task dependencies are expressed in four relationships: Finish-to-Start, Start-to-Start, Finish-to-Finish, and Start-to-Finish, although the last one is rarely used.

It is virtually impossible to manually handle all the challenges of scheduling a project, but fortunately, powerful automated systems are available. Project schedules are often depicted in such forms as activity lists, bar charts, and networks. The critical path method (CPM) is a way of estimating the project completion date by identifying time-critical dependent activities.

Criterion 7 requires the identification of project indicators for progress measurement. If used, milestones should be set frequently so that fewer estimates of completion are required at the EVMS status points. Work packages (WPs), too, should be small enough to eliminate as much estimation as possible.

Criterion 8 mandates a time-phased budget baseline at the control account (CA) level. The baseline, called the performance measurement baseline (PMB), is created by associating CAs with dollar estimates to components of the work schedule. The PMB has a variety of uses, including measuring performance to contract, judging the value of investments, improving resource usage, providing a basis for progress payments and incentives, and identifying performance trends. Work that is too far in the future to define for CAs can be held in summary-level planning packages (SLLPs). If for uncontrollable reasons the PMB becomes so obsolete that meaningful reporting is no longer possible, a reconstruction of the plan might be necessary. The new plan, called an over-target baseline (OTB), must be done only in very unusual circumstances and only after every other alternative has been considered.

DISCUSSION QUESTIONS

1. Why is it so difficult to obtain accurate and realistic estimates for task durations?

2. Discuss the four dysfunctional behavior traits that waste time when completing project activities.

3. What are the pros and cons of project crashing, and how is it accomplished?

4. What effect should probability theory have on our thinking about the project schedule?

5. What factors might control the sequence in which project tasks are performed?

6. Name the four task dependencies, and discuss their meaning and relative frequency of use.

7. What is the most common form of project bar chart, and what does it depict?

8. Describe the elements of the AON and AOA project network diagrams.

9. Discuss the most important benefits of PERT. Are there any weaknesses?

10. What is a PMB, and why does EVMS require one?

11. When can project replanning be performed, and what is the new plan called?

CHAPTER 8

The Budget
(Criteria 9–15)

This chapter on budgeting concludes Part III on project planning, probably the most important and most neglected part of any project. Saving budgeting until the final phase of planning must be saving the best for last—doesn't everyone love preparing budgets? Regardless of your previous experience with budgeting, we intend to make project budgeting as painless as possible. The budgeting process for projects is very similar to budgeting in general, and the basic concepts discussed here can be applied in any situation requiring fiscal control.

Budgeting is the third step in an iterative three-step planning process where the first step involves defining the work (in a work breakdown structure, or WBS) and the second step is scheduling the work (a time-phased baseline showing task dependencies). Budgeting completes the planning phase and is the basic foundation on which EVMS is built, setting a standard against which future progress is measured. Therefore, using estimates that are as realistic as possible—given the uncertainty and limited time to accumulate information—will minimize unexpected and unfavorable variances as work progresses.

Criteria 9 through 15 cover establishing budgets—how they are prepared and controlled, what they include, how they are stated, and to whom they are assigned. Previously, we pointed out that the project plan cost estimate should include the basis for estimates and formal acknowledgment of assumptions made in deriving the estimates. Clearly stating assumptions is a good practice in preparing any budget, but it is especially necessary in the uncertain project world. We also discuss the importance of including provisions for contingency in the project budget and include some techniques for estimating costs.

EVMS CRITERION 9

Establish budgets for authorized work with identification of significant cost elements (labor, material, etc.) as needed for internal management and for control of subcontractors.

Criterion 8 (see Chapter 7) required the establishment of a time-phased baseline that shows the sequence of tasks and the time period in which the tasks are to be accomplished. Criterion 9 requires that budget values representing the total resource effort, as determined in the baseline of work to be accomplished, be assigned to the responsible organizational units. All significant direct costs must be identified. Such costs would normally include direct labor, materials, subcontractor costs, and other costs directly attributable to the work package (WP). (Overhead or indirect cost is covered later in Criterion 13.)

To comply with Criterion 9, a management process must exist or be created within the performing organization. That process must be capable of determining the effort to be completed, identifying the responsible organizational units, and authorizing effort and expenditures by those units. If the organization currently does not use work authorization documents, we highly recommend that such a system be implemented to properly assign the budgeted effort of each task in terms of time and cost, to minimize miscommunication, and to prevent unauthorized work.

In many cases, the work authorization document should specify a "start no earlier than" start time to discourage *frontloading*. Accelerating a schedule by passing on early finishes of time- and resource-dependent tasks is desirable because the work value is earned appropriately. On the other hand, frontloading involves performing work out of sequence to keep workers busy or to obtain credit for work in a period earlier than that in which it was scheduled for completion. This practice causes problems in earned value measurements and incurs costs at unscheduled points in the project or results in other variations that inevitably lead to preventable rework. Unauthorized completion of work that is scheduled for a later time period distorts the EVs of both periods and must be strenuously discouraged. (See Chapter 16 for a description of a "P-factor" that formally recognizes rework caused by tasks performed out of sequence.)

Most projects use physical materials for which costs must be planned, controlled, and reported. A simple project bill of materials document can be used to support material acquisition requirements. Several good automated software products include the capability of generating a bill of materials in their project management modules. Several can be found by searching the Internet with terms like "project accounting" and "bill of materials." Material requisitions for projects are handled in much the same way as a manufacturing materials requisition, except that the uniqueness of the project environment probably will increase the requisition staff's work.

Much of the work of many projects involves subcontracting work to other organizations or entities. This outsourced work must be budgeted and controlled as strictly as the work performed in-house. Regardless of whether project work is outsourced, every project can be envisioned as a type of contract. Figure 8.1 illustrates the elements of a contract budget base that shows the relationships of some of the topics covered in this chapter. For projects intended for internal use and authorized by a charter rather than a contract, there would, of course, be no profit component to the project budget.

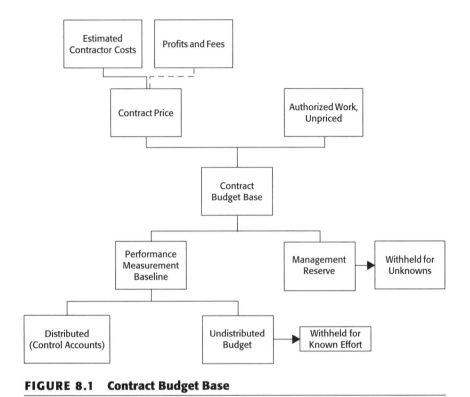

FIGURE 8.1   Contract Budget Base

Figure 8.2 illustrates an organization project control structure where several WPs fold into one general ledger control account (CA) that tracks budgeted and actual costs. Authorization and broad guidelines for the work are embedded in the contract or project charter. Work budgeted and accomplished, along with cost details, is accumulated in the work packages and control accounts.

EVMS CRITERION 10

To the extent it is practical to identify the authorized work in discrete work packages, establish budgets for this work in terms of dollars, hours, or other measurable units. Where the entire control account is not subdivided into work packages, identify the far-term effort in larger planning packages for budget and scheduling purposes.

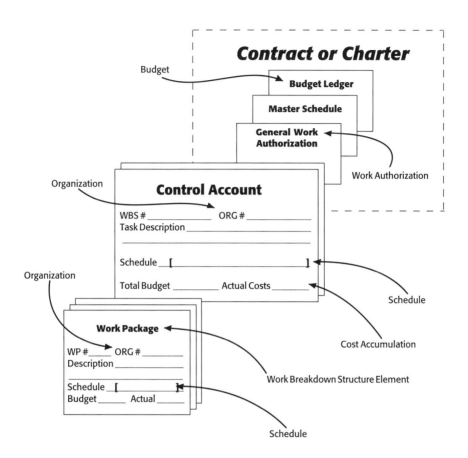

FIGURE 8.2   Organization Project Control Structure

This criterion requires that budgets be established in measurable units. EV is usually tracked by work accomplishment expressed in the cost of expended hours, but it may be in any measurable unit. The performance indicators, such as package milestones or discrete deliverables, must be scheduled to relate directly to a CA and reflect a specific quantity of that CA. That is, the sum of all expended hours (cost) of a CA's WPs and planning packages must reflect the total expended hours (cost) shown in the CA. Sometimes progress on a certain portion of the project cannot be concluded from the direct reporting of expended hours of effort. In those cases, hours may be apportioned based on the progress of related efforts.

During the breakdown of the project, all the project effort must be included in the *control account plan* (CAP). The CAP consists of CAs that are set up at the intersection of elements of the WBS and the organizational breakdown structure (OBS) (see Chapters 5 and 6). The CAs are subdivided into WPs (both internal and external) or planning packages.

Work Packages and Planning Packages

A WP is a subdivision of the CA and is an assignment of project control to a specific organizational unit at a lower level of the WBS. It defines a discrete deliverable (or activity) and should be of short duration so that work-in-progress does not need to be assessed. Typically, a WP requires 10 to 14 days of work. This generally ensures that WPs in process at the end of an accounting period are minimal.

Sometimes, however, the WP may require enough time that it will not be completed in its entirety at a point when EV measurements are requested. In those cases, the detailed description of the WP should contain intermediate objective milestones so that an accurate assessment of progress can be made. The idea is to minimize subjective estimates of completion of the WP, such as percent complete. (A common saying in project management circles is, "There are lies, darn lies, and percent complete!")

A *planning package* (PP) is also a subdivision of a CA. It is a holding account with an estimate of effort for which WPs cannot be fully determined when the project is initiated. The PP must be subdivided into WPs as soon as feasible. The description of the PP must contain as much detail as possible so that task and cost integrity can be maintained when the PP is restructured into WPs.

Special Packages

WPs also should be established for materials that will be used during the project. These may also be PPs if any required design effort has not yet established a complete requirements definition. The packages may be a part of the same CA that holds the packages for the activities that will use the material. As with all budgets, there should be controls to ensure that material budgets are not used for other elements, and in most cases they should be charged at the same rate as the activities progress.

CAs are required for outside activities such as subcontracts; the activity for those CAs may also be distributed to WPs. An internal control account manager should be assigned to monitor the efforts of the subcontractor and ensure the integration of the subcontractor's schedule with the project schedule. It would be best to require EV measurements from the subcontractor; where that is not feasible, however, the CA manager should be responsible for accurate progress reports, which may include the estimation of progress when the subcontractor is not able to provide timely information.

The relationship between WPs, CAs, the WBS, and the OBS (Figure 6.4) is repeated in Figure 8.3.

EVMS CRITERION 11

Provide that the sum of all work package budgets plus planning package budgets within a control account equals the control account budget.

The CA must have an approved budget, schedule, and organizational unit assignment. As discussed in Criterion 10, CAs can be subdivided in several ways, including WPs, PPs, and particular items for material usage and subcontracting. Criterion 11 requires that the sum of these subdivisions always equal the approved and assigned budget for the CA. The CA manager should use the performance measurement and budget documents to verify the reconciliation.

EVMS CRITERION 12

Identify and control level-of-effort activity by time-phased budgets established for this purpose. Only that effort that is unmeasur-

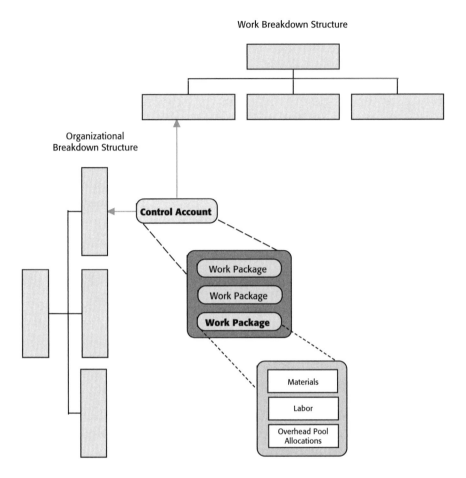

FIGURE 8.3   Work Packages, Control Accounts, WBS, and OBS

able or for which measurement is impractical may be classified as level of effort.

We have found few activities or services that can be justified as *level of effort* (LOE), and thankfully so. LOE is that part of the project scope that is general or supportive and for which progress measurement is impractical or for which there is no intermediate objective or deliverable. Of course, there can be many activities for which specific assignment to the project is difficult to measure, but most of those activities are a part of the indirect or overhead costs that are covered under Criterion 13.

Some examples of LOE might be the project manager, some project staff, and some elements of security. They can be LOE if they are assigned to only this one project. In that case, the cost would not be classified as overhead because none of their cost is apportioned to any other organizational activity. Even though the cost is attributable to only one project, it still might be difficult to assess their EV with any criterion other than elapsed time. In any event, LOE should be budgeted only when absolutely necessary and then segregated and strictly controlled.

Because there is no actual progress measurement for LOE, its EV is calculated only by the passage of time. For LOE work, the EV (budgeted cost of work performed) will always equal the planned value (budgeted cost of work scheduled) because it is impossible to measure what was accomplished. Thus LOE EV presents the possibility for corruption in the measurements if LOE costs are not actually incurred over the measured amount of time. Again, LOE should be budgeted only when absolutely necessary and then segregated and strictly controlled.

EVMS CRITERION 13

Establish overhead budgets for each significant organizational component of the company for expenses that will become indirect costs. Reflect in the program budgets, at the appropriate level, the amounts in overhead pools that are planned to be allocated to the program as indirect costs.

Every organization with which we have worked has a category of expenses that consists of overhead or indirect costs. These are costs that are not directly attributable to specific project deliverables. They are costs incurred to generally maintain the organization, such as costs for senior management, organizational units that support the entire organization (accounting, information systems, human resources), and the physical site and its infrastructure (power, water, environmental controls). Overhead generally is allocated to various organizational units by an arbitrary scheme. The allocation process must be considered arbitrary because the costs are *indirect*; by their nature, there is no direct way to attribute such costs.

Criterion 13 recognizes the potential problems with the allocation of overhead costs and the accompanying project management risk. To partially counteract this risk and expose all potential project costs, the criterion first requires that all of the organization's indirect costs be accounted for in overhead budgets. The costs should be collected in pools of similar costs. This grouping helps in the allocation process. The portion of each pool that is allocated to the project must then be budgeted at appropriate levels of the baseline. The methods for the allocation of indirect costs are covered in detail in Chapter 9 on EVMS accounting requirements.

EVMS CRITERION 14

Identify management reserves and undistributed budget.

EVMS requires careful control and accounting of all project costs. Two of the costs most vulnerable to manipulation are management reserves (MR) and undistributed budget (UB). These terms are sometimes confused with *summary-level planning packages* (SLPPs). An SLPP differs from an MR and a UB in that the SLPP is identified with a specific work element that has not yet been allocated to a CA because it is a far-term effort without sufficient detail for a complete definition.

An MR is included in the total project budget, but not initially as part of the project measurement baseline. Because projects are unique events, there is considerable uncertainty about unplanned costs, and an MR provides a way to deal with this type of uncertainty. This reserve is not to be used for authorized but undefined work or for authorized project modifications, both of which will have approved budgets. Nor should the MR be used for known conditions with uncertainties that can be reasonably estimated, such as a percentage of rework. Budgeted amounts for those uncertainties should be included in the measurement baseline.

The MR is a contingency budget, and the state of the project's uniqueness and other special conditions will affect the contingency rate. When estimating the project cost and especially the contingency, the estimator should be aware of the availability and productivity level of the organization's staff and the expected working conditions. Special working conditions include security requirements, weather conditions, and hazardous circumstances. The estimator also should consider market conditions and how market fluctuations might affect costs. Although an MR of 10 percent of the total project cost is fairly common, almost all sponsors of EVMS projects carefully examine contingency estimates and are especially concerned if the MR exceeds 15 percent in the final budget.

The U.S. Department of Energy (DOE) defines *contingency costs* as:

> costs that may result from incomplete design, unforeseen and unpredictable conditions, or uncertainties within the defined project scope. The amount of the contingency will depend on the status of design, procurement, and construction; and the complexity and uncertainties of the component parts of the project. Contingency is not to be used to avoid making an accurate assessment of expected cost (Department of Energy 1997, ch. 11.2.A).

An MR should be maintained and accounted for at the total project level; that is, the MR is part of the total project cost. When it becomes necessary, some portion of the MR can be allocated to the performance baseline for a specific CA and removed from the MR. Therefore, it will do exactly what it is designed to do, and the total project cost will remain unchanged.

Abundant useful information on the MR is available, such as *An Analysis of Management Reserve Budget on Defense Acquisition Contracts* (Christensen and Templin 2000).

The MR is maintained separately from the UB, which is included in the performance baseline for effort related to a specific and planned work scope but not yet identified in a WP. It would not yet be part of a CA, but it is maintained as a separate budget item until it can be allocated appropriately. Typically, items in this category would not be scheduled for completion in the near term.

An allocation of UB should be made as soon as possible to an element of the WBS and organizational unit. As with MR, the undistributed budget is maintained and accounted for at the total project level.

EVMS CRITERION 15

Provide that the program target cost goal is reconciled with the sum of all internal program budgets and management reserves.

The program (project) target cost goal is the negotiated or estimated contract cost. The contract may be a legal and formal document with another organization, such as a government contract, or an internal agreement made between the project sponsors and the project management. The two basic elements in the total cost are the performance measurement baseline (PMB) and the management reserves.

The PMB is the total of all the work packages and planning packages in all cost accounts and the overhead or indirect budgets. In the discussion of Criterion 10, PPs were described basically as undistributed costs. The MR is not included in the PMB because that account is not assigned to any authorized work. It is added to most project budgets and becomes a part of the total project target goal, but it is not measured in the PMB.

Criterion 15 requires that the sum of all the items in the PMB and the MR must always be equal to the original total project target. (Authorized changes are discussed as parts of other criteria.) EV will be calculated using progress in completion of baseline tasks and the budgeted costs reflected in the PMB.

For a simple example of a project with task budgets, see Figure 8.4. Assuming a 10 percent MR and no undistributed budget, the 52-week project (as illustrated in Figure 8.4) would have a total project cost of $228,800—$208,000 budgeted for the tasks plus $20,800 in MR.

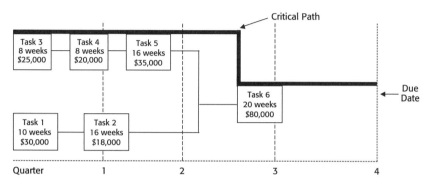

FIGURE 8.4   Activity in Box Budget Baseline

PROJECT COST ESTIMATION

The seven EVMS criteria on budgeting give project managers many rules but no real assistance in how to estimate the cost of a project. Cost estimation is a very difficult task. It comes on the heels of project scheduling and uses many assumptions and estimates. Many organizations have professional estimators, and for large EVMS projects the help of professionals might be indispensable. Project managers should find the subsequent discussion of various cost-estimating methods and common estimating terminology beneficial. DOE's Directive G 430.1-1 is very helpful, but it is a complex document. A description and full list of its chapters can be found online (Department of Energy 1997).

You also might be interested in using cost estimation software. You can locate vendors easily by using a Web search engine. A brief discussion of cost estimation software can be found at http://www. p2pays.org/ref/01/00047/00047c.htm#3.1.

Cost Data

In forming the project cost estimate, data may be compiled from many sources, such as costs from similar projects, cost reports, databases of historical and current product costs, and the organization's purchasing department. The collected cost data must be adjusted based on their source and time. Some differences, such as inflation factors, different quantities, and varying quality, might be fairly apparent, but geographical differences and possible regulatory changes must be considered as well.

Some adjustments may be facilitated by the use of a cost index such as an inflation index. Several indices that can help the estimator determine current project costs by applying an index to the known costs from another time, project, or location may be available.

Project Controls

Project controls are all the systems used to plan, schedule, budget, and measure the performance of a project. A few applicable components of project controls are discussed in the following sections. The cost estimation package sets the baseline for EVMS project controls. A spreadsheet profiling the funding schedule over the life of the project should be a part of that package; one can be constructed as the cost estimation package is developed.

Cost Estimation Package

DOE states that a cost estimation package consists of "the estimate, the technical scope, and the schedule" (Department of Energy 1997, ch. 2, 1). This means that the estimator must begin with the WBS (and the imbedded CAs and the time-phased schedule). The cost estimation package establishes the project budget, provides the cost baseline, and becomes a major document for performance measurement.

As the estimate is developed, the package should contain not only all the documentation to support the costs but also an analysis of how the costs were developed. This information will discuss what is included in indirect costs, a justification for the overhead rate, and the consideration of project contingencies.

Basis of Cost Estimate

Good documentation provides reliability for the project's cost estimate and contributes to the success of future estimation efforts. That documentation should include all supporting data, the assumptions used, and the environment that is assumed to exist. Not all projects require the same level of detail in their cost estimates; even within a project, the detail might not be the same for different legs of the WBS.

The Federal Aviation Administration suggests four factors that should be considered to determine an appropriate level of detail (Federal Aviation Administration 2003, 1):

1. *Dollar value of the project.* High-value programs require more extensive detail in cost estimates.
2. *Purpose of the estimate.* Early planning estimates require less accuracy than a final approved budget estimate.
3. *Nature of the project.* Regardless of dollar value, the cost estimate for a project with few intermediate objectives (less activity) can usually be prepared at a more cumulative level.
4. *Data availability.* If the technical details of a project are not completely available, an aggregate estimate with budgeted uncertainty might need to be prepared.

Estimating Methods

Several techniques can be used to estimate the cost of a project deliverable or the cost of the entire project. The estimator can choose one or a combination of these techniques based on the size and nature of the project, the estimator's experience, the time available to prepare the estimate, and the availability of information and other resources.

Different types of estimates may be required at different points in the contract process. Some estimates must be very detailed; others may be considered order-of-magnitude (ballpark) estimates that are prepared using only very basic decision factors.

Bottom-Up Method

The *bottom-up method* can be used effectively when all activity to be estimated is clearly detailed. It is especially useful if the bottom-up scheduling technique was used to schedule the project. Estimates are made at the lowest level of detail and summarized as the estimator works up the levels of the WBS until a total is accumulated for the entire project or the unit to be estimated.

These low-level estimates can be very accurate, but be aware that duplication is possible:

- Work that is performed in one organizational unit may satisfy the requirements of deliverables that might have been assumed by more than one organizational unit during the estimation process.
- Cost estimators at lower levels of the organization may not be aware of efforts in other parts of the organization.
- During a roll-up of costs, assumptions that may not account for possible duplications at lower levels of the estimation are often used.

Rolling Wave Method

Sometimes there is not enough detail in the initial planning stage to completely break down the project, which can undermine the ability to estimate cost in the far term. If the project sponsors agree to a certain level of uncertainty, the *rolling wave method* can be used. This technique shortens the initial planning effort while producing more accurate plans. As we are all aware, there are many cases in which weeks are spent to produce a very careful and complex plan that quickly becomes obsolete because of unforeseen circumstances.

The rolling wave technique means doing the detailed planning in cycles (waves). The cycles can vary from two to nine months, depending on the certainty of events and the amount of time necessary for advance support requisition. The plans for the short term (current cycle) are produced in great detail, and an overall plan is estimated for the rest of the project. Near the end of the first cycle, the next cycle is estimated and planned in detail. The current-cycle estimates are expected to have a very tight margin of error, while the remaining project estimates may be expected to vary to a wider degree.

Parametric Method

If none of the available information is very detailed, the *parametric method* may be the only way to arrive at reasonable estimates. One would not expect such estimates to be in the same range of accuracy as a more direct estimate, but the method has been increasingly used in the aerospace industry with great success. Parametric estimating relies on historical data from similar endeavors or the ability to model the current objective. Regression and other statistical analyses are performed on the historical data to discover correlations between the cost drivers and the system parameters. The technique focuses on the cost drivers and not on the details of the project. It is complex and multifaceted.

NASA's *Cost Estimating Handbook* (National Aeronautics and Space Administration 2008a, 1-27–1-30) gives a very complete explanation of parametric cost estimation (as well as other estimation methods). In addition to showing the estimating process steps and examples of output, it reviews the strengths and weaknesses of the method. Statistically sound predictors, ability to apply sensitivity analysis to results, and nonreliance on opinion are its major strengths; data acquisition, communicating results to non-mathematicians, and assumption that past experience will hold in the future are its major weaknesses.

Analogy Method

For a specific analogy to work at all, the costs of items in a similar project must be known. The estimate starts with the cost of a similar element for a different project, and adjustments are made for known differences in the projects. In using the *analogy method*, the estimator must look for differences in the characteristics of the design and expected performance of the projects or project elements. This method is a top-down method that estimates the overall cost of a project based on the known properties of a similar completed project.

Expert Opinion Method

The *expert opinion method* involves consulting with several experts or specialists and establishing a consensus. Although many view this technique as one of last resort, if the project activity is within the domains of the experts' expertise, such estimates can be reliably substituted for ones from more empirical methods. The estimates can be viewed with an even higher degree of dependability if the expert opinions have been verified previously with empirical evidence.

Criterion 9 requires the establishment of budgets that identify all significant cost elements for the work established in the time-phased baseline. Criterion 10 covers the budgeting for work packages (WPs) and planning packages (PPs), which are the subdivisions of control accounts, and Criterion 11 requires that the sum of the subaccount budgets equal the total control account budget. Criterion 12 states that any level-of-effort (LOE) activity must be identified and controlled.

Criterion 13 establishes the initial guideline for controlling overhead costs—a very vulnerable component of the project budget. Criterion 14 requires the identification of management reserves (MR) and undistributed budget (UB). MR are held outside the project measurement baseline as a way to deal with project uncertainty. UB is part of the baseline and represents planned work that has not yet been detailed in WPs. Criterion 15 states that all the elementary project budgets plus the amount budgeted for management reserves must equal the total project budget.

All the criteria concerning project budgeting establish many rules and requirements, but they don't provide very much help in arriving at a budget for the project. Estimators must consider all the available cost data and should provide project control information, such as a cost estimation package, appropriate control accounts (CAs), and a basis-of-cost estimate. Cost-estimating methods include bottom-up, rolling wave, parametric, analogy, and expert opinion.

DISCUSSION QUESTIONS

1. How does your organization authorize work? What would you recommend?

2. How should outsourced work be budgeted and controlled?

3. How could frontloading distort EVMS measurements?

4. Discuss why you might or might not have an LOE component in a project budget.

5. Describe the difference between direct and indirect costs, and list some examples of each.

6. Describe an overhead pool, and give examples of the contents of a pool.

7. In what circumstances can actual project expenses be charged against the budget for MR?

8. What data sources would you use in estimating the project budget?

9. How would you determine an appropriate level of detail for a project budget?

10. Defend one of the five cost-estimating techniques.

PART IV

Project Status

> *"Unless the PM understands the organizational accounting system, there is no way to exercise budgetary control over the project."*
> —MEREDITH AND MANTEL (2003, 338)

As previously noted, EVMS was developed from a standard cost model. Because of this close association, many if not most of the deficiencies of traditional standard cost systems also attach to EVMS. Nonetheless, accounting metrics play a large role in EVMS and the formal 32 criteria requirements. Our intent is to make the material clear and understandable for managers with little or no accounting training or background.

The first 15 criteria discussed in earlier chapters specify planning requirements for detailing elements of the project objectives, the organization, the work schedule, and the budgeting process. The next 12 criteria cover management and accounting requirements, including those for identifying, summarizing, recording, and reporting actual project expenses and their variances from the project plan.

Chapter 9—Criteria 16 through 19—discusses estimation, recording, tracking, and allocation of project costs. The chapter includes a discussion of some special circumstances for projects with manufacturing components and an analysis of the requirements of a formal material accounting system, as required in Criteria 20 and 21. Chapter 10 deals with the specific requirements of Criteria 22 through 27 concerning project variances.

CHAPTER 9

Tracking Performance (Criteria 16–21)

> *"I think it is an immutable law in business that words are words, explanations are explanations, promises are promises—but only performance is reality."*
>
> —HAROLD S. GENEEN

Criteria 16 through 19 are concerned with recording project costs and, although they seem simple enough, are critical in maintaining an EVMS-compliant system. These four criteria, along with Criteria 20 and 21, however, usually are assumed to be difficult to understand and implement. The detail required in accounting for projects, not the concepts themselves, cause this misunderstanding. The most important aspect of the accounting criteria is the requirement for accurate progress measurement—knowing how to account reliably and accurately.

All the criteria concerned with accounting for ongoing project work are designed to establish minimum standards and do not require use of a particular accounting system. Although accountants do the actual recording and processing of data, the project manager is charged with reporting the input data and establishing communication links between parties. Becoming familiar with these criteria will enable you to funnel appropriate and timely information into the accounting system and assist the organization in capturing required information and following established procedures. In addition, the accounting department will be able to provide feedback that will alert you to problems or opportunities.

EVMS ACCOUNTING

The great value of EVMS is that with the required accounting reports, those interested in the project are not dependent upon subjective feelings or vague assurances. EVMS also relieves project managers from time-consuming explanations of their current positions so they can concentrate on running projects. We pointed out earlier that reliable estimates of a project's total time and cost are essential for the organization to make appropriate and successful project decisions. Sometimes projects require additional resources; however, there are projects, through no fault of the project manager or the project team, that need to be put out of their misery. Accounting information aids in making these difficult decisions, as well as in making numerous other tradeoffs.

Specialized documents required for EVMS include a detailed control (or cost) account (CA) structure (the project's chart of accounts) and the data requirements stipulated by the contract or charter. In addition, an accounting manual containing the organization's accounting policies and procedures, including allocation methodologies, should be maintained and available. Project managers will find that even vague familiarity with these policies and procedures can avoid many missteps and communication problems.

For federal government projects, a formal Cost Accounting Standards Board Disclosure Statement that details the procedures that will be followed must be submitted. The purpose of the statement is to provide assurance that costs are properly recorded and there is a timely and accurate transfer of actual cost information from the general accounting system into the EVMS. Although this document is not required for nonfederal EV implementations, similar care should be taken to ensure that accounting best practices are observed.

An acceptable accounting system should be capable of accounting for all resource expenditures as the resources are consumed. As discussed in the section on Criterion 21, there is considerable variation in accounting for material usage, and consistency in treatment becomes quite important.

One of the biggest complaints we hear from project managers is that their accounting systems seldom reflect up-to-date (real-time) performance. It is in the project manager's best interests to form a good working relationship with the accountant(s) handling his or her project so that the project manager can assist in timely recording of transactions, which, in an EV system, translates into project performance metrics.

EVMS CRITERION 16

Record direct costs in a manner consistent with the budgets in a formal system controlled by the general books of account.

The organization's accounting procedures must follow generally accepted accounting procedures (GAAP). A very real concern is that the accounting system be able to transfer accurate information into the EVMS with appropriate timing. If the system adheres to standard accounting procedures and follows consistent planning procedures, it will be EVMS-compliant and facilitate the audit of all of the project's direct costs.

Direct Costs

Criterion 16 requires that the accounting methods used to collect direct costs and post them to the CAs are the same as those used when the baseline budget was established. (You may find a quick review of Chapter 8 helpful at this point.) Criterion 16 relies heavily on appropriate establishment of CAs and specific budget allocations during the early phases of project planning. As discussed earlier, even with direct costs, there may be some activity apportionment. The actual costs of apportioned effort must be collected in the same manner as budgeted to ensure accurate EVMS measurements (Figure 9.1).

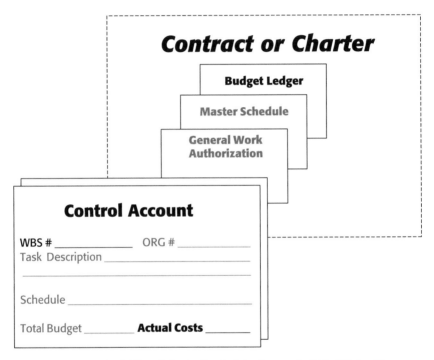

FIGURE 9.1   Actual Direct Costs Posted to Accounts Established in Budget

Chapter 7 of a Department of Energy (DOE) directive, DOE G 430.1-1, defines direct costs as "any costs that can be specifically identified with a particular project or activity, including salaries, travel, equipment and supplies directly benefiting the project or activity." The directive further explains that *activity* should be interpreted as being the same as a CA (Department of Energy 1997, 7.2.A).

(You may want to refresh your recollection of CAs by reviewing the discussion of them in Chapter 5.)

Imagine direct costs as having invisible strings that are tied to the place where the direct costs are consumed. These costs do not have to be allocated, just traced to their users. For example, materials used in one work breakdown structure (WBS) would be assigned to the CA for that WBS number. Labor—other than that classified as level of effort (LOE)—is traced easily by its invisible string to the CA for the WBS benefiting from the labor.

Although direct costs most commonly relate to one CA, two or more CAs can share a direct project cost. An example might be a specialized piece of equipment that is dedicated to three different WBS numbers within one project. In this case, the total cost would be allocated to the three WBS numbers on the basis of their consumption of the activity driver.

For the specialized piece of equipment, the activity driver or basis of allocation might be the ratio of equipment time used by each WBS to the total equipment productive time available. The resulting ratio multiplied by the cost of the equipment would be the amount to be charged to the individual WBS CA. Productive time available but not used would represent excess capacity that should not be allocated immediately to the WBS elements using the asset. Depending on individual situation circumstances, this excess capacity cost might or might not be allocated ultimately to the project, along with other indirect costs, but individual WBS elements should not have to bear this excess capacity cost.

Special Circumstances

Control of work performed by subcontractors is the responsibility of the prime contractor. Subcontract costs must be recorded in the same accounting period as the associated primary effort. If the subcontractor cannot supply timely information, the project manager must establish estimates of subcontractor costs to comply with period reporting requirements. Additionally, some subcontract costs must be separated into the appropriate cost elements for accurate posting to appropriate CAs. Therefore, the more detail the project manager can supply, the better.

For projects involving the Department of Defense, special rules govern material management and accounting systems (Department of Defense 2008c). Criterion 21, discussed later in this chapter, details some of these requirements.

EVMS CRITERION 17

When a work breakdown structure is used, summarize direct costs from control accounts into the work breakdown structure without allocation of a single control account to two or more work breakdown structure elements.

This criterion exists simply to require that costs do not become duplicated as they are summarized up through the levels of the WBS. (Remember that Criterion 5, presented in Chapter 6, required that performance measurements be the same, whether from the WBS or the organizational breakdown structure [OBS].) This requirement depends heavily on a carefully developed WBS and CAs. It also relies on the accounting system's ability to collect and allocate the costs in a consistent and reliable manner. For an illustration of how actual costs incurred are traced to the WBS, see Figure 9.2.

The most care is necessary when costs need to be apportioned from one CA to another. The organization's accountants handle the actual accounting, but it is the project manager who provides a reality check on the reasonableness of accounting department distributions.

EVMS CRITERION 18

Summarize direct costs from the control accounts into the contractor's organizational elements without allocation of a single control account to two or more organizational elements.

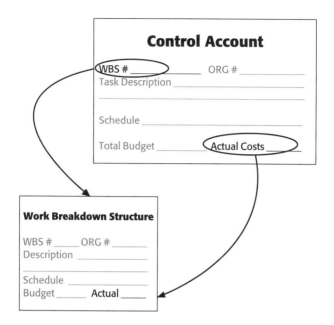

FIGURE 9.2   Control Account Actual Costs Match Those on Its Related WBS Element

This is the same requirement as that for Criterion 17, only as it applies to the organizational breakdown structure. Cost data integrity must be maintained as the data are summarized from the CA to the highest unit level of the OBS. This requirement heavily depends on the careful assignment of project elements to organizational units. Figure 9.3 illustrates how actual costs are assigned from the CA to the OBS as well as the WBS.

Thus far, we have addressed three criteria (16, 17, and 18) that concern direct project costs. Now we turn our attention to indirect costs.

EVMS CRITERION 19

Record all indirect costs that will be allocated to the contract.

Indirect costs (overhead) represent expenses that are attributable to more than one project or organizational entity. Criterion 4

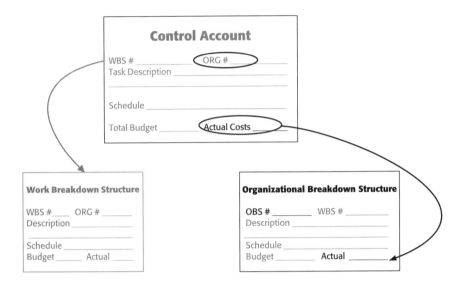

FIGURE 9.3   Control Account Costs as Summarized in the WBS and OBS

(Chapter 6) requires identification of the organization's function responsible for controlling indirect costs, and Criterion 13 (Chapter 8) requires establishment of the budget for indirect costs. Now Criterion 19 requires the allocation of indirect costs in the same manner as they were planned in the budget. They should be allocated often (at least monthly) to maintain accurate EVMS measurements. Some contracts require dividing the indirect costs into *recurring* and *nonrecurring* costs. Recurring costs, for example, might include supervisory or administrative costs, while property taxes are an example of a nonrecurring (one-time) cost.

Indirect costs do not have invisible strings connecting the cost source to the user as described earlier for direct costs. The DOE directive defines *indirect cost* as "any cost not identified specifically with a single final cost objective but with two or more final cost objectives, e.g., heat, light, and power" (Department of Energy 2004, 42.1, 2). A good example of such an indirect cost is the chief executive officer's (CEO's) salary. The CEO is charged with setting the direction of the entire organization, including projects that support that direction.

Cost Pools

Rather than accumulating all indirect costs in a single account, or pool of costs, a far better approach is to establish a cost pool for each group of related activities. Then the costs of each pool are allocated to the users of the pool according to some rational allocation basis, or driver.

If several candidate drivers exist, cause-effect criteria can usually be invoked to select the best driver. That is, the driver that is the best candidate is the one whose changes most directly cause costs in the pool to change (assuming all other things are equal). (Caveat: As the project manager, you should consider whether the employee behavior likely to result from using a particular driver is the behavior desired.)

For example, resource costs first might be assigned to various pools using relevant resource drivers (allocation bases), and then the pool costs would be assigned to users based on relevant cost pool drivers (allocation bases). For an illustration of how this might look for a simple three-pool environment, see Figure 9.4.

Cost Pool Drivers

Only totally variable costs have unique drivers. If the overhead pool consists of purchased travel costs, for example, most (if not all) of the costs will vary with the number of trips taken or the number of miles traveled. That is, as long as commercial travel is used, travel costs are variable with the number and/or type of trips.

If cost pools contain fixed costs as well as variable costs, there is no perfect driver that can be selected to allocate the costs of the pool. Therefore, if the organization has a permanent travel department, a certain amount of costs is fixed in nature; moreover, there

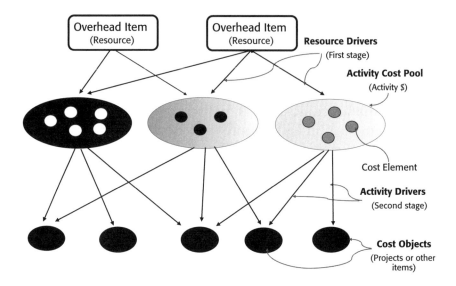

FIGURE 9.4   Overhead Cost Pools with Their Sources and Allocations

is no absolute base or driver for the travel pool that can be defended against all other potential drivers. Therefore, the allocation of these fixed costs, to some extent, would be arbitrary.

Selection of the pool driver is important because cost allocations can change dramatically from use of one driver versus another candidate driver. The solution to the driver-selection problem is to select rational cause-and-effect drivers that have the least undesirable unintended consequences. That is, the drivers should minimize attempts to "game" the system. The project manager's expertise is invaluable in helping accounting personnel select appropriate drivers for indirect cost allocation pools.

COST ALLOCATION METHODS

One of three basic methods—known as *direct, step-down,* and *reciprocal*—may be used to allocate indirect costs. Many government agencies and private organizations highly regard a specific allocation system known as *activity-based costing* (ABC); therefore it, too, is covered briefly in this section.

Of the three basic methods, the direct method is simplest. It is accomplished by using some rational allocation base or driver, such as number of staff involved, to allocate a pool's costs to the users of that pool. The example in Table 9.1 reflects three overhead pools where resource costs of $80,000, $60,000, and $40,000 have been traced to the accounting, human resources, and maintenance pools. The table also shows drivers selected for each overhead pool, the number of hours worked, the number of employees, and the number of square feet occupied by each of the overhead departments and the three projects. The three projects are the only "productive" activities of the organization.

TABLE 9.1   Example of Overhead Costs and Consumption

	Overhead Pools			Projects		
	Accounting	Human Resources	Maintenance	1	2	3
Costs	$80,000	$60,000	$40,000			
Driver	work hours	number of employees	square feet			
Quantity						
hours	1,000	5,000	500	20,000	8,000	12,000
employees	2	10	20	250	150	90
square feet	250	500	100	2,500	3,000	1,550

Direct Allocation Method

With the *direct allocation method*, any interdepartmental services provided to other overhead pools are ignored, and each overhead pool's costs are allocated only to projects and production areas, if they exist. This allocation is accomplished by forming a simple ratio of the allocation base or driver consumed by a project to the total consumed by all users of the overhead pool. The resulting project costs in the direct allocation method would be as follows:

Overhead Pools			Projects		
Accounting	Human Resources	Maintenance	1	2	3
$80,000	$60,000	$40,000			
($80,000)			$40,000*	$16,000	$24,000
	($60,000)		30,612+	18,367	11,020
		($40,000)	14,184#	17,021	8,794
- 0 -	- 0 -	- 0 -	$84,797	$51,389	$43,815

*20,000/(20,000 + 8,000 + 12,000) * $80,000 = $40,000
+250/(250 + 150 + 90) * $60,000 = $30,612
#2,500/(2,500 + 3,000 + 1,550) * $40,000 = $14,184

Step-Down Allocation Method

When overhead pools provide significant services to themselves as well as to projects and production areas, such as the human resources department handling all personnel needs of the other pools as well as for the projects, the direct method, which ignores this reciprocal service, is inappropriate. In this situation, the indirect costs of supporting activities might use a *step-down allocation method* to distribute costs to other overhead pools and projects more equitably. That is, the overhead pool providing the most service to other pools is allocated to other pools as well as to projects and producing areas (including manufacturing areas, if they exist).

Assuming that accounting provides the most service to the other pools (this selection is debatable and is part of the problem of using this methodology to allocate overhead pool costs), the accounting department costs first would be allocated to the other overhead pools and the projects. Then the pool that provides the next "most" service would have its costs, including the amount allocated to it by accounting, allocated to the remaining pool and the projects. Finally, the last pool costs, now increased by their share of the other two overhead pools, would be allocated to the projects. In this example, human resources costs are allocated following the accounting department costs, and the maintenance costs are allocated last.

Using the data from Table 9.1, the costs would be distributed as follows using the step-down allocation method:

Overhead Pools			Projects		
Accounting	Human Resources	Maintenance	1	2	3
$80,000	$60,000	$40,000			
($80,000)	8,791	879	$35,165	$14,066	$21,099
	($68,791)	2,698	33,721*	20,233	12,140
		($43,577)	15,453	18,543	9,581
- 0 -	- 0 -	- 0 -	$84,339	$52,842	$42,819

*250/(20 + 250 + 150 + 90) * $68,791 = $33,721

Notice that once again a total of $180,000 ($84,339 + $52,842 + $42,819) ended up in the project accounts. The amounts, however, are slightly different from those found using the direct method. Whereas the differences in allocations between the two methods in this example may not appear to be material, it should be clear that under certain circumstances, the amounts allocated using the two methods might be significantly different. Also, the choice of with which overhead pool to begin the step-down allocation procedure is somewhat arbitrary, and performing the allocation using a different sequence would result in different allocations to projects.

Reciprocal Allocation Method

Both the direct and step-down methods of allocation of overhead pool costs are susceptible to charges of bias, whether intentional or unintentional. The only equitable method of overhead pool cost allocation is one in which each area pays for exactly what it uses in providing its output—including consumption of services provided by other overhead pools. *The reciprocal allocation method* (sometimes called the *simultaneous equation method*) fulfills this requirement. It uses a set of simultaneous equations to determine the total costs of an overhead pool that includes its fair share of other overhead pools' costs.

Before the widespread availability of personal computers and spreadsheets, this method, while theoretically superior, required mastery of some formidable mathematics involving the inverting of a sometimes sizable matrix. With a spreadsheet such as Microsoft Excel, however, the mathematics are inconsequential. An example of the application of the reciprocal method using the same example data used for the direct and step-down methods is presented in Appendix 9-A at the end of this chapter.

Whereas the allocated costs using the reciprocal method in this simple example do not differ significantly from those using the theoretically unsupportable direct method, it should be obvious that the reciprocal method can be logically defended as the method that is most fair to all parties. Once the matrices are established, only the current department costs and possibly the usage quantities must be changed to find the appropriate allocations for a new period.

Activity-Based Costing Method

In addition to the standard overhead pool costs (e.g., purchasing, personnel, information systems), other indirect activities might need to be applied to functional areas or overhead pools as well as to projects.

Implementing ABC

ABC is a method of applying indirect costs by establishing multiple cost pools, each of which contains the costs of certain activities. By carefully selecting an activity driver whose use causes the pool costs to increase, a pool's costs can be allocated to entities using the activities provided by the pool. (If this description sounds very much like traditional overhead allocation procedures with more cost pools, it is.)

The activities captured in a pool, such as material movement or engineering services, might span the entire organization. Because this allocation procedure appears to charge indirect costs on the basis of "only users pay," the federal government encourages its use. For example, based on time spent on each activity, an engineering resource might be allocated to three activity pools: design and design changes, maintenance repairs and modifications, and a lead time reduction program (Figure 9.5). Other costs, such as supplies, also would be allocated to these pools. Once the costs are accumulated in the pools, projects using the activities provided by the pools would be charged based on their use of the selected activity drivers.

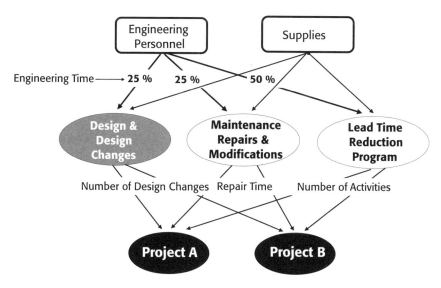

FIGURE 9.5   Engineering Cost Pool Allocations

Problems Associated with ABC and Other Indirect Allocation Methods

A detailed discussion of ABC is beyond the scope of this book. However, several caveats concerning ABC and other indirect allocation methods are in order.

First, the activity and other overhead pools typically contain both variable and fixed costs. The *fixed costs* represent the costs that must be incurred in lump sums to support the provision of the activity, while the *variable costs* are incurred as the activities are provided. Computing one rate for the entire pool treats all costs as if they are variable with consumption of the pool driver.

The pool must be geared up to provide for demand for its activities based on projected demand. Because details of projects, as well as details of individual project tasks, are inherently uncertain, over-capacity and undercapacity conditions occur frequently. Further, allocating pool costs based on driver quantity consumed means that one project's costs are influenced by the use of the pool by other projects. One way to eliminate this bias is to separate each pool into two subpools—one containing the variable costs of the pool and the other containing the fixed costs. Then the variable-cost subpool can be allocated based on actual use, and the fixed-cost subpool can be allocated based on original projected demand.

Finally, the project budget will reflect the portion of overhead that is planned for allocation to the project. The allocation will be based on some cost driver or allocation base, as described earlier. The rate is usually predetermined for a particular accounting period. Because there are usually several cost pools, there will be different rates for each pool. It is very important points for EVMS that an appropriate allocation rate is established and that the rate used in the budgeting process is the same as the rate used in the operating cycle.

EVMS CRITERION 20

Identify unit costs, equivalent units costs, or lot costs when needed.

For projects that contain a manufacturing component with multiple units being produced in a production or similar-type environment, a contractor might be required to have an accounting system that is capable of providing unit costs, equivalent unit costs, or lot costs.

Unit costs consist of direct costs (e.g., materials and perhaps labor) plus indirect (overhead) cost. The cost of one unit, therefore, includes direct materials and direct labor for the unit, plus manufacturing overhead.

Computing unit costs in some production environments, specifically on a continuous production or accelerated assembly line basis, is extremely difficult. This situation also might occur where substantially comparable units are produced for more than one customer. In these situations, it is acceptable to use *equivalent unit costs* (a quantity of units produced during a single period by assuming a particular flow of units) as computed in a process-costing environment. In process costing, production consists of basically fungible (identical) units produced in multiple (and usually sequential) departments or processes. In this situation, direct costs (materials and labor) are traced to the process (department), and indirect (overhead) costs are allocated to the process. Then a process's costs for the period, including transferred-in costs, are divided by the equivalent whole units of production for the period to find the process unit cost. For example, if the ending inventory consists of 90 units one-third completed, the equivalent whole units would be 30.

The weighted-average method of computing equivalent units (units transferred out plus the equivalent whole unit portion of ending inventory completed but still in process) is most commonly used. Alternatively, the first-in first-out method may be used. That method counts only the work completed during the current period (beginning inventory work completed, transferred-out units, and work performed on the ending inventory).

Where units are produced in batches or lots, the total costs (materials, labor, and overhead) of the batch or lot are traced or assigned to the group of items produced. Then the total cost of each batch or lot is divided by the number of good units to yield a unit cost.

EVMS CRITERION 21

For EVMS, the material accounting system will provide for:
(1) Accurate cost accumulation and assignment of costs to control accounts in a manner consistent with the budgets, using recognized, acceptable costing techniques
(2) Cost performance measurement at the point in time most suitable for the category of material involved, but no earlier than the time of progress payments or actual receipt of material
(3) Full accountability of all material purchased for the program, including the residual inventory.

Criterion 21 establishes recording and reporting requirements for materials to ensure that data used in computing project performance, including cost and schedule variances and other metrics, in addition to being accurate, are assigned to appropriate periods. Without proper alignment in time, interpreting performance metrics is extremely difficult, if not impossible.

The first part of this criterion is designed to ensure that generally recognized and acceptable costing techniques are followed and that actual material costs are posted in the same CAs for which amounts were budgeted. There also should be adequate internal control procedures in place to find and correct any errors made in postings, either in amount or to appropriate accounts. Although this responsibility belongs to the accounting department, project managers should make every effort to see that they are provided accurate and timely information and should review accounting reports for reasonableness.

The second part covers the timing for expensing project material. Should actual costs not be available in a timely manner, the project manager should assign estimated costs. When actual amounts become known, the estimated amounts can be corrected, if necessary. However, to recognize a material cost for which an invoice has not been received, the goods must be received. There is some latitude in the timely costing of material—the material may be recognized when it is accepted from the supplier or when it is consumed—as long as the system is consistent. Indirect material and other costs are addressed in Criterion 19.

The value and significance of materials should determine detailed procedures followed, with this information formally documented. Because the significance and materiality of various types of material purchases can vary dramatically, it is permissible to follow different procedures for different values of materials. There is considerable variation, in practice, concerning when material costs are recognized. The time most suitable for the type of material involved is acceptable. Formal entry into the accounting system, however, should occur no earlier than when the material is received or progress payments are made.

A critical issue is making sure the cost of the materials is recorded no later than when the materials are used; otherwise, the EV metrics may be meaningless. Chapter 10 discusses variances of actual material costs from those planned in the budget, as well as projections of future material requirements.

The third part of Criterion 21 requires full accountability of all material purchased for the program. In many organizations, project managers are permitted to borrow (or "steal") material that was ordered for another use. Construction-type industries, in particular, find this a common problem. This practice, if not controlled, makes it extremely difficult to track the inventory and consumption of materials.

If materials are purchased for one program or project, any amounts not used for their intended purpose must be tracked. This residual inventory may or may not have a market value; nevertheless, it should be tracked and reported. The *Material Management and Accounting System* (Department of Defense 2008c) documents some detailed instructions on a material loan/payback technique that might be useful if borrowing materials is common in your industry. *Caution*: New materials-management rules with some major proposed changes will be finalized sometime in 2009. We suggest you check online for the latest version of the DoD Federal

Acquisition Regulation on materials management and subsequent modifications.

In addition, there are literally hundreds of voluntary consensus standards bodies, none of which are specifically endorsed by the U.S. government. A quick Internet search can provide links to government requirements on their use and specific standards groups.

ACCOUNTING AND EARNED VALUE SOFTWARE

Even small companies now have access to sophisticated accounting software. Just as accounting is no longer a manual operation, EVMS also can be automated to remove much of the drudgery of keeping track of performance.

Because the software industry is expanding and developing at such a hectic pace, it would be ineffective to review accounting or EV software here. Most enterprise resource management (ERM) programs now include optional EV modules. In addition, there are many standalone software programs capable of sophisticated drill-down access to detailed EV performance. Most project management scheduling and control programs also deal more or less successfully with EV metrics. A simple Internet search for "EVMS software" will provide enough leads to occupy several hours.

If your organization uses Microsoft Office Project, you might be interested in Dayal's *Earned Value Management Using Microsoft® Office Project* (2008).

> The six criteria on accounting covered in this chapter closely follow the principles of the budgeting criteria presented in the previous chapter. EVMS makes a very strong statement that the actual project expenses must be charged in accordance with the principles used in the planning process. EVMS accounting provides information to make management decisions; moreover, it does so in a more objective way than do subjective progress estimates.

Direct costs and *indirect costs* make up the two general cost categories. Direct costs can be specifically identified with a particular activity,
but even direct costs may need to be apportioned if the direct activity
is shared by multiple users or cost objects.

Criterion 16 deals with direct costs. It requires that the EVMS accounting be accurate, timely, and consistent with the organization's
formal accounting system. Criteria 17 and 18 prevent the duplication
of entries and summarization errors by prohibiting the allocation of
control accounts (CAs) to more than one work breakdown structure
(WBS) or organizational breakdown structure (OBS) element.

Criterion 19 regulates indirect cost allocations. It, too, stresses following processes and procedures established during the budgeting
phase. Indirect costs cannot be identified with a particular activity
and are generally allocated through cost pools based on rational, but
arbitrary, cause-and-effect determinations (cost drivers). Overhead can
be allocated using one of the three basic methods—*direct, step-down*,
or *reciprocal*. Many government agencies and private organizations
highly regard a specific allocation system known as *activity-based
costing* (ABC).

Criteria 20 and 21 establish standards for two areas not involving
direct and indirect costs specifically, but rather procedures. Criterion
20 relates to projects with manufacturing components and stipulates
the generation of unit costs, equivalent unit costs, or lot costs when
appropriate. The details necessary for an appropriate material accounting system are specified in Criterion 21.

Professional accountants, of course, provide the actual accounting
work, but the project manager's cooperation ensures not only that
criteria are followed but that information is provided to all project
stakeholders, including the project team, on a timely basis.

DISCUSSION QUESTIONS

1. Why should a project manager be concerned with criteria devoted to
   work that is the primary responsibility of others in the organization?

2. Summarize, in your own words, the four criteria dealing with assignment of costs to project elements.

3. When may Criterion 20 safely be disregarded? When may it not?

4. Under what circumstances might a project manager borrow materials designated for another project?

5. Describe your organization's system for assigning costs to projects.

6. Comment on the following statement: "Once the budget has been prepared and approved, there is nothing a project manager can do but use the dollars allocated without deviation."

7. What are a project manager's responsibilities for establishing communication links with accounting?

8. Describe some of the problems you have encountered with subcontractors.

9. How might the accounting department make your life easier?

10. Describe the three basic overhead cost allocation methods.

11. Briefly describe an activity-based costing system.

12. Describe your organization's overhead allocation method.

Appendix 9-A. Reciprocal Allocation of Overhead Costs

For convenience, the details of this example are the same as those used to illustrate the direct and step-down methods for allocating indirect costs, repeated here as Table 9-A.1.

TABLE 9-A.1   Reciprocal Example

	Overhead Pools			Projects		
	Accounting	Human Resources	Maintenance	1	2	3
Costs	$80,000	$60,000	$40,000			
Driver	work hours	number of employees	square feet			
Quantity						
hours	1,000	5,000	500	20,000	8,000	12,000
employees	2	10	20	250	150	90
square feet	250	500	100	2,500	3,000	1,550

Forming equations for the total cost of an overhead pool (its own cost plus its share of the other overhead pool costs), where its use of another overhead pool is the ratio of its use of that pool's driver to the total use of the driver by all other pools, we have the following system:

A = Accounting
HR = Human Resources
Mnt = Maintenance

A =	80,000	+	2/512	**HR +**	250/7,800	**Mnt**
HR =	60,000	+	5,000/45,500	**A +**	500/7,800	**Mnt**
Mnt =	40,000	+	500/45,500	**A +**	20/512	**HR**

The next step is to rearrange these equations into matrix format (A * X = B), where each column of the A matrix represents the pools for accounting, human resources, and maintenance, respectively. (Remember that moving the coefficients to the opposite side of the equal sign reverses their values from positive to negative and that each variable has an implied value of 1.)

A			X	B
1	−0.003906*	−0.0320513	A	$80,000
−0.10989011	1	−0.0641026	HR	60,000
−0.01989011	−0.039063	1	Mnt	40,000

*-2/512

Once matrices containing the equations are in this form, Excel matrix inversion formulas can be used to find A⁻¹, the inverted matrix. [The formula for the first row, first column, below is =INDEX(MINVERSE(A49:C51),1,1), where A49:C51 locates the A matrix and 1,1 refers to row 1, column 1. (The formula for the second row, first column, would be =INDEX(MINVERSE(A49:C51),2,1), and other cell locations would be identified in a similar manner.)]

The inverted matrix is displayed below, along with the variables and the original amounts of the three pools:

A Inverse			X	B
1.000924973	0.005176	0.03241272	A	$80,000
0.110974712	1.0030842	0.06785715	HR	60,000
0.015334125	0.9392399	1.00300685	Mnt	40,000

The next step is to multiply the A Inverse matrix by the B matrix to find the amounts that must be allocated from each pool. Multiplying the A Inverse matrix by the B matrix (Excel command =INDEX(MMULT($A$55:$C$57,$E$55:$E$57),1,1), where the matrix begins in column A, row 55) for the first row, first column (Accounting Pool), value results in the enhanced costs for each overhead pool. The amounts to be allocated are:

Accounting	$81,681
Human Resources	$71,777
Maintenance	$43,701

When costs are allocated back and forth between the overhead pools and projects, the total costs of each overhead pool will equal zero. (For convenience, the allocation bases and usages by each department and project are repeated at the top of Table 9-A.2.) Using this method, the allocations (all amounts rounded to the nearest dollar) are shown in the lower part of Table 9-A.2.

TABLE 9-A.2 Reciprocal Allocations

	Service Departments			Projects			Totals
	Accounting	Human Resources	Maintenance	1	2	3	
Accounting hours	1,000	5,000	500	20,000	8,000	12,000	45,500
Employees	2	10	20	250	150	90	512
Square feet	250	500	100	2,500	3,000	1,550	7,800
Mfg. overhead charged to service departments	$80,000	$60,000	$40,000	N/A	N/A	N/A	$180,000
Accounting allocation	$(81,681)	$8,976	$898	$35,904	$14,362	$21,542	$0
Human Resources allocation	$280	$(71,777)	$2,804	$35,048	$21,029	$12,617	$0
Maintenance allocation	$1,401	$2,801	$(43,701)	$14,007	$16,808	$8,684	$0
Totals	$0	$0	$0	$84,958	$52,198	$42,844	$180,000

Overhead pool costs have now been allocated to all users in a logical and defensible manner.

CHAPTER 10

Reporting Variances (Criteria 22–27)

> *"Things are going to get a lot worse before they get worse."*
> —LILY TOMLIN

Several assumptions underlie the material presented in this chapter. They include (1) costs have been appropriately budgeted and (2) costs incurred for project work have been accurately recorded and summarized to the proper control accounts. Quite simply, all the previous EVMS criteria are in place to support the next six criteria.

Criteria 22 through 27 establish specific metric reporting requirements and additional management actions triggered by those measures. Criteria 22 through 24 dictate the required basic metrics and how they should be analyzed, while Criteria 25 through 27 discuss how the basic metrics are used to gain additional performance insights.

More specifically, Criterion 22 requires reporting of basic schedule and cost variances, and Criterion 23 requires an explanation of reasons for the differences (variances) in planned and actual performance. Criterion 24 discusses information on project charges for indirect costs and their differences (variances) from plan.

Criterion 25 mandates that variances be summarized through the organizational structure and/or the work breakdown structure (WBS) in order to meet management information needs. Then, Criterion 26 looks at the implementation of management changes required to address computed variances. Using original projections, actual results, and calculated metrics, Criterion 27 requires revised estimates of cost and expected variances at completion, as well as any additional funding requirements.

EVMS CRITERION 22

At least on a monthly basis, generate the following information at the control account and other levels as necessary for management control using actual cost data from, or reconcilable with, the accounting system:

(1) Comparison of the amount of planned budget and the amount of budget earned for work accomplished. This comparison provides the schedule variance.

(2) Comparison of the amount of the budget earned and the actual (applied where appropriate) direct costs for the same work. This comparison provides the cost variance.

The measurements of EVMS were introduced in Chapter 3. *Actual cost* (AC) is the cost of all work completed as of the status date. *Planned value* (PV) is the cost that was budgeted for the work that was scheduled for completion for that same period. *Earned value* (EV) is the cost that was budgeted for the work that actually was completed during the period. Confusion often arises here because the EV metric is the result of a calculation using a planned value and an actual value while the other two measures, AC and PV, are total actual or total planned amounts.

EV is a measurement of the actual work performed, but only at the amount budgeted (planned) for that amount of work, not its actual cost; therefore, EV constitutes the "earned" amount of the project budget. These relationships are easy to see in the EVMS metrics triangle (Figure 10.1), which was first presented in Chapter 3.

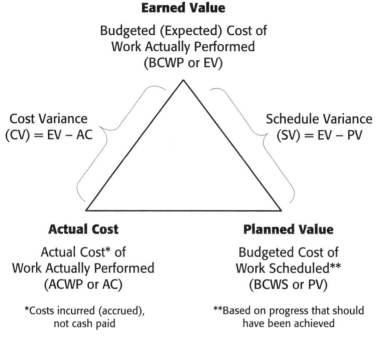

Earned Value

Budgeted (Expected) Cost of
Work Actually Performed
(BCWP or EV)

Cost Variance
(CV) = EV – AC

Schedule Variance
(SV) = EV – PV

Actual Cost

Actual Cost* of
Work Actually Performed
(ACWP or AC)

*Costs incurred (accrued),
not cash paid

Planned Value

Budgeted Cost of
Work Scheduled**
(BCWS or PV)

**Based on progress that should
have been achieved

FIGURE 10.1   EVMS Metrics Triangle

Criterion 22 requires information on the *schedule variance* (SV) and the *cost variance* (CV). SV is the difference between the EV and the PV (see Figure 10.1). Both variances are calculated in dollars. SV measures the difference between the budget for work that was actually performed (EV) and the budget for work that was scheduled (PV); budgeted costs are held constant in both measures. The CV is the variance between the EV and the AC; it is the difference between the budgeted cost for the same amount of work—the work actually performed during the period being reported—and the actual costs incurred for the same period. When beginning either equation with EV, if the variance is negative, it is unfavorable.

Determining the SV for the current status period, along with the cumulative SV since the start of the project, provides a valuable indicator of the project's overall schedule status in terms of dollars. However, it may not clearly indicate whether scheduled milestones are being met, especially if some work has been performed out of sequence or is ahead of schedule. SV does not indicate whether a completed activity is *critical* (where a positive or negative variance could affect the project's completion date) or *noncritical* (having no effect on project completion).

As we indicated earlier, this is a weakness of EVMS, and it reinforces the necessity of a formal, time-phased scheduling system. The status of critical activities and milestones, and therefore interpretation of variances and appropriate management response, must be determined through the diligent application of other sound project management techniques.

It is critical that the same basis used in budgeting be used for accumulating ACs. In Chapter 8, we stressed the use of a cost estimation package that includes the basis of the cost estimates as well as the cost baseline. To ensure valid comparisons to the baseline, the objective methods used during the estimation process must be employed during the project's progress. The accounting department should confirm that any estimates and assumptions used to accrue estimated costs for the budget baseline, such as indirect allocations, also are used in accruing ACs.

Determining the EV of work packages that are only partially completed at the time of the project status may pose some difficulty. There are many ways to estimate how much work has been completed, but none of them are very defensible. Work packages generally encompass one to two weeks of work, which minimizes this estimation problem, but some may be longer. Accurate progress will be easier to measure if discrete milestones are imbedded in larger work packages so that you need not use an algorithm to determine the percent completed.

Actual cost data from the organization's accounting system, or data that can be reconciled with the accounting system, must be used for calculating the EVMS metrics. Analyzing the CV in detail can reveal factors causing the variance, such as a higher cost for labor and materials, a requirement for additional resources, lower-than-expected efficiencies, the use of different budget and actual rates, or even poor budget estimates. The budget amounts should be scheduled in conjunction with project events and then earned and actual costs applied when the event occurs. A problem often is encountered when there are delays between the end of a project status period and the availability of cost data from the accounting system. In that case, estimates must be used so that artificial variances are not created solely by lags in recording transactions.

Correct data availability for variance computations is the key to complying with Criterion 22. Once the variances are identified, they must be analyzed. Criterion 23, discussed in the next section, requires this natural follow-up.

EVMS CRITERION 23

Identify, at least monthly, the significant differences between both planned and actual schedule performance and planned and actual cost performance, and provide the reasons for the variances in the detail needed by program management.

EVMS provides the evaluation and feedback loop for management action, so that management can evaluate variances and make informed decisions for corrective action. There may be activities that can bring a project back on plan or compensate in other ways for the variances in cost, schedule, or project scope. Sometimes the management decision may be to discontinue the project if the deviations are great enough and compensatory actions are not deemed viable.

This criterion requires the identification of significant variances and their reasons. Determination of what *significant* means depends on the organization, the size of the project, task and project risk, and a number of other factors. The amount of detail required for the variance report depends on the margin of deviation from the plan.

Schedule Variance

Comparing the project schedule with milestone completion reports, critical path or critical chain data, and other information such as the WBS is sufficient to discover the reasons for schedule variances. The perceived significance of the variance will depend on its severity and expected schedule impact. Even severe variations in individual task durations may not be considered significant if they are caused by factors that will not delay the project or increase costs.

If subcontractors are involved in the project, the primary organization must have processes in place to check and verify the subcontractors' progress. It is good practice to have a responsible manager in the primary organization who reviews and analyzes the subcontractors' reports. The information then must be integrated into the primary progress report and EV data. In EVMS, the subcontractors' progress payments will usually depend on EV calculations that must be verified by the responsible primary manager. Some items to check carefully are the consumption of any reserves, changes in the apportionment of manpower, or a baseline change in the subcontractors' schedules.

Cost Variance

Material usage generally accounts for a major part of a project's cost variance. Analysis of material accounts should focus on *significant* variances and may include variances above or below the expected usage, as well as above or below the expected cost per item. For example, comparing budget and AC information on material usage should enable you to determine whether the variance results from a change in material cost (usually called a *price variance*) or a change in consumption (sometimes called a *quantity* or *efficiency variance*).[1] Often, a project will require more material than was expected because of unexpected destruction during testing and scrap

---

[1]The left side of Figure 3.1 shows the cost/budget and quantity/volume variances of a standard cost system.

resulting from quality problems. Complete variance records with identification of causes will help significantly in providing accurate estimations for future project plans.

The accounting department will compute these price and efficiency variances, but you might be wise to consider keeping a journal record of selected (major) situations of rising costs or more-than-expected usage to aid in explaining variances that may not be computed until weeks after the events occurred.

Explaining Variances

First, be aware that Criterion 23 does not require an explanation for every variance in the EVMS calculations. Note that the criterion specifically mentions the "reasons…in the detail needed by… management"; management's interest should always be one of the guiding factors. Other factors include the level of risk in achieving the project's technical objectives and significant variances in high-cost elements.

Although there are many methods for setting variance reporting thresholds, we consider three the most helpful:

1. Analyze any variance that exceeds a predetermined threshold in dollar or percentage terms. This method usually results in more variance analyses, particularly as the project progresses.
2. Analyze the top five or ten (or any number) largest dollar variances. This method usually reduces the number of variance analyses and focuses attention on the most significant problems.
3. Preselect high-cost or high-risk areas for analysis. As the project progresses, the risk areas will change, so the areas selected for analysis also should change.

Keep in mind that variances can be positive or negative, current, cumulative, or at completion.

EVMS CRITERION 24

Identify budgeted and applied (or actual) indirect costs at the level and frequency needed by management for effective control, along with the reasons for any significant variances.

The differences in and examples of direct and indirect costs were presented in Chapter 9. In general, *direct costs* are those that can be directly traced to a project (materials and labor, for example), while *indirect costs* are shared overhead-type costs that must be allocated. Criterion 24 requires a thorough examination of the entire process for establishing and allocating indirect costs to individual projects. Indirect cost allocation often is more difficult in organizations that do not have a project-oriented organizational structure (see Chapter 6), because the organization that is structured around projects will incur most of its costs by project and typically has lower overall shared indirect expenses.

Indirect costs may be variable with some level of activity, fixed regardless of activity, or some combination of the two. For example, the human resources department may be able to handle a 10 percent increase in the current level of employees with its current staff, but if additional project workers are required, the department must hire additional staffers.

Indirect fixed costs are planned and experienced based primarily on the passage of time; there should be little variance between project budgets and actual allocations, with the exception of changes in costs (such as an unexpected change in the local property tax rate). Some other causes for variances include changes in corporate structure, changes in number of projects using the same organizational elements, and differences between the timeframe or driver used for planning and that used for the allocation.

The variances must be reported accurately so that they can be analyzed and the project manager can determine appropriate corrective action. Sometimes corrective action is not appropriate, but the variance report also is important for developing revisions to the estimated cost at completion (EAC) and for more accurately estimating future indirect project costs.

EVMS CRITERION 25

Summarize the data elements and associated variances through the program organization and/or work breakdown structure to support management needs and any customer reporting specified in the contract.

The summarized data elements and associated variances should include all the points shown on the EVMS metrics triangle (see Figure 10.1). Calculations for PV, AC, EV, and the two variances should be made at appropriate levels and summarized (aggregated) for the entire organization involved in the project.

The level of summarized data for a contractual report is usually well defined in the contract. The more difficult aspect of this criterion is ascertaining the level of information required for internal management needs. Management reports generally are considered adequate when constructed from the summary information at level two or three of the WBS. However, reporting must recognize that a high-level manager may have a large oversight scope where positive and negative variances at lower levels cancel each other in the manager's summarized report and may not indicate a problem. Immaterial variances at a top summary level, though, do not necessarily mean that managerial action is not required.

The appropriate summarization starts at the control account (CA) level. CAs have been established in conjunction with the accounting department at the lowest level of the organization where a specific organizational unit was responsible for a specific piece of the WBS (see Control Accounts in Chapter 5). As a requirement of Criterion 25, this summation must continue upward through both the organizational breakdown structure (OBS) and the WBS, but the summations must reconcile. That is, the total variances must be the same whether summarized through the WBS or the OBS.

Management needs are satisfied and appropriate corrective actions can be identified when all levels of management receive and evaluate EVMS metrics at their level. This approach also will allow an appropriate evaluation in cases where small variances at lower management levels may not merit attention but cumulatively signal a problem.

EVMS CRITERION 26

Implement managerial actions taken as the result of EV information.

This criterion generally requires that management at the various levels of the organization have authority for corrective action. As pointed out earlier, a significant variance at the CA level may be cancelled out by other variances when it is included in the summarized report. Corrective actions may not be taken at the various levels at which problems have occurred unless the managers at those levels of responsibility have commensurate authority. The CA level can be the primary management control point for the project.

Caveat: This is an excellent time to review the caution expressed in Chapter 3. EV metrics are informational as opposed to motivational: They may indicate a problem, but they do not pinpoint the reasons for the problems. Project decisions must be based on sound project management practices, and personnel evaluations should not be based on EV metrics. The practice can elicit unproductive responses. EV metrics, however, can give a fairly reliable forecast of the project's final cost performance. (Schedule variance is less useful for predicting final status. At least during the last third of a project's duration, schedule variance will reconcile to zero.)[2]

---

[2]Earned schedule, discussed in Chapter 16, attempts to overcome this shortcoming of the EV schedule variance.

EVMS CRITERION 27

Develop revised estimates of cost at completion based on performance to date, commitment values for material, and estimates of future conditions. Compare this information with the performance measurement baseline to identify variances at completion important to company management and any applicable customer reporting requirements, including statements of funding requirements.

This criterion states three considerations in developing revised cost EAC. They are "performance to date, commitment values for material, and estimates of future conditions." Those three elements are examined first; then the second part of this criterion, reporting, is discussed.

Performance to Date

Performance to date is primarily a calculation of EV metrics and a review of how well the technical requirements are being met.

Earned Value Measurements

One way to develop an EAC is first to calculate an estimate to complete (ETC) with the formula provided in Chapter 3. You must know the total budget at completion (BAC) or total value (TV), the current EV, the cost performance index (CPI), or alternatively, the CPI and the schedule performance index (SPI). The CPI is the EV divided by the AC. The SPI is the EV divided by the PV. (You may want to review the EVMS metrics triangle in Figure 10.1.)

To calculate the ETC, subtract the EV from the BAC and divide the result by the CPI. Alternatively, if both the CPI and the SPI are taken into consideration, the result is divided by the product of the CPI times the SPI. Once the ETC has been calculated, it is easy to develop an EAC by simply adding the AC and the calculated ETC. The formulas are:

Estimate to Complete:

$$\text{ETC} = \frac{Budget\ at\ Completion - Earned\ Value}{Cost\ Performance\ Index} \quad \text{or}$$

$$\frac{BAC - EV}{CPI} \quad \text{(for an ``optimistic'' estimate) or}$$

$$\frac{BAC - EV}{CPI * SPI} \quad \text{(for a ``pessimistic'' estimate).}$$

Estimate at Completion (revised total estimated final cost):

EAC = *Actual Cost (to date) + Estimate to Complete,*
or EAC = *AC + ETC.*

To discover what level of performance must be achieved on the remaining project work in order to complete the project within some specified financial goal such as the original budget, the total project price, or another maximum amount, a to-complete index (TCI), may be computed. This ratio, when greater than 1, reflects performance at a higher level than that previously demonstrated as required; when less than 1, it means that performance can be less than that previously experienced and still meet the desired goal. This index is computed by dividing the value of the remaining work by the remaining funds. *Remaining funds,* however, may be defined in several ways: BAC less costs incurred to date, EAC less ACs incurred, or total contract price less ACs incurred.

Here is one commonly used version where funds are limited to those originally budgeted:

$$\text{TCI} = \frac{Remaining\ Work}{Remaining\ Funds} =$$

$$\frac{Budget\ at\ Completion - Earned\ Value}{Budget\ at\ Completion - Actual\ Costs\ Incurred}$$

To demonstrate these computations, we use the simple example from Chapter 4, repeated here as Figure 10.2.

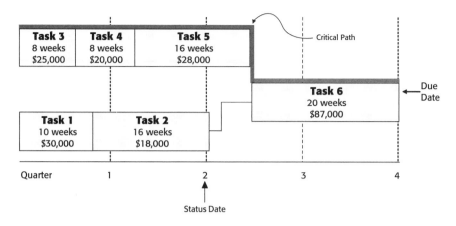

FIGURE 10.2   A Project Network

Assume the status date is now the end of the second quarter. By this date, Tasks 1, 3, and 4 should have been completely finished, along with about 93 percent of Task 2 and 57 percent of Task 5. Although Tasks 1, 3, and 4 are finished, however, Task 2 is only 75 percent complete and Task 5 is estimated at 25 percent complete. Materials are added only in Tasks 1, 3, and 6; costs for other tasks are incurred uniformly over time. Costs incurred thus far total $101,500. Figure 10.3 displays this situation on the EVMS metrics triangle, and Figure 10.4 contains EVMS calculations for the example project.

We can see from the example calculations in Figure 10.4 that the project is estimated to complete at a cost of $221,181 (or $235,973) rather than $208,000, as originally budgeted. It also is clear from the TCI that future efforts must be more productive than exhibited thus far if the project is to be completed within the original budgeted amount.

At each status reporting date, an SV and a CV should be calculated for each control account before being rolled up for the entire project. CA managers need to be aware of variances that will affect the EAC, because authority and responsibility for corrective action begin at that level.

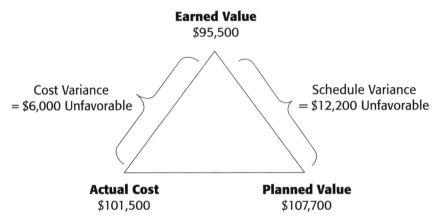

Earned Value
$95,500

Cost Variance = $6,000 Unfavorable

Schedule Variance = $12,200 Unfavorable

Actual Cost
$101,500

Planned Value
$107,700

FIGURE 10.3   EVMS Metrics Triangle for Example Project at Halfway Point

Interpreting the Variances

It is obvious that the second-quarter results are continuing the trend established in the first quarter: Cost and schedule variances remain negative. While the cost variance remains unchanged at $6,000 unfavorable, the schedule variance has increased an additional $2,200 unfavorable. However, the EAC has decreased by a minimum of $7,390 from the first quarter (from $228,571 and $265,781 to $221,181 and $235,973 for optimistic and pessimistic estimates, respectively). Thus, performance is improving.

Nevertheless, to complete the project on budget, performance must increase by a factor of 0.06. Or, negotiations may be entered to increase the baseline budget to a more realistic amount closer to the current EAC.

Technical Performance

Variances in cost and schedule are often caused by technical problems; however, the absence of significant budget variances does not necessarily mean that the project is achieving its objectives. The

A status is taken at the end of six months for a one-year project. The total planned budget for the project is $208,000. The project staff has completed Tasks 1, 3, and 4 but only 75 percent of Task 2 and 57 percent of Task 5. Expenditures to date equal $101,500.

TV (BAC) = $208,000 = $30,000 + $25,000 +$18,000 + $20,000 + $28,000 + $87,000

AC = $101,500

PV = $107,700 = $30,000 + $25,000 + $20,000 + (.93 x $18,000) + (.57 x $28,000)

EV = $95,500 = $30,000 + $25,000 + $20,000 + (.75 x $18,000) + (.25 x $28,000)

CV = $6,000 Unfavorable = $95,500 – $101,500 = ($6,000)

$$CPI = 0.94 = \frac{\$95,500}{\$101,500}$$

SV = $12,200 Unfavorable = $95,500 – $107,700 = ($12,200)

$$SPI = 0.89 = \frac{\$95,500}{\$107,700}$$

"To complete" calculations considering only the CPI ("optimistic" estimate):

$$ETC = \$119,681 = \frac{\$208,000 - \$95,500}{0.94}$$

EAC = $221,181 = $119,681 + $101,500

$$TCI = 1.06 = \frac{\$208,000 - \$95,500}{\$208,000 - \$101,500}$$, using the original BAC, shows that additional

effort must be expended to complete the project on budget.

Alternative calculations taking into account both the CPI and the SPI ("pessimistic" estimate):

$$ETC = \$134,473 = \frac{\$208,000 - \$95,500}{0.94 \times 0.89} = \frac{\$112,500}{0.8366}$$

EAC = $235,973= $134,473 + $101,500

Another alternative calculation is TCI using a consultant's *independent* ETC of $118,500 and EAC of $220,000:

$$TCI = 0.95 = \frac{\$208,000 - \$95,500}{\$220,000 - \$101,500}$$, which probably would be deemed credible,

even though it is not within the optimistic and pessimistic estimates. (The TCI index is slightly more than 1 percent different from the CPI, and the acceptable variation usually is ± .5 percent.)

FIGURE 10.4   Sample EVMS Calculation

quality of the project work can be determined with appropriate testing, inspections, and mechanical measurements. A narrative report by the project members sometimes can be helpful in determining the technical performance status. Reports from team members, whether solicited or not, should be read carefully and special attention given to suggestions.

One problem we have encountered repeatedly is that a project manager belatedly will discover a lack of required resources. The project is rolling along right on schedule, and suddenly no one is available for the next critical task. Project managers must be aware of remaining work on the project and must predict both the requirements for and availability of resources.

The critical chain methodology provides an early warning device for critical resources (Leach 2005). Chapter 17 explains the essential elements of critical chain.

When corrective action or necessary project changes are required, project managers should carefully consider the alternatives. Some work-arounds or fixes for a technical problem may involve substantial changes in the project cost and schedule. If changes are considered necessary and an alternative action is chosen, the changes must be reflected in the project plan. New work packages might need to be added or existing packages altered.

Our experience indicates that projects get into the most trouble when changes are not fully documented and communicated. Project managers must be certain that all project changes are fully authorized, accounted for, and clearly shown in a revised project baseline. (See Chapter 11 for Criteria 28 through 32 and a more thorough discussion of project revisions.)

Updated Values for Materials

For each periodic EVMS measurement, there is a requirement to determine the amount and cost of materials needed to complete the project. This estimate becomes a part of the ETC, and it should be based on the actual costs to date, actual usage to date, estimates of future usage, commitments for additional material, and projections of future prices. Any variance with the material budget must be documented and reported for possible corrective action. Just as a project manager must be concerned with providing for future human resource requirements, he or she must also be concerned with the future material requirements and must communicate and coordinate updated information with the organization's purchasing department in a timely manner.

Estimates of Future Conditions

When considering the "performance to date" and "commitment values for materials" cited in this criterion, some additional facets of future conditions must be taken into account in developing the most accurate EAC. For example, the estimates made from performance to date should acknowledge probable changes in future performance. The cost of materials should include both future price changes and future changes in usage. This criterion, however, adds a further general category of "future conditions."

This might be considered an unnecessary catch-all category, but some conditions outside the project parameters might not be considered if it were omitted. Examples of possible factors include the following:

- Overall anticipated business volume
- Estimates of general economic changes
- Organizational changes contemplated by management.

Performance Reporting

The second part of Criterion 27 requires the generation of information important to management and any reporting required by the contract. To maintain a cost-effective system, the federal government encourages contractors to report only enough information for adequate management control. Although we have tried to present all the standard metrics, it is possible that particular contracts might require additional measures, such as quality performance, time required to implement approved changes, or number of changes accepted versus those requested. The project manager must be alert to these requirements and ensure that data are recorded so contractual obligations are met.

The use of electronic data interchange (EDI) is recommended (mandatory in many cases), using the American National Standards Institute (ANSI) Accredited Standards Committee (ASC) X.12 standard for EDI. Requirements for submitting reports by electronic means may be included in the contract (Department of Defense 2006a, section 2.2.5.5.2). The primary report for EVMS projects has been the contract performance report (CPR); however, a proposed EVMS revision now includes the integrated master schedule (IMS).

Contract Performance Report

The contract performance report (Defense Acquisition University 2005a, chapter 11.3.1.4.1) is a contractually required report, prepared by the contractor to provide a status of progress on the project. The report must be made for all contracts that require compliance with EVMS, but it also may be requested on contracts that fall below the dollar thresholds for EVMS compliance. It is intended to provide an early indication of cost and schedule problems and to show the effect of any management actions implemented to correct such problems.

The CPR is subject to tailoring by the contracting agency, but it basically details the project's cost/schedule status and trends using five formats. A government agency may request data in Formats 1 through 4 from the contractor to "get the numbers" while the narrative (Format 5) is being prepared. In some cases, such as when a narrative is given during regular project status reviews, the agency may forgo Format 5.

Sample formats can be seen on the Department of Defense's website for the Directorate for Information Operations and Reports (DIOR):

1. Format 1 reports EVMS metrics on elements of the WBS (http://www.dior.whs.mil/forms/DD2734-1.pdf).
2. Format 2 is a similar report from the viewpoint of organizational categories (http://www.dior.whs.mil/forms/ DD27342.pdf).
3. Format 3 reports performance data concerning the performance measurement baseline (http://www.dior .whs.mil/forms/DD2734-3.pdf).
4. Format 4 deals with performance data and forecasts for staffing (http://www.dior.whs.mil/forms/DD2734-4.pdf).
5. Format 5 is a narrative that reports explanations and problem analysis (http://www.dior.whs.mil/forms/DD27345.pdf).

Integrated Master Schedule

A section of the *Defense Acquisition Guidebook* (Defense Acquisition University 2005a, chapter 11.8) concerns *integrated product and process development* (IPPD), which is the Department of Defense management technique that integrates all essential acquisition activities through the use of multidisciplinary teams called *integrated product teams* (IPT). These teams coordinate all the activities related to a product. The primary documents of IPPD that are now being required for all Department of Defense acquisitions are the *integrated master plan* (IMP) and *integrated master schedule* (IMS).

The IMP describes the events, significant accomplishments, and accomplishment criteria for all the activities that were specified in the contract work breakdown dictionary and other documents that were a part of the government solicitation. The completed IMP then usually becomes the defining project document and part of the final contract.

The IMS places the events and significant accomplishments (the accomplishment criteria specify the conditions for completion of a significant accomplishment) on a time scale as schedule milestones. Tasks are added to the IMS to support the events and significant accomplishments (milestones). The tasks and milestones are linked to produce the IMS. EVMS metrics can then be generated from the IMS to provide the required performance measurements.

Other Requirements

Criterion 27 also requires the reporting of contract funding requirements. The Contract Funds Status Report (CFSR) (DD Form 1586) is designed to supply funding data about defense contracts to program managers for:

- Updating and forecasting contract fund requirements
- Planning and decision-making on funding changes to contracts
- Developing fund requirements and budget estimates in support of approved programs
- Determining funds in excess of contract needs and available for deobligation
- Obtaining rough estimates of termination costs.

See Figure 10.5 for an example form provided by the Defense Acquisition University.

Your project might not require the formality of the various government report formats, but these reporting criteria were designed so that the reported information is meaningful. Any report prepared must provide accurate and timely information that can inform management decisions. It should be noted that the previous admonition is also an excellent guideline for nongovernmental projects.

Four primary characteristics of *significant information* are:

1. *Relevance*: The information has accurate, confirmatory, and predictive value.

CLASSIFICATION

CONTRACT FUNDS STATUS REPORT *(Dollars in)*

1. CONTRACT NUMBER	3. CONTRACT FUNDING FOR FOR FY	5. PREVIOUS REPORT DATE	7. CONTRACTOR *(Name, address and zip code)*	9. INITIAL CONTRACT PRICE a. TARGET b. CEILING
2. CONTRACT TYPE	4. APPROPRIATION	6. CURRENT REPORT DATE	8. PROGRAM	10. ADJUSTED CONTRACT PRICE a. TARGET b. CEILING

11. **FUNDING INFORMATION**

LINE ITEM/WBS ELEMENT a	APPRO-PRIATION IDENTI-FICATION b	FUNDING AUTHORIZED TO DATE c	ACCRUED EXPENDITURES OPEN COMMITMENTS TOTAL d	CONTRACT WORK AUTHORIZED: DEFINITIZED e	CONTRACT WORK AUTHORIZED: NOT DEFINITIZED f	CONTRACT WORK AUTHORIZED: SUBTOTAL g	FORECAST: NOT YET AUTHORIZED h	FORECAST: ALL OTHER WORK i	FORECAST: SUBTOTAL j	TOTAL REQUIRE-MENTS k	FUNDS CARRY-OVER l	NET FUNDS REQUIRED m

12. **CONTRACT WORK AUTHORIZED** *(With Fee/Profit)* **- ACTUAL OR PROJECTED**

	ACTUAL TO DATE									AT COMPLETION
a. OPEN COMMITMENTS										
b. ACCRUED EXPENDITURES										
c. TOTAL *(12a + 12b)*										
13. FORECAST OF BILLINGS TO THE GOVERNMENT										
14. ESTIMATED TERMINATION COSTS										

15. **REMARKS**

Page _____ of _____ Pages

CLASSIFICATION

SAMPLE FORMAT 1. Contract Funds Status Report Page 7 of 7

Source: Defense Acquisition University 2004, *Defense Acquisition Guidebook,* Chapter 11.3.2.4.

FIGURE 10.5 Contract Funds Status Report

2. *Reliability*: The information is complete and as error-free as possible.
3. *Comparability*: A strict following of the requirements of EVMS will ensure that report information has a base with which current performance can be compared.
4. *Comprehensibility*: Information is fully explained and free of biased or misleading representations.

This chapter presents the results of establishing all the EVMS metrics—the performance reports that reveal the differences between projected and actual performance. All previous criteria were established to ensure that reliable data are recorded and summarized so that reliable variances can be reported, analyzed, and addressed.

Criterion 22 stipulates that cost and schedule variances must be computed and reported at the control account and other levels necessary for management control. Criterion 23 requires that variances between planned and actual schedule and cost performance, combined with reasons for the variances, be described at a level of detail that will satisfy management and contractual needs.

Criterion 24 prescribes that differences in budgeted and applied indirect costs, as well as reasons for significant variances, be reported at the level and frequency needed by management. These are costs that cannot be directly traced to a project, and they must be allocated using some rational and reasonable formula. They pose a bigger problem for functional organizational structures than do project-oriented structures.

Criterion 25 requires that data elements and resulting variances be associated with the work breakdown structure or organizational structure to support management's need for information or to comply with contractual obligations. The amounts thus associated are then combined for all elements to generate project totals.

Actions to remedy unfavorable variances are stipulated by Criterion 26, while Criterion 27 requires revised estimates of cost at completion, estimates of future conditions, comparisons with the project baseline, and implications of funding sufficiency. The contract performance report and the integrated master schedule are the primary reports for federal EVMS contracts.

PRACTICE CALCULATIONS

Exercise 1

Assume the following project (Figure 10.6) is being prepared for progress review at the end of the third quarter.

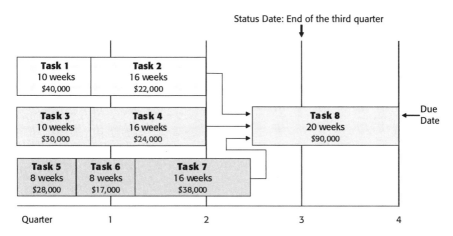

FIGURE 10.6   Exercise Project Layout

According to the budget baseline, all tasks should be completed except Task 8, which should be about 30% complete at this time. The project manager reports, however, that all tasks are finished except the last one, which is about 50 percent complete.

Required: Assuming that actual costs to date total $240,000, compute the following:

   a. BAC

   b. BCWS (PV)

   c. EV

   d. AC

   e. CV and CPI

   f. SV and SPI

   g. ETC and EAC

   h. TCI.

Exercise 2

Evaluate the variances computed in Exercise 1.

See Appendix B for solutions to Exercises 1 and 2.

PART V

Handling a Project's Changes and Termination

These two chapters cover the criteria for handling project changes and an important part of the project life cycle that is not covered by EVMS—terminating a project. Because every project is a unique event, meeting the project's objectives of schedule, cost, and quality is a very risky proposition. The uncertainties always result in some project modification, but managing risk can mitigate the probabilities and consequences of major change. The last five criteria, explored in Chapter 11, detail the requirements for controlling, making, and documenting project changes.

Because finishing a project is sometimes difficult and almost always precipitates undesirable effects, Chapter 12 covers project termination. The project must first be completed and its objectives met before initiating the activities and reports that will officially close the project. One of the important documents of project termination that will help guide future projects is the "lessons learned."

CHAPTER 11

Time for a Change (Criteria 28–32)

The last five EVMS criteria cover change—how and when to change, what to change, controlling change, and reporting change. Because the need for change results from the high degree of risk involved in projects, we begin with a look at the implications and ramifications of risk. Then we address the management of change, present a formal change control process, and finish with some specific information about each of the criteria.

UNCERTAINTY MAY BE THE ONLY CERTAINTY

You probably have heard about the 1995 Standish Group's study of information technology projects and their horrendous failure rate (Standish Group International 1995). Even though an update showed significant improvement over the next decade (Standish Group International 2004), failures still occur far too often and cost too much. We believe that more professional practices, such as using EVMS, are contributing to better project success rates. Yet if anything can go wrong during the project's life span, it will—Murphy's

Law in action. We can minimize the frequency of Murphy's visits by addressing and managing risk.

Risk management is a very complex process and is the responsibility of the entire organization. If the organization has an enterprise risk management process or practice, the project manager should be able to align the project's risk management with the organization's risk activities. If not, the project manager should promote an enterprise risk management framework. However, the project manager must operate solo for the current project.

We provide some suggestions and tools in this chapter, but risk management depends on several key factors, such as the level of the organization's capacity for risk tolerance. Therefore, please keep in mind that our suggestions and examples will need to be modified for your specific organization's environment.

If your organization would like assistance in establishing an enterprise risk management practice, we highly recommend *Enterprise Risk Management—Integrated Framework* written by PricewaterhouseCoopers, LLP (Steinberg et al. 2004). The framework was commissioned by the Committee of Sponsoring Organizations[1] of the Treadway Commission, commonly referred to as COSO. The framework is designed to assist organizations in determining how much risk their entity is prepared to accept and how it can proceed to handle risks and opportunities effectively. This analysis and a companion document, *Application Techniques*, are available at https://www.cpa2biz.com.

---

[1]COSO members include the American Accounting Association, American Institute of Certified Public Accountants, Financial Executives Institute, Institute of Management Accountants, and Institute of Internal Auditors.

UNDERSTANDING THE ELEMENTS OF RISK

> *"I know you think you understand what you think I said, but I'm not sure you realize that what you heard is not what I meant."*
> —Unknown

The Department of Defense (DoD) defines *risk* as:

". . . a measure of future uncertainties in achieving program performance goals and objectives within defined cost, schedule and performance constraints and has three components: (1) a future root cause that, if eliminated, would avoid a potential consequence (2) the *probability* of failing to achieve a particular outcome and (3) the *consequences* of failing to achieve that outcome [emphases added]" (Department of Defense 2006b, 1).

Risk management is the process of applying resources to mitigate future potential root causes and their negative consequences, and it should occur from a project's earliest planning stage to its conclusion. An investigation of project risk should include a statement of the future root cause of a risk event and a categorization of its probability and consequence; for example, a computer failure is only a concern and cannot be considered a risk unless and until the event's probability and consequence can be specifically defined.

Another misunderstanding often occurs when people talk about *high* risk. They might mean there is an increased probability for the event to occur, or they might mean that the consequences will be severe. It is a *combination* of these two factors of probability and impact that determines the overall level of risk. Figure 11.1 illustrates four levels of probability and impact for the acceptability of project risk (left half) or the potential contribution of an opportunity (right half). If the risk event's probability and impact intersect in the lower-left quadrant, the risk would be considered low. The determination of the ratios of low, medium, and high risk could be adjusted to reflect the organization's overall risk tolerance. Similarly, if an opportunity's probability and impact intersect in the far-right lower quadrant, it would not warrant further attention. Thus, the four side-by-side quadrants are mirror images of each other, and the probabilities and impact that intersect in either of the "high" regions require careful follow-up.

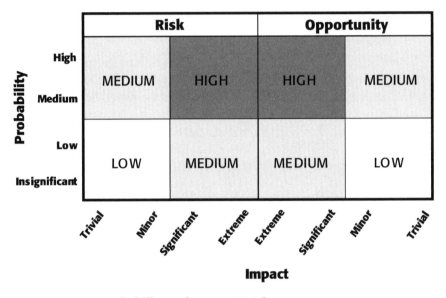

FIGURE 11.1   Probability and Impact Matrix

The Department of Energy (DOE) recognizes both threats and opportunities: "Threats are risks with negative consequences, and opportunities are risks with positive benefits" (Department of Energy 2008b, 1).

RISK MANAGEMENT

The latest version of DOE's *Risk Management Guide* (Department of Energy 2008b)[2] focuses on the continuous nature of risk man-

---

[2]This guide describes suggested nonmandatory approaches for meeting requirements. It does not establish requirements, and its suggestions are not to be construed as requirements in any audit or appraisal for compliance.

agement. The guide lists five risk management responsibilities of a contractor project manager:

1. Apply a continuous, iterative risk management process.
2. Document and manage risks.
3. Develop, maintain, and provide required risk documentation and reporting to appropriate project and program management personnel. This includes providing configuration management for this documentation.
4. Ensure a tailored approach to risk management.
5. Verify acceptance and closure of key program/project risks.

A complete responsibility assignment matrix for risk management roles and responsibilities should be included in the risk management plan.

The risk management process involves risk (1) identification, (2) analysis, (3) mitigation planning, (4) mitigation implementation, and (5) tracking. Our general model of risk management includes three phases: risk assessment (identification and analysis), disposition (mitigation planning and implementation), and monitoring (risk tracking). Figure 11.2 reflects these relationships.

Risk Assessment

Risk assessment is a multiphase process of examining the three project *constraints* (cost, schedule, and technical requirements) and other areas and factors surrounding a project in order to *identify* and *evaluate* potential problems. Identifying every possible problem is virtually impossible, but by using a variety of techniques, most of the significant project risks can be exposed. It is helpful to combine some elementary assessment during the identification phase so that immaterial problems can be quickly eliminated.

One of the major difficulties in risk identification is surfacing all the possibilities, because there are so many subconscious assumptions we never question in planning a project. In the Identifying

Risk section, some techniques specifically designed to surface and explore assumptions are described.

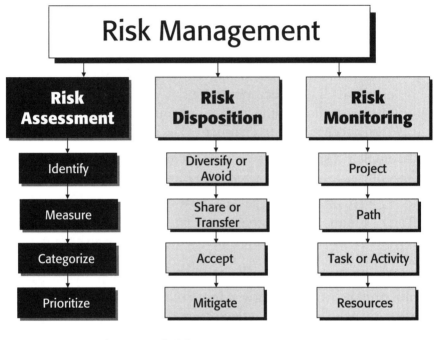

FIGURE 11.2   Elements of Risk Management

Identifying Risk

Risk identification will be more complete if you include in this activity as many appropriate stakeholders as possible, including the project manager, all members of the project team, end users, and outside experts on the project deliverables or risk management. The following techniques have proven useful for identifying risk:

- *Brainstorming*. A trained facilitator should lead this group activity in an unrestrained atmosphere. The idea is to generate as many ideas of risks (and opportunities) as possible, with no "idea ownership," so group members can feed off one another. The contributions should be made without judgment—at least in the beginning—so that potential ideas are not suppressed. The real challenge comes in validating the items from an unrestricted list so that only the best ones survive.

- *Surveys.* This technique is a great way to solicit a lot of input, but it has at least two weaknesses. One is that many people simply do not respond to surveys, while others tend always to do so, biasing the results. Another problem is that survey results are often tainted by the way the survey is presented, the way questions are asked, or the fact that questions contain various ambiguities subject to different interpretation by respondents.
- *Checklists.* A checklist of previous risk events can be very helpful when the organization has managed projects similar to the one being assessed. Be sure to allow room for additions, because reviewing previous events likely will trigger thoughts about additional possibilities.
- *Personal interviews.* This technique can elicit many possible risk events if the interview is conducted in a relaxed environment by a trained facilitator, but it has weaknesses similar to those of the survey. In addition, the facilitator must be knowledgeable about the project, because there will be no other assistance during a one-on-one interview.
- *Lessons learned* (*previous projects*). This technique is very similar to the risk checklist in that it presents a starting point. It differs in that it is not specific to risk events and therefore allows for more freedom of thought; however, it may lead to some irrelevancy.
- *Examination of the work breakdown structure (WBS) elements.* This is a very thorough but time-consuming way to assess the project for potential risk. The examination should be done in stages corresponding to the levels of the WBS. Major risk events may be associated with the top levels of the WBS, but the "devil" is usually in discovering the detailed information so that a solution strategy can be formulated.

We found a number of alternative techniques for identifying risk proposed by Dr. David Hillson (the "Risk Doctor") in his Internet papers (Hillson 2009). One of our favorites involves encouraging imagination through the use of *fantasy questions* to expose risks in a nonthreatening way. One of his fantasy questions is, "If you were dreaming about your project and it turned into a nightmare, what would be happening?" He notes that "this question encourages people to talk about perceived threats" that would not be articulated with more conservative thinking.

An appendix to the DOE's *Risk Management Guide* provides a detailed "Risk Identification Checklist" (Department of Energy 2008b, appendix 8).

Evaluating Risk

Although some risk analysis is accomplished while identifying potential project risk, a more thorough evaluation must be completed after the risks have been recognized. The process begins by expanding the depiction of the risk to establish its probability of occurrence and the possible severity of its consequences (see Figure 11.1). Identifying probable causes for each event helps with the process and provides additional insight. Because there are always a great number of potential events, they cannot all be handled in the same manner or with the same level of effort. They must be differentiated. The risk analysis process provides a basis for determining the priority and disposition method for each event.

Categorizing risks according to sources of the risk, which portion of the project is affected, or which resources might be involved may assist in the risk evaluation process. Grouping risks according to common causes also helps generate some focused and creative responses.

Although analyzing a risk's probability and consequences, which produces the comparative level of risk, is a difficult process, it can be made somewhat easier with the use of a rating scheme. The rating should include the probability of the event's occurrence and the possible consequences for the three project constraints—schedule, cost, and specifications.

Figure 11.3 is an example of a matrix using a rating scheme to prioritize potential risks. Each of the descriptions can be assigned a weighting factor, and a matrix can be used to assess the overall threat the risk poses to achieving the project's objective and to assist in prioritizing the risk events to facilitate the selection of appropriate disposition methods.

Risk Event	Occurrence	Schedule	Cost	Specs
Vendor fails to deliver software	Remote	Major slip in project date	Initial monetary problem	Some adjustment to specs
Loss of in-house trainer (resignation, illness, etc.)	Unlikely	Some project delay	Low monetary consideration	Minor adjustment to specs
Loss of network server	Unlikely	Some project delay	Some monetary consideration	No change in specs
. . .	. . .	. . .	. . .	. . .

FIGURE 11.3   Risk Rating Form

One complex, but productive, method particularly useful for analyzing risk is the *Delphi technique* developed by Brown and Dalkey of the Rand Corporation during the 1960s. It is a method of achieving consensus through an iterative and anonymous survey of experts. One of its first applications was technological forecasting, but it can be a valuable tool for analyzing possible risk and consequence. The method is "commonly used when a group must develop a consensus concerning such items as . . . uncertain future conditions or events" (Meredith and Mantel 2003, 77).

Risk Disposition

Once the risk events have been identified, analyzed, categorized, and prioritized, the next activity in risk management is to decide on an appropriate disposition method for at least the medium and high risks. Evaluation parameters should include the cost/benefit tradeoffs, the potential effectiveness of the method, and the consequences for the project's schedule and deliverables.

The Project Management Institute devotes an entire chapter to project risk management in *A Guide to the Project Management Body of Knowledge*. The guide is an invaluable tool for project management, and we recommend it for all project team members. When it comes to the disposition of project risk events, it describes four terms that are often misunderstood or misapplied—*avoid, transfer, mitigate*, and *accept* (Project Management Institute 2008a, 303–304):

1. *Avoid* "involves changing the project management plan to eliminate the threat entirely." This method requires cooperation and acceptance from the project's end users because changing the plan will affect some aspects of the schedule, cost, scope, and/or resources. Root cause analysis, sometimes called effect-cause-effect analysis, is a good way to acquire the information needed to avoid a risk.

2. *Transfer* is "shifting some or all of the negative impact of a threat, along with ownership of the response, to a third party." This is a form of risk sharing that is most effective in dealing with financial risk since the risk itself is not eliminated. Although contracts may be used to accomplish the transfer, a risk premium is usually required. Transfer also may apply to elements within the organization, such as transferring a function from hardware to software in the event of a failure.

3. *Mitigate (sometimes referred to as control)* "implies a reduction in the probability and/or impact of an adverse risk event." This method usually requires additional time and resources, such as operating a parallel plan or running modeling and screening processes.

4. *Accept (sometimes referred to as assumption)* "indicates that the project team has decided not to change the project plan to deal with a risk or is unable to identify any other suitable response strategy." Risks for which an appropriate disposition method cannot be determined until they occur generally fall into this classification. The most planning that may be done is to arrive at some estimate of the resources that might be required if and when the risks occur.

Any of these methods, or some combination of them, may be used in response to risk exposure. The most important point is that a risk plan must be developed prior to initiation of the project, and it must be continuously updated as the project progresses.

Risk Monitoring

Risk monitoring is intended to provide a warning of impending risk events and a basis for improving the risk management process. Effective risk monitoring should identify the weak and strong points of the risk management plan and forecast new risk events. It depends on a comprehensive risk plan and a reliable cost, schedule, and performance evaluation system. Fortunately, we know of such a performance evaluation system.

Earned value calculations provide periodic comparisons of the actual work accomplished with the work planned. EVMS is useful in monitoring the effectiveness of the risk-handling plan. The periodic cost/schedule variances supplied by the EVMS status data can provide for both the detection of risk events and the assessment of the effectiveness of the disposition methods. The data can be analyzed to determine the cause of variances and to suggest improvements for risk handling.

There are two additional important points in risk monitoring and for risk management in general. The first is that all monitoring activity and results should be documented. A requirement for formal documentation encourages a more comprehensive effort and provides a history for future risk management activities. The documentation is most important because it records the circumstances of risk events and provides substantiation for risk decisions. The second point is that risk monitoring and the entire risk management process must be continuous.

Continuous Risk Management

Although no longer used, a former DoD website illustrated the concepts of risk management. The site had an animated logo with the four words *Plan, Assess, Handle,* and *Monitor* emphasized around the center of a circle containing the word *Document.* That DoD logo encapsulated the fact that awareness of and planning for the inherent risks in project management must be continuous. We have attempted to model that theme of continuous risk management in Figure 11.4.

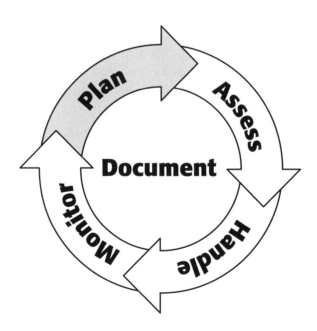

FIGURE 11.4   Continuous Risk Management

Risk Management Tools

Both government and commercial tools that can assist in risk management activities are available. We'll mention a few, but even a cursory search will yield several.

- *@RISK for Project* is a tool we have used frequently for modeling project schedules. It is a risk analysis and simulation add-in for Microsoft Project. There is also a module for Microsoft Excel that is useful in analyzing probability/impact matrices. @RISK is a product of the Palisade Corporation (http://www.palisade.com).

- The *Program Evaluation and Review Technique* (PERT) (described in Chapter 7 as a project network representation) was originally developed as a risk management tool. It uses a probabilistic model based on three time estimates—"optimistic, most likely, and pessimistic"—to plan and control a project. This technique generally has been eclipsed by newer methods but is still favored by some. (Most project software generates a PERT chart automatically, but the minimum and maximum times may need to be added.)

- *Critical chain* (described in Chapter 17) is a project management system in which one feature is an attempt to reduce the risk of project overruns. To control task completion risk, critical chain removes the individual protection time built into task estimates—where it is often wasted—and strategically relocates it to protect critical points (at feeding path mergers and at project completion) in the overall project schedule.

- The Defense Acquisition University features a risk management website with links to various systems and tools (Defense Acquisition University 2005b).

- You can find a full list of guidebooks at https://akss.dau.mil/Lists/Guidebooks%20%20Handbooks/AllItems.aspx, including four dealing with risk. The list includes the *Risk Management Guide for DoD Acquisition* (6th ed). Much of the guide could be applied to any organization.

- The Mitre Corporation developed a risk matrix that helps to identify, prioritize, and manage key risks, but it is available only to employees of the federal government and contractors under a current government contract. If you have or expect to have a government contract, check with Mitre.
- The U.S. Army Communications Electronics Command (CE-COM) Software Engineering Center (SEC) developed the *Software Insight Tool for Risk Mitigation.* It has an assessment questionnaire with detailed questions to identify software acquisition program risks (http://www.sed.monmouth.army .mil/sit).
- Carnegie Mellon University, Software Engineering Institute, has developed acquisition risk management practices, processes, methods, and tools (Software Engineering Institute 2009).

Risk management tools may assist in addressing and controlling risk, but they do not lighten the burden of responsibility. Nor do these activities eliminate the need for change and a formal change control process.

WHEN CHANGE BECOMES NECESSARY

We have encountered very few projects that did not require some changes to the budget, schedule, and/or objectives. Whenever changes are authorized, they should be made within a control account (CA) and first attempted within the constraints of the original CA budget and schedule. If the changes cannot be made within the original budget, management reserve may be used. When work must be transferred between CAs (to other functional units), the transfer must be carefully controlled and documented, making sure that the budget amount is transferred along with the scheduled work.

Project changes must not be made for work already completed; they may be made only for future work. Because of the pressure to circumvent change procedures, even changes for effort scheduled in the near future should be discouraged. Government agencies encourage *replanning activity* that is designed to reduce costs, improve efficiency of operations, or otherwise enhance the completion of the project. Appropriate replanning can be the consequence of several factors:

- A review of project specifications that modifies the objectives
- A major change in resource availability that will affect the schedule
- Budgetary restrictions that necessitate a change in resources or deliverables
- Significant changes in the rates that were used to calculate the original cost.

Replanning should never be done just to eliminate variances or to change a cost or schedule index. Generally, replanning is permitted to internally revise the project plan as long as it is within the original baseline. Inappropriate replanning terminates the project's status as an EVMS-compliant system. Even when change appears to be valid, excessive change indicates a lack of sufficient initial planning and can cause the entire system to be suspect.

EVMS CRITERION 28

Incorporate authorized changes in a timely manner, recording the effects of such changes in budgets and schedules. In the directed effort prior to negotiation of a change, base such revisions on the amount estimated and budgeted to the program organizations.

EVMS Criterion 8 required the establishment of a time-phased budget baseline, which we described in Chapter 7 as the *performance measurement baseline* (PMB). Criterion 9, discussed in Chapter 8, required establishing budgets for all the authorized work of the project.

Both the PMB and the authorized budget are critical for valid EVMS metrics. When changes are authorized, they must be incorporated into the PMB and the project budget as soon as possible to maintain legitimate EVMS measurements and reporting. Other documents, such as work authorization forms, also may be affected.

If feasible, the change should be detailed at the work package level, but at the very least within a CA, to maintain reporting integrity. Changes that encompass more than one CA should be documented by writing multiple change requests.

Authorized Changes

Any interested party should be allowed to initiate a change request, but changes must be authorized. An item in the project charter should cite the organization's change control system and specify how changes may be requested and on whose authority changes may be made. The documentation should also have specific limitations for the scope of any change authorization. The limitations can be set at different levels for different levels of authority and can be expressed in both dollars for budget changes and time for schedule changes. Change authority usually is not vested in any one person but is the franchise of a small group of people in the organization.

Change Control Board

With one exception, every organization with which we have worked had a formal change control process and a change control board or change review committee. The committees were a functional mix of organizational personnel who were primarily from the upper management level.

In one large organization, different committees reviewed potential project changes within their own structural elements. The committees were charged to review and either approve or reject requests for project changes. In most cases, the change control system allowed emergency changes and other minor plan modifications without committee review. When such changes were made, the committee still reviewed and endorsed the change or recommended additional activity and/or documentation.

The duties and responsibilities for reviewing, approving, and documenting change requests vary a great deal, but Figure 11.5

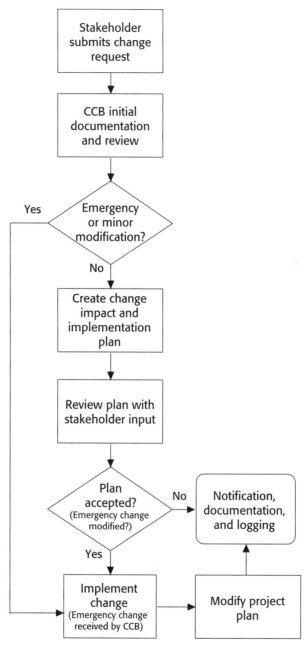

FIGURE 11.5   Change Control Board (CCB)

illustrates the activities and decision results of a typical change control board or committee.

The committee is charged with an immediate inspection of all change requests to check for emergency needs or minor modifications that will not require changes to the project budget or baseline. The committee prepares the initiating documentation, and if the change is an emergency or involves only minor modification, it sends the change request directly to the project team for implementation. Otherwise, the committee requests a change implementation plan from the project team. The committee then reviews the plan with other stakeholders for feasibility and acceptance.

If the plan is not acceptable, the committee notifies affected stakeholders and documents and logs the change request denial. A new change request with some modifications can always be resubmitted for consideration. If the plan is acceptable, the project team implements the plan and modifies the project plan accordingly. When the changes are complete, the team notifies the committee, which can notify stakeholders and document and log the change request results.

Documentation of Change

We cannot overemphasize the need to have standard forms for change requests and to authorize budget and schedule changes. The documentation can include change request forms, budget revision records, change authorization records, change control documents, and logs to maintain traceability of all change documentation.

A log of every change request form (CRF) should be maintained in order to schedule and monitor the change requests. Although we have seen many formats for a CRF, its design depends on the environment of the organization. The form should have at least the following elements:

- CRF number or identification and date
- Project identification

- Identification of the affected WBS element and control account (number and title)
- Description of the change and a revised CA plan
- Reason for the change request
- Requested cost and schedule changes and their impact
- Signatures of the requestors with dates
  - –At a minimum, the signatures should include those of the CA manager, a functional or business unit manager, and the project manager.
  - –Signatures also may be requested from one or more of the following: an accounting department manager, a scheduling department manager, and a project management office manager.
- List of documents to be changed and the impact
- Supporting documents as attachments to the request form
- Rejection or approval, with authorized signature and date.

After a CRF has been approved, several other documents must be generated, modified, and tracked. Budgets must be revised, work authorization forms modified or generated, notifications sent to all parties involved, and logs updated.

Directed Effort

Sometimes, project changes are directed by the customer (or other stakeholder) before the impact on cost, schedule, or requirements can be fully determined. These directed changes are usually emergency reactions to cost pressures, but they certainly affect the schedule and other planning and reporting elements. The final effect of such changes must be negotiated with the customer, but estimates of the change impact should be used until replanning can be completed. The intent is to maintain an accurate and legitimate PMB at all times.

EVMS CRITERION 29

Reconcile current budgets to prior budgets in terms of changes to the authorized work and internal replanning in the detail needed by management for effective control.

Because of imperfect views of the future or changing conditions, making project plan adjustments is a normal process. One of the most important EVMS requirements for change is that the overall project objectives be supported in a way that the performance metrics are not compromised. The documentation must be detailed enough to track the current project values back to the original plans. A formal change control process is necessary to ensure proper control of replanning and to enable accurate reconciliation.

The original budget is the target against which project progress is measured, and this base can be modified only by authorized changes. When changes have been detailed, negotiated with project sponsors, and authorized, the target is adjusted by the authorized amount. For detailed changes that have been authorized, but for which a final cost has not yet been fully negotiated, the target may be adjusted by a reasonable estimate. Special care must be exercised for adjustments when a "not-to-exceed" amount has been contracted for the project. Adequate documentation must be maintained so that reconciliation is both possible and valid.

EVMS CRITERION 30

Control retroactive changes to records pertaining to work performed that would change previously reported amounts for actual costs, earned value, or budgets. Adjustments should be made only for correction of errors, routine accounting adjustments, effects of customer- or management-directed changes, or to improve the baseline integrity and accuracy of performance measurement data.

Earlier, we warned that changes should not be made to work that has been completed, but there are a very few cases in which retroactive changes may be made. An organization must be able to correct errors and make routine accounting adjustments. Accounting adjustments are often made when performance estimates had to be used before actual data were available. Corrections may and should be made if incorrect data are hampering management decisions. Constant change, however, is an indication of an improperly planned or managed project. This is doubly true when changes are made to previously published historical data.

EVMS CRITERION 31

Prevent revisions to the program budget except for authorized changes.

Some rescheduling in future or current work packages is expected and acceptable, but the organization must have a change control procedure that limits changes to be made to the original budget baseline. The accounting department should record any changes in the project budget log. A budget base change should not be made without an accompanying contract modification, project charter revision, or authorization of the change control committee. Any baseline change, especially a budget change, should be limited to certain ranges as established in the change control process.

EVMS CRITERION 32

Document changes to the performance measurement baseline.

When we defined PMB in Chapter 7, we likened it to a baseline in a sporting event, where it is used to measure progress. If the baseline kept moving, we would never be able to tell who was "in bounds" or who was winning or losing. The same is true of the project PMB. Its validity must be maintained, or EVMS metrics become meaningless. The PMB is a reflection of management's current plan to achieve project objectives. All changes must be documented, and the links for all changes must be derivable.

The contractor's management system should include procedures for the disciplined incorporation of authorized contract changes and internal replanning. These procedures should ensure that:

- Budget is not transferred independent of work scope.
- Budget and schedule changes are incorporated simultaneously.
- Retroactive changes are strictly controlled.

Although these processes should result in disciplined management of the baseline, they should not be so strict as to preclude any adjustment to the PMB. Changes occur throughout the life of any contract, and the baseline should be adjusted to incorporate authorized changes or replanning as necessary (Department of Defense 2006a, Sec. 2.5.2.3).

We all know Murphy's Law will strike—we're just never quite sure where, when, and how. It is imperative to have risk management plans in place, and risk planning should be an effort throughout the entire organization. Projects often involve opportunities as well as threats, and a process similar to that of risk analysis should be designed to position the organization to take advantage of opportunities that become feasible and desirable.

No project plan can be considered complete and reliable unless it has at least a risk management component. The first task must be to ensure that risk is understood. Risk events must be defined in terms of the probability of their occurrence and the severity of their impact. In consideration of these two characteristics, the intensity level of each risk, and an appropriate reaction, can be determined in line with the risk tolerance of the organization.

The method for handling a risk when it occurs can be formulated from one of four general risk disposition categories: avoidance, transference, mitigation, or acceptance. EVMS is a very effective risk management instrument, particularly for risk monitoring. Risk monitoring should be a continuous activity in order to warn of impending risk events and to improve the risk disposition methods.

Not meeting the completion date is one of the most recurring project risks, and we recommend critical chain (Chapter 17) as an effective solution. The total risk management process must be continuous; there are many available tools to help.

Changes become necessary because of many factors; however, replanning should be done cautiously. Changes should first be attempted within the original parameters and never done just to eliminate plan variances. When changes are authorized, they must be incorporated in a timely manner and their effects recorded in the project plan. The use of a change control board or a change review committee is a good way to authorize changes and enforce change controls.

All changes must be reconciled from the original plan to the revised plan, and any retroactive changes must be tightly controlled. In fact, all changes must be controlled to prevent unauthorized changes and to ensure appropriate documentation. DoD requires internal procedures to establish acceptable practices and established discussion points for use in maintaining the validity of the PMB.

DISCUSSION QUESTIONS

1. Describe the three major activities of risk management.

2. Discuss the following statement: "Since project problems are only potential events, it is much more profitable to spend time on managing the project for success and not worry about risk management."

3. What are the parts of a complete risk description?

4. Describe some risk identification techniques, and identify the most likely effective method for your organization.

5. What kind of risk rating system is in use, or what kind would you like to see in use for your organization?

6. Describe the four general categories for risk disposition.

7. Why is EVMS useful in risk monitoring?

8. When is replanning appropriate and when is it not?

9. What kind of documentation would you recommend for project changes?

10. What retroactive changes can be made to project records?

CHAPTER 12

Are We There Yet?

Whew! Now that the project is complete and everyone is totally exhausted, one important final task remains: formally closing the project. No EVMS criterion requires a closing process—instead, the impetus is common sense and the desire to continuously improve.

This chapter deals with project termination. It is often said that "all things must end," but that saying doesn't seem to apply to all projects. Some old projects that should have been terminated long ago are still hanging around on the books of many organizations. On some projects, work slows down to an eventual crawl but never quite ends completely. Unless the organization is intentional, such projects may never disappear.

Evaluation of the many reasons for terminating a project, and when to do so, is beyond the scope of this book. Instead, we focus in this chapter on covering the important steps required to close a project properly. Without carefully monitoring the project plan and properly closing the project, the organization may suffer several adverse effects and lose an important improvement opportunity.

> Recently, we worked with an organization that had many inactive projects that were still on the books years after their inauguration. Many staff members were reluctant to start work on yet another project that might also just run off into the sands of time. Other staff members were grateful that they were never accountable for the project deliverables. We saw old projects carry over into new projects without the original project ever "finishing." In all of these circumstances, the consequences were the same: low morale, no acknowledgment of effort, and the loss of many valuable lessons.

PROJECT TERMINATION

One of the primary calculations in EVMS is the estimate at completion (or the estimate to complete). This periodic measurement is helpful in focusing attention on project completion and ensuring that the project is "finished"—either completed and delivered or prematurely terminated for cause. Without appropriate controls, a project might drift into unintended (and unnoticed) overspending, or the unused funds from an incompletely closed project might be misapplied to other projects. It is not unusual for us to find charges to a project continuing long after it has ended.

Some government units dictate the full and appropriate termination of projects; others are less formal. The Department of Energy (DOE), for example, states its requirement this way:

> When the project nears completion and has progressed into formal transition and commissioning, which generally includes final testing, inspection, and documentation, the project is prepared for operation, long-term care, or closeout. The nature of the transition and its timing depends on the type of project and the requirements that were identified subsequent to the mission need (Department of Energy 2006, 7).

Additional details are provided in guides such as DOE's *Information Technology Project Guide* (Department of Energy 2008a).

Figure 12.1 illustrates the main closing activities and their relationships. We like to divide the project closing into two primary functions: (1) ensuring that the project is complete and is ready to be accepted by the owner or customer and (2) conducting some postproject activities.

Completing the Project

As shown in Figure 12.1, closing tasks begin with a pre-close audit to determine the completion of project deliverables and to review actual performance compared with the estimates generated to justify the project. If the project is not complete, additional work must be done. If the project is complete, various resources must accomplish a whole series of actions, culminating in a project closing report, which includes a history of the project.

We emphasize that the project closing is a major phase of a project's life cycle and consists of all the activities and events that must occur before the project is considered complete. Figure 12.2 illustrates the project's life cycle (discussed previously in Chapter 2). The arrows in Figure 12.2 from "Closeout" to "Execution" and back indicate the recycling activity frequently required between the major phases of a project.

Project Review

A project should not be considered complete until a physical, financial, and functional audit that compares the expectations of the project charter or contract to the actual project deliverables is performed. In addition to ensuring that the project delivered on its expected objectives, this audit should examine the original cost/benefit analysis and the original risk assessment against the actual project results. The results of the final assessment (sometimes referred to as the postmortem autopsy) should be documented in the project closing report.

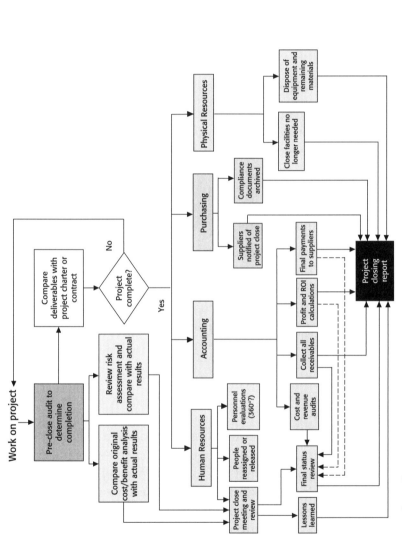

FIGURE 12.1   Project Closeout

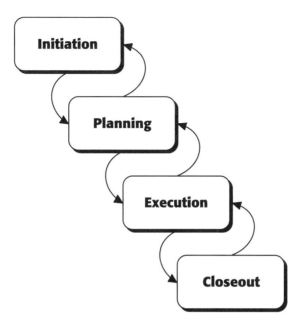

FIGURE 12.2   Project Life Cycle

While the project team is still intact, all members should be involved in the final project review. A group discussion elicits the most information, with contributions by some team members stimulating thought among others. We highly recommend a period for individual reflection prior to the meeting. Distributing a questionnaire before the review discussion should generate some helpful participation. We have used several versions of project review questionnaires (a Google search for "project review questionnaire" pulled up more than 1.7 million hits), but one we found especially interesting was from Chris Everett Project Management (http://www.spottydog.u-net.com/guides/close/frameset.html).

The object of the project review is twofold: (1) to gather data for a complete and accurate final status report and (2) to document the lessons learned (good and bad) in this project to improve future projects. There are many topics to examine during the project review. Some, such as the financial data, are required; but the team's group discussion can generate several more. We suggest that the meeting agenda items include the following to be sure that all aspects of the project are addressed:

- How well the project objective was met
- Resource availability and utilization
- Means and effectiveness of communications
- Usefulness of project meetings
- Work that went well and why
- Work that didn't go well and why
- Any disasters, what caused them, and how they might be avoided in the future.

Reporting

The project closing report signifies the formal end of the project and is the final status report. The report should be sent to the project sponsor, to all other project stakeholders, and especially to the accounting department. The accounting department will have been involved in generating the final metrics and closing the control accounts, but there should be a formal notification to terminate any further entries for the project.

The report should document what worked well and what processes could be improved. It needs to specify the level of success in meeting the project goals and relate the impact of management activities, variance analyses, and changes during project execution. It should also identify the items that will be a part of the operation and maintenance of the project's deliverables. The end users should have details of their responsibilities after their acceptance of the deliverables. The report should be in the same format and follow the same processes as all the preceding project reports.

Many organizations, including several state agencies, require a *post-implementation evaluation report* (PIER) at the conclusion of a project. The PIER usually provides a picture of the project management results. It covers such issues as staffing, scheduling, and the management of cost, risk, quality, communications, and user expectations. The report often has sections for lessons learned and all the project sign-offs; if a formal PIER is not required, we recommend separate activities and reports to complete these latter elements.

Also, in separate reporting, performance evaluations should be completed for all project team members. Sometimes we have seen evaluations performed by each team member for each of the other members, including the project manager. This "360-degree" approach provides a wealth of feedback that can be used to improve future performance. Most often, however, the project manager prepares evaluations for each team member. Especially in functionally structured organizations, copies of evaluations are usually sent to the member's direct supervisor.

Project Deliverables

Another task for project closeout is to ensure that all contracts and subcontractor contracts have been completed and acceptance signatures obtained. Some claims or outstanding issues might need to be settled before the final report is prepared. The accounting department also is involved as final postings are made, accounts are reconciled, and all control accounts are closed. The final status report should disclose the degree of variance from the planned schedule, budget, and technical scope, along with a brief description of causes.

Several project objective concerns should be addressed before the project is considered complete. First, the project deliverable must be transitioned to complete and successful use by the end user. Second, there should be evidence that the user can depend on and maintain use of the deliverable. Sometimes, especially for government contracts, sign-offs and clearances must be executed to ensure that all the project's terms and conditions have been met before the end user issues a formal acceptance of the project deliverable. Even without a contractual obligation to do so, these final steps build significant goodwill for future endeavors and are good policies to have in place.

Lessons Learned

Documenting lessons learned in the management of a project is one of the most important contributions that can be made to the success of future projects. Some of the best practices that might be identified in the lessons-learned document are:

- Effective communication with project stakeholders
- Ways to obtain support for the project
- Team-building and consensus-building techniques
- Improved cost and schedule processes
- Effective ways to identify and obtain resources
- Determining an appropriate balance between the need for detailed plans and the cost of producing that detail
- Effective scope and change management systems
- Vendor management techniques
- Ways of disseminating project knowledge.

A lessons-learned review with all project stakeholders present is the best way to get a complete picture of the project's successes and problems. Attendees at a review meeting should include the project team, executive management, external audit or oversight personnel, end users, and operations staff. This lessons-learned meeting is sometimes combined with a closing or celebratory event (described in the next section, Post-Project Activities).

On large projects, if too many people are involved for an effective meeting, the meeting can be held with a representative from each major group. If for some reason a meeting is deemed inappropriate, the review can still be conducted through the use of surveys. In any case, there must be a broad and inclusive view from all perspectives to provide the most value for future projects.

Post-Project Activities

Once the project is considered to have met its goals, a few more tasks should be performed for the project to contribute to meeting future needs. These activities include acknowledging the efforts of the project staff, releasing project resources, and archiving project documents.

Holding a Closing Event

A celebration of the project's completion can be an excellent way to notify everyone of the official close of the project and to recognize the team members. Many team members will be going back to functional assignments or starting new endeavors. Positive reinforcement is an effective management tool, and the closing event presents an opportunity to foster a positive attitude that can carry into new engagements. Many organizations host a celebratory dinner or party; however, even recognition for the team at a regular meeting provides some incentive and reinforcement for team members.

Even if the project was not considered a success, there must be some recognition of its completion. We heard of one group that held a "wake" for its project. It's true that most of us do not want to reward failure, but we should take the time to recognize effort and learn what we can from the experience. Thomas Edison is well known for the invention of a commercially successful light bulb, but few know about the thousands of failed attempts, his many other unsuccessful ventures, or his fervent denial that his unsuccessful endeavors were failures—he learned from each of them. The most important thing is to take away lessons learned from the project that will help with the next project.

There are several ways to reward team members for a job well done. Money always works! Although financial compensation is important, recognition can be equally effective—sometimes even surpassing monetary reward. If executive management shows its appreciation, it not only rewards the project participants but also reinforces the organization's emphasis on effective project management. Recognition is most effective when it is shown at a key organizational meeting or any large gathering. (And when you have a celebratory party, be sure to invite the accounting department.)

Releasing Resources

The redeployment of project resources may begin even before the project is complete. As the project winds down, fewer staff and less space and equipment may be required. It is important that the project manager release unneeded resources as soon as possible without adversely affecting the project schedule and technical requirements. Project team members can be assigned to other projects or continue their functional assignments. At the end of a project, one of the final steps is to make sure that remaining materials and other resources are put to other use or appropriately discarded.

For government projects, these final activities may include the decommitment of unused funds and the proper disposal of government-furnished property. Government contracting officers may also need assistance in checking the conditions of the contract, settling any unresolved issues, and completing the contract documentation.

Archiving Project Documents

All projects, especially EVMS projects, accumulate a flood of reports, documentation, and correspondence. All the essential records of a project need to be securely stored in a manner that will allow reasonable access when information is required. There may be inquiries concerning the project decisions or business audits that necessitate the retrieval of project records. Part of the initial project plan should detail the organization, storage, retention schedule, and retrieval strategy for project documents.

The amount and type of archival records will vary from project to project depending on size and complexity. The accounting department will archive the detailed accounting records, but a usual list of other documents would include:

- Requests for proposals (RFPs), proposals, and procurement documents
- Project plans (e.g., work breakdown structure, organizational breakdown structure, performance measurement baseline)

- Contracts and invoices
- Technical documents specifying design and test details
- Change request and change order documents
- Critical correspondence
- Minutes of project meetings
- Copies of reports and logs
- Lessons-learned document
- Audit results.

Most organizations have a record retention center and record retention guidelines. The project archive should include a list (with brief descriptions) of the documents that are held in the archive and contact information if further inquiry is needed. The project records can be invaluable as a training tool for project managers and in planning new projects. Although retaining some document hard copies may be desirable, most information is more easily accessed in a computer database.

Because the last days and weeks of most projects are chaotic and hectic, it is tempting to do a quick wrap-up and move on to the next challenge. A formal closing process led by the project manager will avoid the loss of extremely valuable information that can greatly enhance future performance of the project team and the organization. Formally notifying all interested parties of the project's closing also can prevent future unauthorized charges to the project.

A pre-closing audit to determine project completion and to review and compare project results with those planned can improve planning processes. If the project is complete, four areas—accounting, purchasing, human resources, and physical resources—are involved in closing out the work and archiving the records.

Accounting must wind up its project work by auditing all accounting, collecting receivables, paying suppliers, and computing profit and return on investment. All or major portions of this work are shared with the project team so it can analyze project performance.

One of the most critical areas of closing concerns human resources. People who have worked on the project have the best intuition for analyzing their performance. If they have access to financial information, they are in a position to evaluate the entire project and document lessons learned for the organization as well as for themselves. Feedback is essential for team members' personal growth; appreciation of their efforts provides motivation for future productivity.

Duties for the purchasing department include notifying suppliers of the project's close so they will not expect future orders. Purchasing also has the responsibility of archiving any required compliance documents.

Finally, physical resources must be detached from the project. Facilities no longer needed must be closed or returned. Any equipment and remaining materials must be disposed of properly. All information pertaining to the project is accumulated in the project's closing report, which is then distributed to all interested parties to formally notify them of the project's close.

In effect, closing a project provides an excellent opportunity for a project health check that addresses the level of project control, compliance with contractual obligations or company policies, and validation of the original business case. It also enables examination of team interactions, including communication success. Risk issues shrouded in uncertainty at the beginning of the project can now be compared with actual results.

All this ensures that mistakes will not be repeated and that even unsuccessful efforts can contribute to future success.

DISCUSSION QUESTIONS

1. Discuss the best example of how you have closed a project in the past. Was the project labeled a "success" or a "failure"? Did the close process change that perception?

2. Closing a project appears to be a project in itself. Discuss the characteristics of this closing project and how it is different from other projects.

3. Describe some common effects of not properly closing a project.

4. Would use of a closing process template be beneficial for all projects? Why or why not?

Earned Value
Implementations

Part VI presents information about EVMS government implementations in particular and EV implementations in general. Chapter 13 starts with a discussion of a complete EVMS implementation. Chapter 14 presents some EV certification issues and covers more of the requirements of government acquisition contracts. Chapter 15 presents a spectrum of implementation levels for organizations or particular projects when strict adherence to EVMS criteria is not required.

CHAPTER 13

Implementing EVMS

In this chapter, we look at the reasons for implementing a complete earned value management system and discuss the challenges of implementing any innovative procedure. Projects often use resources and processes across the entire organization. Therefore, when you change the way you handle projects, you also affect the entire organization. If you are responsible for implementing EVMS in your organization, you will need to plan the activity as a project and use all of your project management skills.

You cannot appreciate all the specifics of managing a project with EVMS until you actually start a project that will adhere to all the criteria, but there are several activities that should be undertaken first. Trying to implement EVMS on a project without first implementing the concepts throughout the organization is not a good idea. We have found it best to have a future project in mind so that there is a reference point for the issues you will be addressing, but managing an active project while implementing a new process on that project has not worked well for us in the past.

The first important step is having or developing a compelling business case to implement the new system.

REASONS TO IMPLEMENT EVMS

There are several reasons to implement an EVMS. Often, an organization must use EVMS because of contractual requirements with entities such as the Department of Defense (DoD) or other federal agencies. Other times, internal management would like the control and reporting mechanisms of an EVMS, perhaps to better comply with the Sarbanes-Oxley Act (Sarbanes and Oxley 2002) or to improve internal reporting. Your organization's requirements for implementation may differ significantly from those of other organizations. Depending on technology, processes, and procedures currently in place, some management systems will necessitate a great deal of change, whereas others may satisfy the EV criteria fairly well in their existing state.

In fact, many federal agencies analyze the extent of modification that must be made to an organization's system when EVMS is adopted. Their analysis indicates the maturity of the organization's management process. A mature system already captures cost and schedule performance data, conforms to the spirit of EVMS, and satisfies the following criteria:

1. Relates time-phased budgets to specific contract tasks and/or statements of work
2. Indicates work progress
3. Properly relates cost, schedule, and technical accomplishment
4. Captures and processes valid data in a timely and auditable manner
5. Supplies managers with information at a practical level of summarization. (Department of Defense 2006a, section 1.2).

If an organization has a system in place (level 3 or above in project management maturity) that provides all the above basic capabilities, an EVMS implementation flows fairly smoothly. Otherwise, the organizational changes and investment in time and dollars may be significant.

THE IMPLEMENTATION PLAN

It would be highly unusual for a new management system to integrate seamlessly with existing systems and to perform successfully from the outset without considerable advance planning and careful execution.

When we were called in toward the end of a very late project, we overheard a member of the project team say, "We need to find that plan we made when the project was authorized!" There are many great plans in file folders that have never been used. Like strategy, projects often have difficulty not in their conception or planning, but in their implementation. Implementing EVMS is much like any other project—following the best practices of project management is required. Of course, an excellent source for project management knowledge is *A Guide to the Project Management Body of Knowledge (PMBOK® Guide)* (Project Management Institute 2008a).

Some of the most important activities in the implementation plan are:

- Setting up your communication system
- Promoting the purpose and benefits of EVMS
- Establishing appropriate expectations
- Providing and scheduling EVMS training
- Investigating and choosing software support
- Developing a method, with strong support from the accounting staff, to establish and use control accounts.

DETAILS OF IMPLEMENTATION

A project team cannot implement an EVMS alone; the entire organization must be involved. As you undoubtedly are aware, the first principle of any new system implementation is to have unequivocal and overt top management commitment.

Organizational Support

Every organization has been through several of the latest and greatest management improvement processes; some were successfully implemented, but many were not. Without strong management commitment, team members may view EVMS as another improvement process that can be safely ignored and eventually will fade away. Senior management's commitment must be written and well publicized, and the project manager must have the support of several departments as well as methods to encourage positive reactions and behavior.

Resource Managers

In a functionally designed organization, where project teams include members from various functional areas, project work performance is usually considered only incidentally and informally (if at all) in evaluations by functional heads, often referred to as resource managers. The selection of persons for project assignments also falls under the resource manager's purview. When functional duties collide with project requirements, the project team member faces a difficult dilemma. Part of the implementation process may include the formal incorporation of performance evaluations by the project manager.

Functional heads, especially if they do not have a clear understanding of project priorities, may not be in the best position to assign resources to individual project work packages. Functional heads either must be far more involved in project work or must share responsibility for work assignments with someone familiar with the organization's project portfolio. The project manager should nurture relationships with department managers and promote the establishment of a project management office.

Because accounting personnel will have the responsibility of gathering, aggregating, and reporting EVMS data, their role requires the project manager's special attention.

The All-Important Accounting and Finance Team

Possibly the most important team that the project manager must deal with is the accounting and finance team. In many organizations, the accounting and finance roles are intertwined and overlapping; in others, accounting reports to the chief financial officer. On the other hand, accounting and finance may be independent functional areas. In any event, accounting personnel will be charged with accumulating project data and preparing reports. It is extremely important for project managers to understand the accounting positions and the positions to which they report, and then to work with them to ensure the speedy capture and reporting of all relevant data.

We are not suggesting that project managers learn accounting. It is vital, however, to cooperate with the accountants and appreciate the work they do. EVMS evolved from a standard cost system, and accountants are able to readily master the intricacies of both systems, as well as understand the systems' deficiencies. In addition, they are willing and able to answer questions and help project managers master the requirements for their inputs. The vast majority of accountants do not relish their perceived role of "enforcer."

Everyone wants up-to-date information. As a project manager, you can help or hinder the work performed by accountants. EVMS reports provide valuable information. Therefore, we urge you to make friends in the accounting department and forgo attempts to game the system. Accountants can explain the importance of acknowledging project commitments prior to receipt of transaction documentation and the need to keep up-to-date records.

Education and Training

To effectively apply the concepts of EVMS and to generate and report all the information that a compliant system should produce, training is absolutely necessary. Education and training of everyone charged with providing input for EV metrics should be included as part of the comprehensive implementation plan. Besides those intimately connected with responsibilities that affect EVMS reports, entire project teams should be informed about why the new system is being adopted and how the teams will be affected. In addition, their individual contributions to the system's successful implementation must be explicitly addressed.

On-the-job training, self-learning, and internal training are opportunities for acquiring EVMS knowledge that have an advantage in convenience and cost, but they may not provide the necessary level of rigor and acceptance outside the organization. Many companies and several universities, including U.S. government departments and agencies, offer formal EVMS training. Also, the majority of government contractors with approved EVMS systems offer in-house training that in some cases outsiders may attend.

Most of the federal government's training courses are specific to their staff needs, such as an Internet-based course designed to provide knowledge and comprehension of applying EVMS to evaluate contractor cost and schedule performance. Most government classes are restricted to their personnel or the staff of active government contractors; however, if you qualify, the training opportunities are excellent. The Defense Acquisition University (http://www.dau.mil) maintains an earned value management department and provides a list of member organizations as well as other recognized educational institutions. The Air Force Institute of Technology (http://www.afit.edu) has a course designed for all personnel who will be involved in reviewing EVMS systems.

Eliciting Desired Behavior

"Any change, even a change for the better, is always accompanied by drawbacks and discomforts."
—ARNOLD BENNETT

Most of us underestimate the level of overt and covert resistance to change. It may be necessary to spend what might seem to be an extraordinary effort on the change management process. We have guided many change initiatives and have developed an innovation empowerment model (Figure 13.1) that has helped greatly when implementing change. We designed the model in a circular pattern to indicate that one must continually build a sense of momentum and cover all requirements at least once.

Notice, in the center of the diagram, that activity may go on for some time before sufficient motivation for change is developed. If there is not enough motivation for change and an agreement among all interested and affected parties, the change will be short-circuited long before it has a chance to be successful.

In Chapter 5's section on Defining the Project, we mentioned our version of how to surface obstacles and required conditions. We must do a similar set of exercises in steps 5 and 6 of the empowerment model. Get everyone involved, and make sure there is complete understanding of what should happen when EVMS is implemented. As changes are identified and made in the organizational processes and procedures (step 7), continually evaluate the intermediate results (step 8). Sometimes it is necessary to return to step 5 and change some part of the process.

When new processes or procedures are put in place to support a change initiative, new performance metrics designed to support the change also must be in place. EVMS metrics are designed to evaluate a project, not the people working on the project. The organization must expend effort developing a personnel evaluation system that encourages the desired behavior and minimizes or eliminates dysfunctional actions. We know of no simple solutions to this issue; however, the organizations that recognize the problem and apply their best efforts to find a solution will find themselves in a better long-term competitive position. It is important for the project manager to recognize who controls and administers staff evaluations. In many organizations, this duty falls solely to functional or resource managers.

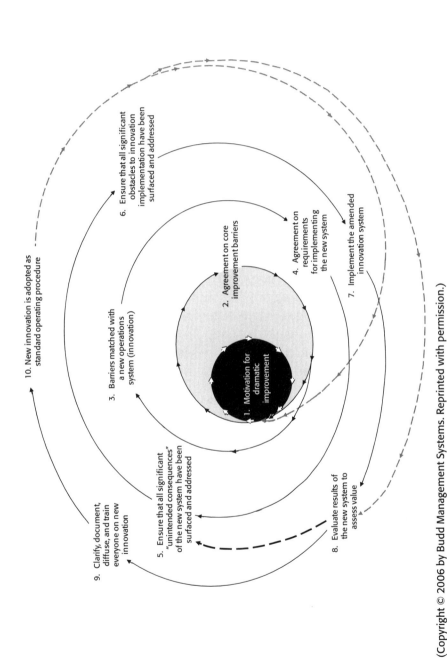

(Copyright © 2006 by Budd Management Systems. Reprinted with permission.)

FIGURE 13.1   Innovation Empowerment Model

DO YOUR OWN THING, BUT CAREFULLY

No organization produces its project deliverables in exactly the same way as another organization. The many differences in an organization's objectives and projects will not produce identical systems. Working relationships are different and depend a great deal on the organization's culture. During attempts to bring together organizational units in mergers and acquisitions, difficulties in combining or changing cultural differences have been substantiated repeatedly. No universal EVMS could satisfy the great diversity of management needs.

In fact, there is no universal EVMS. A reasonable or acceptable EVMS is one that adheres to the 32 stated criteria. The EV criteria provide a framework for determining an acceptable project management system. They do not describe specific system requirements, nor do they even provide all the necessary requirements of good internal control and management of project cost, schedule, and scope. The criteria, however, have many years of proven value, and meeting their requirements provides a basis for effective management decisions.

Certain Department of Defense contract guidelines state that the contractor must meet EVMS criteria, but they do not mandate that a specific information system be used. They allow the flexibility to use any project management system or tools that meet the criteria. The prospective contractor, however, must describe the system for planning, controlling, and reporting project performance in sufficient detail to evaluate its compliance with the EVMS criteria.

Whatever systems and processes the project manager uses, it is important to be certain that they integrate with existing organizational systems. It is not cost-effective, nor would it be very popular, to generate additional collection and reporting mechanisms for one project. Within that caveat, government agencies encourage a serious effort in pursuit of the continuous improvement of organizational processes.

There must be a way to capture the cost data for each control account in the project. That means that the organization, collection, and reporting of data can be done manually if that best fits your organizational processes. However, all the EVMS projects with which we have been associated were very complex, so we highly recommend that you use as much automation as is economically reasonable.

SOFTWARE ASSISTANCE

One of the steps in the implementation plan should have been to choose a software system to support the EVMS projects. Because of the size of projects that typically use EVMS, EV metrics can be difficult to gather and manage. The project manager will need as much computerized help as possible.

Several software systems can be used to track and report EVMS data. DoD has a website that lists software tools to assist the program manager at http://acc.dau.mil/simplify/ev.php?ID=52966_201§ID2=DO_ TOPIC. Although we have only some familiarity with the systems listed at the DoD site, we found many positive features in each of them. When working with a major defense contractor, we had the most experience with Dekker, Ltd. (http://www.dekkerltd.com). Nick Dekker has been very helpful and can be reached at n.dekker@dekkerltd.com. Also, wInsight and Cobra, well-known products currently offered by Deltek (http://www.deltek.com), have been helpful in the past.

When evaluating software, the two major considerations should be that the software has the functions and capabilities needed for EVMS compliance and that it is compatible with current tools, systems, and processes. If you are currently using a specific project scheduling tool, the new software must work with it, or you must be prepared to make sometimes significant modifications to one or both of the software programs.

Desirable software also would include certain functionality. Two primary requirements for the software are its ability to (1) differentiate between the baseline and a forecast and (2) handle multiple forecasts, each with its own set of assumptions. In addition, the software must store earned and actual data in a manner that allows the calculation of the required variances and does not compromise the historical metrics if replanning is necessary. Other desirable functionality would include the ability to make global adjustments and to provide statistical forecasts such as predicted funding and staffing.

Just as in any software acquisition, it is important to involve representation from a variety of functional units in EVMS software selection. Rather than using a software provider's data for demonstration purposes, it is wise to use a sample of your own company's data to compare the relative performance of the program offerings of various companies.

IMPLEMENTATION COST

It has been difficult for us to determine the cost of implementing EVMS. First, few organizations have been able to separate the incremental costs of EVMS from their historical project management operations. Second, although there were definite improvements in operations in almost every case in which EVMS was implemented, the value of those improvements was almost impossible to quantify.

An example of cost saving is illustrated by several attestations to the value of an early determination to terminate a project for economic reasons. Rather than continue project expenditures until completion or until it is obvious to everyone that the project will not deliver its objectives, early termination means that valuable and scarce resources can be transferred to more profitable work.

One area in which we found that increased costs are sometimes unnecessarily incurred is in gathering data and reporting at the lowest levels of the work breakdown structure. Extreme breakdown of project details not only adversely affects costs but also encourages undue micromanagement without enhancing the value of the information. Many of the EV criteria involve the calculation and reporting of variances of actual results from those planned. This is a very time-consuming effort for relatively small (in both time and cost) pieces of work, and there is the tendency to overreact and try to fix unfavorable variances that merely reflect the uncertainty involved.

For example, an organization working on a major defense project that had serious problems was spending more than one hour every day reporting status and plans. Every correction attempted simply worsened its performance. When we finally convinced the organization to reduce the level of management detail and concentrate on using good project management practices without trying to manage EV metrics, the project recovered.

Just as in any change initiative, knowing where you want to go (i.e., meet the EVMS criteria) is a required but insufficient first step. Of course, all the members of a project team must know the EVMS criteria thoroughly, but that still will not ensure successful implementation. Although EVMS metrics proclaim the project's progress, metrics alone cannot manage the project. As always, it is the project manager who must possess strong project management skills and must direct the project's progress.

Implementing an EVMS requires a good project plan and a great project manager. Even before creating a plan, there must be a good reason to implement EVMS. In some cases, a project contract requires it; in others, the organization may desire the benefits of a proven system. Important parts of the implementation plan include a promotional effort, a communications system, education and training, effective software, an appropriate accounting method, and the all-important establishment of realistic expectations. Every new implementation requires senior management support, but EVMS especially needs support from the department managers and the accounting team. Education in EVMS methodology and requirements is provided by several software providers, by universities, and particularly well by several government entities. Comprehensive training and appropriate measurement systems can encourage positive reactions from the entire organization.

Because change of any kind is usually difficult, we have included the innovation empowerment model, which was developed and modified over several business process consultancies. An important point about EVMS implementation is that it often can be accomplished within the existing corporate structures without too many serious changes.

There is no universal EVMS. By all means, use the software that conforms most closely to the current management philosophy.

The cost of implementing EVMS varies depending on the existing organizational structures and the required level of the installation. (In Chapter 15, we discuss partial implementations of EVMS.)

DISCUSSION QUESTIONS

For multiple choice questions, select the statement that best describes your understanding of EVMS, and discuss the reasons for your choice.

1. In a functionally designed organization:
   a) Accounting personnel must implement the EVMS.
   b) Department managers usually assign resources to project work packages.
   c) The project manager usually has control over the selection of the project team members.
   d) EVMS project work always takes priority over other duties.

2. An acceptable EVMS requires:
   a) The use of a Gantt project network.
   b) The use of prescribed management objectives.
   c) Substantial revisions to the organization's accounting procedures.
   d) None of the above.

3. What do you think will be your biggest obstacles to a successful EVMS implementation?

4. Your proposed project must use EVMS, but you've heard that one member of the executive management team thinks an EVMS implementation will be too difficult and expensive. What steps could you take to promote the system?

5. How much accounting knowledge or training must the project manager have for an EVMS project?

6. What are some dangers of having too much information?

CHAPTER 14

Government Contracts

"There are only two phases to a big military program: Too early to tell and too late to stop."

—ERNEST FITZGERALD

The bureaucracy of the U.S. federal government is notoriously challenging. James Stevenson used Fitzgerald's *First Law of Program Management,* quoted above, in an earlier book (Stevenson 1993, 305) and recently told us Fitzgerald had used it in one of their conversations.

Although there is far too much information about government contracts to cover in this chapter, we have two primary purposes in presenting it. The first is an attempt to help you through the maze by looking at some helpful websites and publications. Although the various federal departments and agencies have slightly different approaches to earned value management system implementation, they all follow the same basic requirements. The second purpose is to provide a basic understanding of government acquisition policies so that an organization can evaluate recommendations and advice from outside consultants.

INFORMATION SOURCES

EVMS for the Department of Defense (DoD) is documented quite thoroughly under the Office of the Under Secretary of Defense for Acquisition, Technology and Logistics (AT&L). Also, the commercial EVMS product and service organizations provide a great deal of information about government requirements.

DoD Websites

One of the most important websites is http://www.acq.osd.mil/pm. There you will find such information as an earned value management (EVM) contract requirements checklist. DoD's AT&L office also maintains an important website at http://www.acq.osd.mil/organization.html. One of the tabs there, Related Websites, will take you to a list of additional websites of interest. One is the Acquisition Community Connection, where the Acquisition, Technology and Logistics workforce (which could include you) meets to share knowledge. The authors participate in the Earned Value Management Community.

Another link on the Related Websites tab is the AT&L Knowledge Sharing System, which offers the latest DoD news about AT&L, such as the December 2, 2008, announcement of a major revision of the acquisition policy, *Department of Defense Instruction 5000.02* (DoDI 5000.02).

Each military service has its own schools and training institutions. Defense Acquistion University (DAU), however, is part of the Secretary of Defense's organization. The DAU publishes the *Defense Acquisition Guidebook* (DAG), an interactive, URL that covers many of the regulations, requirements, and best practices for members and contractors of the defense industry (Defense Acquisition University 2005a). At that site, the *Functional/Topic View* includes chapter 11, Program Management Activities. Section 11.3.1 of chapter 11 presents information on EVM. The DAG is currently under review as a result of the revisions to DoDI 5000.02 mentioned earlier. The DAU also publishes the EVM Gold Card; a version is illustrated in Figure 14.1

Federal Acquisition Regulation System

A FAR is a Federal Acquisition Regulation; DoD often issues Defense Federal Acquisition Regulation Supplements (DFARS) to notify organizations and agencies of contractual requirements (Department of Defense 2008a).

DFARS 252.234-7000 states that the government will review the program plan, requires the contractor to provide information and assistance for the review, and requires the identification and acceptance of subcontractors or subcontracted work. DFARS 252.234-7001 was published in the *Federal Register* on April 23, 2008, replacing DFARS 252.242-7001. It prescribes the use of a recognized or accepted management system that complies with the 32 EVMS criteria. DFARS 252.234-7001 also requires approval of any EVMS changes, authorizes access to pertinent records and data, and dictates subcontractor requirements.

DFARS 252.234-7002 was published in the *Federal Register* on April 23, 2008. It replaced DFARS 252.242-7002 and established DoD-specific EVM requirements. The complete wording of these DFARS can be found on pages 21846 through 21850 in Volume 73 of the *Federal Register* (Government Printing Office 2008).

DoD encourages contractors and the entire industrial sector to assume a growing responsibility for EVM processes. DoD will continue to review the management systems of contractors, but it would prefer to see industry certification standards, such as those of the International Organization for Standardization, with third-party accreditation. There is certainly a growing number of sources of consulting and training assistance for EVMS. One organization

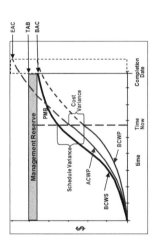

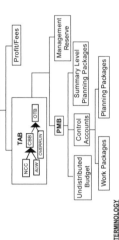

Earned Value Management 'Gold Card'

Defense Acquisition University

TERMINOLOGY

NCC	Negotiated Contract Cost	Contract price less profit / fee(s)
AUW	Authorized Unpriced Work	Work contractually approved, but not yet negotiated / definitized
CBB	Contract Budget Base	Sum of NCC and AUW
OTB	Over Target Baseline	Sum of CBB and recognized overrun
TAB	Total Allocated Budget	Sum of all budgets for work on contract = NCC, CBB, or OTB
BAC	Budget At Completion	Total budget for total contract thru any given level
PMB	Performance Measurement Baseline	Contract time-phased budget plan
MR	Management Reserve	Budget withheld by Ktr / PM for unknowns / risk management
UB	Undistributed Budget	Broadly defined activities not yet distributed to CAs
CA	Control Account	Lowest CWBS element assigned to a single focal point to plan & control scope / schedule / budget
WP	Work Package	Near-term, detail-planned activities within a CA
PP	Planning Package	Far-term CA activities not yet defined into WPs
BCWS	Budgeted Cost for Work Scheduled	Value of work planned to be accomplished = PLANNED VALUE
BCWP	Budgeted Cost for Work Performed	Value of work accomplished = EARNED VALUE
ACWP	Actual Cost of Work Performed	Cost of work accomplished = ACTUAL COST
EAC	Estimate At Completion	Estimate of total cost for total contract thru any given level; may be generated by Ktr, PMO, DCMA, etc. = EAC_{Ktr} / PMO, DCMA
LRE	Latest Revised Estimate	Ktr's EAC or EAC_{Ktr}
SLPP	Summary Level Planning Package	Far-term activities not yet defined into CAs
TCPI	To Complete Performance Index	Efficiency needed from Time now to achieve an EAC

EVM POLICY: DoDI 5000.2, Table E3.T2. EVMS in accordance with ANSI/EIA-748 is required for cost or incentive contracts, subcontracts, intra-government work agreements, & other agreements valued ≥ $20M (Then-Yr $). EVMS contracts ≥ $550M (TY $) require that the EVM system be formally validated by the cognizant contracting officer. Additional Guidance in Defense Acquisition Guidebook and the Earned Value Management Implementation Guide (EVMIG). EVMS is discouraged on Firm-Fixed Price, Level of Effort, & Time & Material efforts regardless of cost.

EVM CONTRACTING REQUIREMENTS:
Non-DoD FAR Clauses – Solicitation – 52.234-2 (Pre-Award (IBR) or 52.234-3 (Post-Award (IBR)
– Solicitation & Contract – 52.234-4
DoD (≥ $20M) DFAR Clauses – 252.234-2 (for solicitations and 252.234-7002 for solicitations & contracts
Contract Performance Report – DI-MGMT-81466A * 5 Formats (WBS, Organization, Baseline, Staffing & Explanation)
Integrated Master Schedule – DI-MGMT-81650 * (Mandatory for DoD EVMS contracts)
Integrated Baseline Review (IBR): Mandatory for all EVMS contracts
  * See the EVMIG for CPR and IMS tailoring guidance.

EVM Home Page = https://acc.dau.mil/evm eMail Address: EVM.dau@dau.mil
DAU POC: (703) 805-5259 (DSN 655)
Revised April 2008

VARIANCES Favorable is Positive. Unfavorable is Negative.

Cost Variance	$CV = BCWP - ACWP$	$CV\% = (CV / BCWP) * 100$
Schedule Variance	$SV = BCWP - BCWS$	$SV\% = (SV / BCWS) * 100$
Variance at Completion	$VAC = BAC - EAC$	

OVERALL STATUS

$\%\ Schedule = (BCWS_{CUM} / BAC) * 100$
$\%\ Complete = (BCWP_{CUM} / BAC) * 100$
$\%\ Spent = (ACWP_{CUM} / BAC) * 100$

DoD TRIPWIRE METRICS Favorable is > 1.0, Unfavorable is < 1.0

Cost Efficiency	$CPI = BCWP / ACWP$	
Schedule Efficiency	$SPI = BCWP / BCWS$	

BASELINE EXECUTION INDEX (BEI) (Schedule Metric)
BEI = # of Baseline Tasks Actually Completed / # of Baseline Tasks Scheduled for Completion

CRITICAL PATH LENGTH INDEX (CPLI) (Schedule Metric)
$CPLI = (Critical\ Path\ Duration + Float\ Duration\ (to\ baseline\ finish)) / Critical\ Path\ Duration$

TO COMPLETE PERFORMANCE INDEX (TCPI) # §
$TCPI_{EAC} = Work\ Remaining / Cost\ Remaining = (BAC - BCWP_{CUM}) / (EAC - ACWP_{CUM})$

ESTIMATE AT COMPLETION #
$EAC = Actuals\ to\ Date + [(Remaining\ Work) / (Efficiency\ Factor)]$
$EAC_{CPI} = ACWP_{CUM} + [(BAC - BCWP_{CUM}) / CPI_{CUM}] = BAC / CPI_{CUM}$
$EAC_{Composite} = ACWP_{CUM} + [(BAC - BCWP_{CUM}) / (CPI_{CUM} * SPI_{CUM})]$

To Determine a Contract Level TCPI or EAC: You May Replace BAC with TAB
§ To Determine the $TCPI_{BAC\ or\ LRE}$ Replace EAC with either BAC or LRE

FIGURE 14.1 DAU EVM Gold Card

has developed an earned value management maturity model. The model and the abbreviation EVM3 are trademarks of Management Technologies (Management Technologies 2004).

DoD Reference Material

A plethora of government (and specifically military) information is available. Helpfully, most of it is available on the Web. The most relevant data are the DAG, the *Earned Value Management Implementation Guide* (EVMIG), and the DoDI 5000.02. An important caveat: Be very careful about the information dates; an old publication is often as available as the new publication that replaced it.

Defense Acquisition Guidebook

We have already mentioned that the DAG covers earned value management in its chapter 11, section 11.3.1. The first subsection, 11.3.1.1, covers applicability. That subsection contains a reference to Office of Management and Budget Circular A-11, part 7. The OMB document has references for performance-based acquisition management and the use of "earned value techniques for performance measurement during execution of the program" (Office of Management and Budget 2008, 4). Subsection 11.3.1.1 also has several references to DoD's EVMIG.

Subsection 11.3.1.2 of the DAG refers to the DFARS clauses for EVM requirements that we discussed earlier. Subsection 11.3.1.3 describes the *integrated baseline review* (IBR) as the "joint assessment of the Performance Measurement Baseline (PMB) conducted by the government program manager and the contractor." The subsection also refers the reader to the EVMIG for additional guidance. Subsection 11.3.1.4 reports that the contract performance report (CPR) provides "contract cost and schedule performance data that is used to identify problems early in the contract and forecast future contract performance." It also describes the integrated master schedule (IMS) as "a time-based schedule containing the networked, detailed tasks necessary to ensure successful program/contract execution." The CPR and IMS are required whenever EVMS is required. Note that the subsection again references the EVMIG.

The last subsection of the DAG, subsection 11.3.1.5, declares that the "Defense Contract Management Agency (DCMA) is DoD's Executive Agent for Earned Value Management. In its role as Executive Agent, DCMA has responsibility for EVMS compliance, validation, and surveillance." The *compliance* paragraph states that the basis for EVMS compliance is ANSI/EIA-748. *Validation* is achieved by assessing the "capability of the contractor's proposed system to comply with the EVMS guidelines . . . ." The *surveillance* paragraph says that "surveillance is required on all contract efforts that require the implementation of EVM . . . ."

EVM Implementation Guide

In October 2006, the DAU issued the revised *Earned Value Management Implementation Guide.* The EVMIG is described as follows:

> The Department of Defense *Earned Value Management Implementation Guide* provides the uniform procedures which have been approved by the Commander, Defense Contract Management Agency (DCMA) under assigned authority as the Department of Defense's Executive Agent for Earned Value Management Systems. The document has been coordinated by SAF/AQ, SAF/FM, ASA (ALT), ASN (RD&A), MDA/PO, NSA/CSS, and DCAA. The document provides guidance to be used during the implementation and surveillance of Earned Value Management Systems (EVMS) established in compliance with DoD Guidelines. Users of this guide are encouraged to submit recommendations for refined procedures, through appropriate channels, to DCMA for consideration. (Defense Acquisition University 2006, 2)

The 99-page document covers all the concepts, guidelines, procedures, and activities for government use of EV. It contains samples of forms and documents and includes an extensive glossary of terms. The electronic version has numerous hyperlinks and bookmarks for further reference. The guide is an invaluable tool for any organization contemplating government projects.

One of the guide's interesting graphics is a roadmap to EVM implementation, which we have reproduced in Figure 14.2. You may notice that the roadmap cites the DAU Gold Card illustrated in Figure 14.1.

DoDI 5000.02

In December 2008, DoD issued Instruction 5000.02 (which canceled DoDI 5000.2, 2003) to establish a management framework for acquisition programs that would achieve cost, schedule, and performance goals. The current instruction applies to all DoD components and all defense technology projects and acquisition programs, including acquisitions of services (Department of Defense 2008b). To give you an idea of its scope, some of the major topics include:

- Procedures
- IT considerations
- Certification approval
- Integrated testing and evaluation
- Resource estimation
- Human system integration
- Acquisition of services
- Program management
- Systems engineering.

Of particular interest to the EVMS world is Enclosure 4. The enclosure contains Table 5, EVM Implementation Policy (Figure 14.3), which delineates the project size requirements for EV. The enclosure also shows Table 4, Regulatory Contract Reporting Requirements (Figure 14.4), which specifies the use of the contractor cost data report and the software resources data report.

Councils and Agencies

The project manager should have some familiarity with government agency contacts, EVMS validation requirements, certain applicable federal regulations, and the general contracting process.

EVM GUIDANCE ROADMAP

	Government		Industry
	Guidebooks	Guidecards	Guidebooks
Implementation	EVMIG	DAU Gold Card	NDIA Application Guide
Compliance Evaluation	DCMA Agency Instruction		NDIA Systems Acceptance Guide—TBD
Integrated Baseline Reviews	The PMs' Guide to the IBR Process		The PMs' Guide to the IBR Process
Surveillance	DCMA Agency Instruction		NDIA Surveillance Guide
Analysis	Guide to Analysis of EVM Data—TBD	Analysis Roadmap	
		EAC	
		Logic Checks	
		Price at Completion	
Over-Target Baseline/Over-Target Schedule	OTB/OTS Handbook	Baseline/OTB	
EVM and Software	NAVAIR Software EVM Toolkit		
Integrated Master Schedule/Integrated Master Plan	IMP/IMPS Preparation & Use Guide		
Schedule Development and Analysis	Office of the Secretary of Defense Guide to Developing, Managing, and Analyzing Program Schedules—TBD		
	DAU Scheduling Handbook		
Standards	N/A		ANSI/EIA-748
	N/A		ANSI/EIA-748 Intent Guide—TBD
EVM and Risk	DoD Risk Management Guide		

(EVMIG — brace spanning the Government Guidebooks column)

TBD = To Be Developed or In Development

FIGURE 14.2 EVM Implementation Roadmap

REQUIREMENTS	SOURCE	WHEN REQUIRED
For Cost/Incentive Contracts[1] ≥ $50 Million[2] •Compliance with EVM system guidelines in ANSI/EIA-748[3] •EVM system formally validated and accepted by cognizant contracting officer •Contract performance report (DI-MGMT-81466A) •Integrated master schedule (DI-MGMT-81650) •Integrated baseline reviews	Part 7 of Reference (c) This Instruction	– At contract award and throughout contract performance – Monthly – Within 180 days after contract award, exercise of options, and major modifications
For Cost/Incentive Contracts[1] ≥ $20 Million[2] but < $50 Million[2] •Compliance with EVM system guidelines in ANSI/EIA-748[3] (no formal EVM system validation) •Contract performance report (DI-MGMT-81466A) (tailoring recommended) •Integrated master schedule (DI-MGMT-81650) •Integrated baseline reviews	Part 7 of Reference (c) This Instruction	– At contract award and throughout contract performance – Monthly – Within 180 days after contract award, exercise of options, and major modifications
For Cost/Incentive Contracts[1] < $20 Million[2]	Part 7 of Reference (c) This Instruction	At the discretion of the PM, based on cost-benefit analysis
For Firm Fixed-Price Contracts[1] regardless of dollar value	Part 7 of Reference (c) This Instruction	Limited use—must be approved by the milestone decision authority (MDA) based on a business case analysis

Notes:
1. The term *contracts* includes contracts, subcontracts, intragovernment work agreements, and other agreements. "Incentive" contracts include fixed-price incentive.
2. Application thresholds are in then-year dollars.
3. ANSI/EIA-748 = American National Standards Institute/Electronic Industries Alliance Standard 748, Earned Value Management Systems.

FIGURE 14.3   EVM Implementation Policy

The top level of federal government contracting is OMB, which established the requirements for the use of EVMS. The Office of Federal Procurement Policy within OMB is responsible for procurement policy, which is documented in OMB Circular A-11. Part 7 of the circular describes the requirements for the use of EVMS (Office

REQUIRED REPORT	SOURCE	WHEN REQUIRED
Contractor Cost Data Report (CCDR)	DoD 5000.04-M-1 Reference (at) This Instruction	•All major contracts[1] and subcontracts, regardless of contracts type, for acquisition categories I and IA (ACAT 1 and 1A) programs and pre-MDAP and pre-MAIS programs subsequent to Milestone A approval, valued at more than $50[2] million (then-year dollars) •Not required for contracts priced below $20 million (then-year dollars) •The CCDR requirement on high-risk or high–technical interest contracts priced between $20 and $50 million is left to the discretion of the DoD PM with approval by the chair, cost analysis improvement group (CAIG) •Not required under the following conditions, provided the DoD PM requests and obtains approval for a reporting waiver from the chair, CAIG: procurement of commercial systems, or for noncommercial systems bought under competitively awarded, firm fixed-price contracts, as long as competitive conditions continue to exist.
Software Resources Data Report (SRDR)	Reference (at) This Instruction	•All major contracts and subcontracts, regardless of contract type, for contractors developing/producing software elements within ACAT I and IA programs and pre-MDAP and pre-MAIS programs subsequent to Milestone A approval for any software development element with a projected software effort greater than $20M (then-year dollars). •The SRDR requirement on high-risk or high–technical interest contracts priced below $20 million is left to the discretion of the DoD PM with the approval by the chair, CAIG.

Notes:
1. For cost and software data reporting (CSDR) purposes, the term *contract* (or *subcontract*) may refer to the entire standalone contract, to a specific task/delivery order, to a series of task/delivery orders, to a contract line item number, or to a series of line item numbers within a contract. The intent is to capture data on contractual efforts necessary for cost estimating purposes irrespective of the particular contract vehicle used.
2. For DSDR purposes, contract value shall represent the estimated price at contract completion (i.e., initial contract award plus all expected authorized contract changes) and be based on the assumption that all contract options shall be exercised.

FIGURE 14.4   Regulatory Contract Reporting Requirements

of Management and Budget 2008). The Government Accountability Office is responsible for the measurement of government program performance and issued a *Cost Estimating and Assessment Guide* in March of 2009. It is available at www.gao.gov/new.items/d093sp.pdf.

In discussions of government contracts and requirements, we often hear the term *component*. A *component* is defined as "a service or agency with acquisition authority" (Department of Defense 2006a, Section 2.1.2). The term *government component* refers to any agency that has authority to acquire goods or services. The head of the component or a designee is referred to as the *executive agent* (EA). The authority of the EA is assigned at the time of the designation, but typically the EA is the responsible agent for conducting the terms of an acquisition contract.

Many government components have an *earned value management support office* (EVMSO) to ensure effective EV management implementation. The EVMSO usually participates in system reviews and can provide training and assistance for the contractor. Many other agencies are involved in government acquisition of goods and services.

The agency definitions in this section are from the DoD EVMIG or the *ACQWeb* (Department of Defense 2004). These definitions are generic in the sense that they more often describe activities than specific organizational entities.

- The office of the *Under Secretary of Defense for Acquisition, Technology and Logistics*, Acquisition Resources and Analysis, Acquisition Management (OUSD/AT&L (ARA/AM)) oversees all EVM policy development within DoD.
- The *Defense Contract Management Agency*, formerly the Defense Contract Management Command (DCMC), is the DoD executive agent for EVMS. The DCMA is responsible for ensuring the integrity and application effectiveness of a contractor's EVMS. DCMA works with various government and industry teams to develop practical EVMS guidance to ensure initial and ongoing compliance with the EVMS guidelines in ANSI/EIA-748. The

agency is also responsible for maintaining the EVMIG and a cooperative relationship with industry.

- The DCMA, as EA, designates a *review director* for all EVMS compliance reviews, including initial validation reviews, post award system reviews, and reviews for cause. The review director is responsible for preparing and executing a review plan, which includes contact information, contract number, dates of the review, and the basis, cause, purpose, and scope of the review.

- The *administrative contracting officer* (ACO) is authorized to execute the advance agreement (AA) or letter of acceptance (LOA) with the contractor. The contractor can choose either of these ways to validate its EVMS system. Both are explained in the next section.

- A *focal point* is established by the DoD component to serve as the principal point of contact for coordination and exchange of information on the implementation of EVMS. Lists of appropriate contacts for component and other agency focal points are available at the Office of the Secretary of Defense EV website (http://www.acq.osd.mil/pm/keypers/keypers.html).

- The *contract management office* (CMO) is responsible for EVMS surveillance and the review of each contract to determine EVMS oversight requirements.

- The *program management office* (PMO) has the assigned authority and responsibility to directly manage a program. It reports evaluations and issues to the CMO. The *contract administration office* (CAO) is assigned to administer contractual activities at a specific facility in support of the PMO.

- The *Defense Contract Audit Agency* (DCAA) is responsible for performing all contract audits for DoD and for providing accounting and financial advisory services.

COMPLIANCE, VALIDATION, AND SURVEILLANCE

The primary reviews are the initial compliance review, the integrated baseline review (IBR), and reviews for cause. The executive agent of the contracting agency appoints a review director to approve and coordinate the review activities. The review director also approves members of the review team, who are administratively responsible to the review director.

Initial Compliance Review

The ACO is responsible for recognizing the contractor's system as compliant with EVMS guidelines. The officer issues a LOA or an AA. An AA may be issued when the EVMS is validated and the contractor commits to using EVMS as part of its management process and documents its use on the current contract and future contracts. The AA remains in effect indefinitely unless surveillance later finds the system noncompliant. The LOA is issued when the system has been validated but the contractor does not wish to enter into an AA (Defense Contract Management Agency 2005).

Integrated Baseline Review

The IBR is conducted by the government and the contractor to assess the validity of the PMB. It is usually conducted prior to the award of a contract. The purpose of this joint assessment is to determine whether the contractor's plan covers all the contract requirements and whether all the activities are scheduled logically. The IBR checks for adequate resources and EV methodologies, and it identifies program risks.

If, for some reason, the preaward IBR was not conducted, one must be scheduled as soon as possible, but no later than 180 days after the contract award. In addition, IBRs may be required if contract options are exercised or the contract is modified.

The government program manager (or designee) leads the IBR team, staffed potentially by CAO personnel, members of the PMO, and EVMS support personnel, as well as the contractor's project manager and technical staff. Participation by members of the integrated surveillance team (IST; see Surveillance section) is also encouraged. The IBR is intended to be a continuous part of the project management process.

Surveillance

The DCMA has the basic responsibility for system surveillance, and recently its auditing role has been increasing. Its assessments are based on the integrated master schedule, as described in DID DI-MGMT-81650 (Department of Defense 2005b). Part of its responsibility is the development of a *standard surveillance plan* (SSP). The SSP establishes the surveillance approach, risk criteria, and schedule and may be conducted independently or jointly with the supplier. Surveillance begins at contract award, continues through validation, and extends through the duration of the contract. The DCMA publishes a standard surveillance process flowchart that illustrates the surveillance process along with the corrective action request process. (Defense Contract Management Agency 2008). The flowchart is reproduced as Figure 14.5.

The DCMA has issued a guidebook (http://guidebook.dcma. mil/79/guidebook_tools.htm) for system-level surveillance of earned value management systems. The guidebook tools include EV templates for verifying adherence to the 32 EVMS criteria (the criteria are called *guidelines* in the templates). The verification points for Guidelines 6 and 7 (EVMS Criteria 6 and 7) include a note to apply the DCMA's 14-point schedule assessment. The DCMA offers a computer-based course in analyzing project schedules using the 14 points at http://guidebook.dcma.mil/79/imp-ims/index.html. Each of the 14 points are defined in the course.

The DCMA's 14-point schedule assessment is becoming much more important in the schedule risk assessments performed by government auditors recently. The metrics, along with explanations, purposes, and goals are presented in Table 14.1.

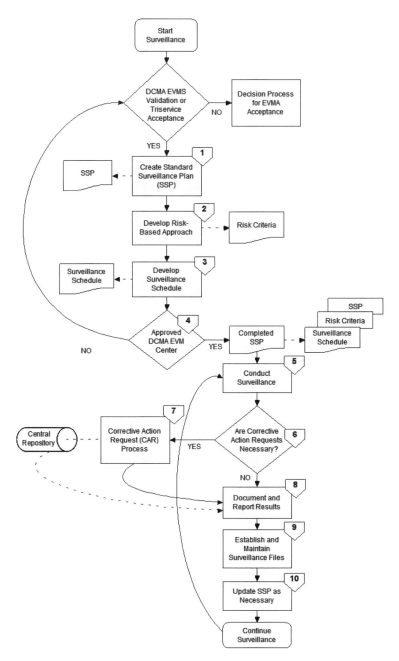

FIGURE 14.5   Standard Surveillance Flowchart

TABLE 14.1 DCMA 14-Point Assessment Metrics (Integrated Master Plan and IMS Schedule Analysis)

Metric	Explanation	Purpose	Goal
1. **Logic** (logic missing)	Any task that is missing a predecessor, successor, or both	Show how well (or poorly) the schedule links together	≤ 5% of tasks without a predecessor and/or successor
2. **Leads**	Any incomplete task that has a lead in its predecessor	Identify leads that distort float and may cause resource conflicts and distort the critical path	None
3. **Lags**	Any incomplete task that has a lag in its predecessor	Prevent adverse effects on critical path and subsequent analysis	Limit lags to less than five percent of total tasks
4. **Relationship Types**	All incomplete tasks that have predecessor(s) should state their relationship to the predecessor (e.g., finish-to-start, or FS)	Identify nontypical relationships (e.g., something other than FS)	Limit nontypical tasks to less than ten percent of total tasks
5. **Hard Constraints**	Any incomplete task that has any type of constraint	Identify constraints that prevent tasks from being logic-driven	Ratio of hard-constraint tasks to total incomplete tasks should not exceed five percent
6. **High Float**	Any incomplete task with float greater than 44 working days (two months)	Check for missing predecessors or successors—checks the stability and logic of the network	Ratio of tasks with high float to total incomplete tasks should not exceed five percent
7. **Negative Float**	Any incomplete task with float less than zero working days	Identify tasks that are delaying completion of one or more milestones	None
8. **High Duration**	Any incomplete task that has a duration greater than 44 working days (two months)	Identify tasks that might be broken into two or more discrete tasks—helps make tasks more manageable and provides better insight	Ratio of tasks to total incomplete tasks should not exceed five percent
9. **Invalid Dates**	Any task that has a forecast start/finish date prior to the IMS status date or an actual start/finish date beyond the IMS status date	Identify future tasks scheduled beyond the IMS status date—identifies inaccurate dates	None

Metric	Explanation	Purpose	Goal
10. **Resources**	Any incomplete task that has resources (hours/budget) assigned	Verify that all tasks with durations of one or more days have assigned resources	All tasks
11. **Missed Tasks**	Tasks that are supposed to have been completed (prior to the status date) with actual or forecast finishes after the baseline date, OR that have a finish variance greater than zero	Identify how well (or poorly) the schedule is meeting the baseline plan	Ratio of missed tasks to the baseline count should not exceed five percent
12. **Critical Path Test**	Assesses overall network logic, particularly for the critical path	Identify illogical path characteristics (e.g., project completion date is not delayed in direct proportion to the amount of intentional slip)	Project tasks or milestones show a very large negative total float number or a revised early finish date in direct proportion to the amount of intentional slip applied
13. **Critical Path Length Index (CPLI)***	Measure critical path "realism" relative to the forecasted finish date	Verify that the critical path makes sense and that the critical path is realistic	Ratio of critical path length plus total float to the critical path length should equal one (greater than one is favorable; less than one is unfavorable)
14. **Baseline Execution Index (BEI)***	Ratio measure of tasks completed to tasks that should have been completed (by the status date)	Gauge the efficiency of contractor performance to plan	Ratio of completed tasks to baseline count should be greater than 95 percent (greater than one is favorable; less than one is unfavorable)

Tripwire metrics

Several agencies may be involved in the surveillance of the contractor's EVMS implementation. These include the CAO with the primary responsibility, as well as the Field Audit Office of the Defense Contract Audit Agency, the PMO, and the EVMSO. The selected grouping of participating agencies is referred to as the IST, and the contractor is encouraged to participate in the surveillance process.

The Program Management Systems Committee (PMSC) of the National Defense Industrial Association (NDIA) published an *Intent Guide* that government or industry communities can use to document "how their EV management system complies with the ANSI/EIA 748 EVMS Guidelines" (National Defense Industrial Association 2006, 1).

Our first and most important point in this chapter is that there is far too much information to cover. Governmental requirements for EVMS are constantly being reviewed and revised and differ greatly depending on the particular agency and the type and value of the contract. The Office of the Under Secretary of Defense for Acquisition, Technology and Logistics provides information and requirements for DoD contracts. We have cited several helpful websites, including the very valuable Defense Acquisition University. On that site, DoD illustrates its earned value management (EVM) "Gold Card."

The Federal Acquisition Regulation system controls government contracts, and the DoD issues Defense FAR Supplements to notify organizations and agencies of their contractual requirements. The DFARS issued in 2008 regulates certain aspects of contracts requiring the use of EVMS.

In December 2008, DoD issued Instruction 5000.02 (DoDI 5000.02), which covers all defense technology projects and acquisition programs, including acquisitions of services. Enclosure 4 of the document contains requirements for the DoD's earned value management implementation policy. The Instruction also refers to the *Earned Value Management Implementation Guide* (EVMIG) issued by the Defense Acquisition University. The EVMIG covers all the concepts for government use of earned value and contains many samples of forms and documents; we have included two of the tables. The other very relevant document is the *Defense Acquisition Guidebook*; EVMS is covered in its chapter 11, section 11.3.1.

For government projects, the project manager must interact with different agencies and authorities, each having a variety of guidelines to follow. The project manager is expected to comply with all of them in just as many different ways. Your EVMS will need to be validated, and there are several avenues available. Among the system reviews are an initial compliance review, the integrated baseline review (IBR), and ongoing surveillance activities. The National Defense Industrial Association (NDIA) published an *Intent Guide* that can be used to document compliance with EVMS guidelines.

CHAPTER 15

Partial EV Implementations

We have shown in previous chapters that substantial effort is involved in implementing and using a full Department of Defense (DoD) EVMS. As EV concepts have become more familiar in the project management world, the value of their objective reporting has become more widely accepted. More project owners are looking to project managers for objective information, and many project managers are looking for convenient and economical ways to provide it. In addition, it is impossible to reach an upper level of project management maturity without an advanced project cost system such as that provided by EV.

In this chapter, we start with a short section about a reduced set of EV concepts and their use on small projects. Then we present four possible EV implementations that are less rigorous than a full DoD-type EVMS. Our suggestions are arranged from the most complete to a minimum implementation, and they include:

- A fully government-compliant EVMS
- A complete EVMS implementation without certain government requirements

- A high-level control-account system
- Basic principles of the guidelines
- The very least that can be done and still be called EV.

Figure 15.1 shows the above-listed phases as a continuum from a fully government-compliant EVMS to the very least system that can still be earned value.

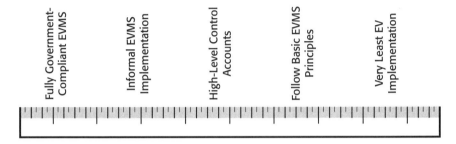

FIGURE 15.1   A Spectrum of EV Implementations

EARNED VALUE FOR PROJECT CONTROL

> Our dog loves to chase squirrels. During our morning walk, it doesn't take long for her to spot one. Off she goes, running to the place where she first saw. But by the time she gets there, the squirrel is long gone. Our dog hasn't caught a squirrel yet! Her information is old by the time she can take any real action.

We have always made the point that EV is a valid, important, and effective device for project reporting. We also believe that sometimes it is not so effective for managing a project (project control). One of the problems is the delay in gathering the data required for reporting EV metrics. We are usually looking at information that is quite dated by the time we receive official results of a reporting period. The delay between the end of a period and receipt of reports can amount to weeks. (We do note that for very lengthy projects, data that may be a month or more old still contains invaluable information for stakeholders who do not have a direct view of project operations.)

We have managed or consulted on many projects, and all of them have been in situations in which parts of the project were developed across multiple divisions of the organization and, in many cases, outside the organization. Data just aren't brought together very quickly. However, if your organization uses an advanced enterprise-wide system or has very tightly contained projects involving a small part of the organization, data collection can be much faster and EV metrics for project control more valid.

For labor-intensive projects, costs are usually more direct (calculated from expended employee hours), and data can be collected more quickly. Therefore, real-time project control information may be available and project data more quickly and easily assimilated into organizational results for external reporting. In any case, for relatively small and/or fast-paced projects, we highly recommend the use of a relaxed implementation of EVMS for "external" reporting, although it would be advantageous to follow as many of the requirements as can be reasonably and economically justified.

ABRIDGED EV IMPLEMENTATIONS

Earned value can be implemented without the complete government-required EVMS, but a minimum of activity must be performed to be called "earned value." We've already covered U.S. federal government requirements, so we present alternative, abridged implementations, starting with the next most complete.

First Alternative: An Informal EVMS Implementation

For EVMS projects, most government agencies have adopted the 32 criteria of the ANSI/EIA-748-A 1998 standard. (The standard was updated to ANSI/EIA-748-B in 2007, but for the most part, the agencies still refer to the ANSI/EIA-748-A.) As you have seen in the previous two chapters, most large government projects are not only required to adhere to the 32 criteria, but there are also sets of guidebooks, guides, instructions, regulations, and recommendations for how to adhere to the criteria, including information that must be provided in reports. An organization can still have a "complete" EVMS implementation, with all of its reporting benefits, by adhering completely to the 32 criteria. The difference from a government-approved EVMS is that the project may be managed and reported in any way the organization desires, without regard to the government prescriptions, as long as all the statements of the 32 criteria are followed.

Second Alternative: High-Level Control Accounts

Some of the EV processes are useful on all projects, but if a full-scale EVMS is not required, it is important to balance the implementation so that the benefits are commensurate with the effort and risks. *Earned value* requires comparing actual costs and planned costs. Collecting detailed actual cost data can be time-consuming and expensive. We have found this process to be the most rewarding area for reducing EV management effort.

Many of the criteria discuss how project costs are planned, accumulated, and reported through control accounts. We have found that a few broad control accounts can be established at a high level, making the collection of costs easier while still enabling EV reporting. The ability to track variances down further into the work breakdown structure (WBS) or organizational breakdown structure (OBS) would be lost, but it could be well worth the savings.[1] In most cases, all 32 EVMS criteria can be satisfied.

If it is important to adhere to all EVMS criteria, some discretion is required. Criteria 17 and 18 specify that a control account not be allocated to more than one WBS or OBS structural element. When

---

[1]One project team stretched the limits by setting up just one control account for its small project to see if it could still follow all EVMS requirements. The team struggled only with some of the summarizing requirements, such as those in Criteria 17 and 18.

setting up control accounts at a high level, special attention must be given to the structure of the WBS and OBS. Criterion 20 requires the identification of unit costs or lot costs. Unless prohibited by the customer, keeping all cost identification at a high level is very helpful.

Third Alternative: Follow Basic EVMS Principles

Even for small, fast-paced projects, we believe there are a few EVM principles that should be followed to sustain any serious EV reporting:

1. Establish complete work and cost details to achieve the project objective (Criteria 1 and 9).
2. Assign work to qualified and responsible parties (Criterion 2).
3. Prepare a stable and comprehensive time-phased project plan (Criteria 6, 7, and 8).
4. Record costs as they are incurred, and compare them to the plan (Criteria 16, 19, and 22).
5. Use relevant and timely information (Criteria 26 and 27).

Principle 1: Project Definition

All the activity and related costs to complete the project must be estimated. Because a project is defined as a unique production event, this can be a difficult task. The WBS becomes a very useful tool and is required by EVMS Criterion 1 for good reason. Remember from Chapter 5 that one of the definitions of a WBS was a complete definition of all the elements of work and their relationship to each other and to the end product.

The first level of a WBS should be a very high-level view of the major components of the project. By starting with these major activities, it is easier to represent all the components of the project work. Each level can then be deconstructed into lower levels of tasks until the plan is adequately detailed for efficient management. The plan must include the estimated costs for each detail of the project. EVMS Criterion 9 requires the establishment of a project budget, and at this point a project budget should be authorized.

Defining and detailing the scope and cost of the project is the first and absolutely necessary principle of EVM and ties into the second principle, discussed next.

Principle 2: Work Assignment

Work scope must be detailed to a level that can be assigned to a person or an organizational area or, if necessary, contracted to an outside party that can be responsible for controlling the three constraints of a project: schedule, cost, and deliverable. The assigned party is responsible for timely and accurate progress reporting. It is at this detailed level of the WBS that control accounts should be established. The accounting department can assist in setting up these accounts for recording project costs. (See the Control Accounts section of Chapter 5.)

In projects that are manpower-intensive with few material purchases, the projected hourly staff costs should have been budgeted in the project definition stage; now they can be paired with the work assignment. As each reporting period is reached, the actual hours and costs of completed activities are compared against the budget to determine the EV.

Project decisions will depend on the accurate calculation of the EV metrics, and it will be important to recognize this responsibility as organizational entities are identified. We covered this topic in Chapter 6, and EVMS Criterion 2 is devoted to this important principle.

Principle 3: Performance Measurement Baseline

This is the scheduling phase. After the work and costs have been defined and the organizational entities identified, all the elements must be integrated as the project plan. We covered this topic in Chapter 7, and project scheduling is required by EVMS Criterion 6.

Many project-scheduling tools can help to automate this process and can provide a variety of project views. (See the Software Assistance section in Chapter 13.)

To create a project network, the durations and relationships of the WBSs must be determined. The scheduling system needs to describe and identify both the sequence and the interdependencies of the project activities. Project scheduling tools typically calculate the critical path or critical chain. Observing progress on the critical path is a critical component in managing the project.

When the project network has been created, ensure that indicators or milestones are included so that progress can be measured accurately. EVMS Criterion 7 requires these indicators, and they are important to calculate EV. EVMS Criterion 8 specifies the establishment and maintenance of a time-phased budget baseline at the control account level. The control accounts should have been established during the Work Assignment phase, and the performance measurement baseline (project schedule) should show activity to at least this level of detail to provide appropriate control.

Once the baseline is established, the primary concern for a small project is reaching the objective quickly. Changes should be incorporated only if they are authorized and minor or absolutely necessary. (EVMS Criteria 28 through 32 concern revisions and data maintenance, but in a small, fast-paced project, however, they boil down to only one mandate: *Control scope creep.*)

Principle 4: Calculate the EV Metrics

EVMS Criteria 16 and 19 require the recording of direct and indirect costs in a formal system. This generally means that the accounting department will need control accounts set up in the corporate general ledger or in a general ledger project-controlling account with a subsidiary ledger detailing various categories of project costs. Recording costs would seem to be an easy and natural part of accounting procedures, but it will depend on your organizational structure. If your accounting has always been performed along functional lines, some additional effort will be required to set up accounts that cut across functional boundaries. Project management will need some accounting knowledge and should take precautions about how costs are allocated to the project.

Recording the project's actual costs is necessary in order to compare them with the planned costs (PV) and calculate the EV. EVMS Criterion 22 specifies that cost and schedule variances (CV and SV) be calculated at least monthly. For small, fast-paced projects, it should be done at least weekly. The weekly collection of cost data and subsequent calculations will require more effort, but it is necessary if the resulting variances and related indices (cost performance index and schedule performance index) are to have management control value. EV metrics can be reviewed in Chapters 3 and 10.

Principle 5: Use the Information

There are two very good reasons to go through the effort outlined in our first four principles of EV. The first is that generating all this information is vital for management decisions. If the project variances are negative, management can decide whether the project should continue without changes, whether more resources should be added, or even whether the project should be canceled. In any case, management can make informed decisions. EVMS Criterion 26 discusses the implementation of managerial actions.

The second very good reason to follow our first four principles is to improve project planning and performance. In fast-paced projects, the EV metrics can provide excellent lessons learned even as the project progresses. The performance data must be gathered and recorded quickly, which adds greatly to their value in project management and control. EVMS Criterion 27 requires revisions of the planned project completion data. The revised information can tell you much about the project-planning process and organizational performance. (See Chapter 10 for more complete information.)

Fourth Alternative: The Very Least EV Implementation

The simplest application of any sort of EV must at least compare the differences in planned cost and actual cost. First, there must be an estimated duration for the project and a schedule of reporting periods over that estimated duration. Second, there must be an estimated cost for the project at each reporting period. Third, there must be a method for determining the actual costs at each reporting period. At each reporting period, then, the EV and related variances can be calculated and reported. The number of reporting periods can depend on the expected length of the project and the frequency of reporting required by management.

Of course, this information will be of little value unless other principles of EV management are followed. We can recommend this minimalist approach only if the intention is to initiate some action toward a more serious implementation. Perhaps this might be the only approach to familiarizing the accounting and project staff with the very minimal, but necessary, planning and data collection processes.

Even in nongovernmental project environments, EVMS is gaining more credibility as an objective reporting mechanism. More project stakeholders are seeking ways to gain EVMS benefits while reducing the substantial effort of implementing and using a full government-approved EVMS. This chapter has presented four alternative types of potential implementations that depend on the organization's requirements.

The most complete implementation of EVMS without the stringent government requirements can still be accomplished by adhering to the 32 criteria but performing them within the organization's current capabilities. Performing all the calculations, following the project management protocol, and using the reporting mechanisms still provides the many benefits of EVMS. Data collection may still be laborious, but other government prescriptions can be avoided.

Collecting cost data for both the project planning and execution phases can be resource-intensive. Our second stage proposes that some projects can be managed using high-level control accounts. Small projects should not require the extensive reporting requirements of a large, complex program. Earned value reporting, however, would also be at a high level.

Our next point on the spectrum suggests that a project can be managed within the *principles* of EV without adhering to all of its 32 criteria. We recommended this implementation for small, fast-paced projects that can still profit from the benefits of EV. Five principles that follow 11 specific EVMS criteria are cited, along with the additional caution to beware of scope creep. The principles are project definition (Criteria 1, 9), work assignment (Criterion 2), performance measurement baseline (Criteria 6, 7, 8), calculating the metrics (Criteria 16, 19, 22), and using the information (Criteria 26, 27).

The very least application of EV still requires some vital steps to gain any benefit from EV. The project must have an estimated duration (project plan) with a schedule of reporting periods. There must be estimated project costs for each reporting period. There must be a method for accruing the actual project costs expended for each reporting period. With these data, the global EV and related variances can be calculated and reported. This minimalist approach can be recommended only as a preliminary introduction to a more complete implementation of EV.

DISCUSSION QUESTIONS

1. How quickly does your organization collect and report financial data?

2. Is that timing helpful or a problem for EV project management and control?

3. Do you or could you affect the collection of financial data?

4. If you were not required to follow government requirements for a full EVMS implementation, but still wanted to use EV, how much of EVMS would you use, and why?

5. In time and effort, what is the most consuming process in order to provide EV project data? Can any of this effort be alleviated during the initial EV implementation?

6. Why (or why not) is creating a performance measurement baseline a critical principle of any meaningful EV-managed project?

7. What are other principles that must be followed if there is to be meaningful EV project management, but without a full-blown EVMS implementation?

8. Why do you believe (or not believe) it would be reasonable to implement the very simplest EV implementation?

Emerging Practices

EVMS has been in practice for a number of years and has had only minor changes since it was originally developed. We are now beginning to see several emerging practices that could become mainstream in a short time.

PERFORMANCE-BASED EARNED VALUE

One of these emerging practices is performance-based earned value, or PBEV (Solomon and Young 2007). Solomon and Young's major contributions are (1) the insertion of product technical requirements and expected quality into a project's plan;[1] (2) recognizing EV for partially achieving product requirements, such as quality; and (3) formally integrating risk management tasks, such as estimated rework, into the EV system. They provide many examples and alternative methods of accomplishing PBEV. They have an entire chapter on level of effort and explain why it should be separated

---

[1]Savvy project managers have been putting deliverables on project schedules for some time, but not to the technical detail recommended by Solomon and Young.

from discrete work packages. The book explains the PBEV approach in detail. If technical requirements are a major issue for your projects (software projects, for example), we recommend that you refer to Solomon and Young's book for additional information on PBEV.

SCHEDULE MARGIN

Another emerging EVMS practice involves placing buffers at designated points of exceptional risk in the project baseline.[2] For example, a margin task might be placed where multiple paths converge to a single task—a known unknown. There is risk at this point because the task is dependent on completion of all the merging paths.

Formally, *schedule margin* is defined as follows:

2.4.1.22 <u>Schedule Margin</u>. A management method for accommodating schedule contingencies. It is a designated buffer and shall be identified separately and considered part of the baseline. Schedule margin is the difference between contractual milestone date(s) and the contractor's planned date(s) of accomplishment (Department of Defense 2005b, 5).

The National Aeronautics and Space Administration refers to schedule margin as *schedule management reserve* or *schedule reserve.* NASA discusses the topic in its *Schedule Management Handbook*:

Schedule management reserve is used for future situations that are impossible to predict (just in case time for unknown unknowns). It is a separately planned quantity of time above the planned duration estimate specifically identified in the schedule as "Schedule Management Reserve" and is intended to reduce the impact of missing overall schedule objectives. This type of reserve must be inserted into the IMS [Integrated Master Schedule] at strategic locations so that it satisfies its intended purpose as overall schedule management reserve for the project completion. To ensure this, it is recommended that this type of reserve be placed at the end of the IMS network logic

---

[2] *Schedule margin* is not the same as the *margin of safety* probability computation provided by some earned value software programs to estimate the risk involved in open tasks when 50/50 earned value is in use.

flow just prior to hardware delivery or whatever the appropriate project completion task/milestone might be (National Aeronautics and Space Administration 2009, section 5.2.6).

Schedule reserve should be easily identifiable and strategically placed within the IMS. Generally, it is recommended to create specially labeled tasks for schedule reserve and place the bulk of reserve at the end of the schedule just prior to project completion so that it will be reflected and easily accounted for and managed as part of the critical path sequence. Other smaller blocks of schedule reserve could also be associated with significant key events in the IMS and placed logically just prior to those events (National Aeronautics and Space Administration 2009, section 7.2.6).

Schedule margin has been used sparingly in the past, but there are several initiatives under way to encourage more widespread government acceptance of schedule margin and other scheduling buffer techniques. Critical chain project management's use of buffers and buffer management is presented in Chapter 17.

EMERGING PRACTICES TO BE TREATED IN GREATER DETAIL

Two additional emerging practices are earned schedule and critical chain. Because of their applicability to all projects, these two practices are discussed in Chapters 16 and 17, respectively.

CHAPTER 16

Earned Schedule

Earned value cost metrics, such as cost variance (CV) and cost performance index (CPI), are intuitively obvious and informative of the condition of a project both during execution and when the project is completed. Derived measures, such as estimate at completion (EAC) and estimate to complete (ETC), likewise provide actionable information during a project and at the end.

EV schedule metrics, however, being in currency, are not intuitively obvious to most users and become absolutely misleading during the last half or two-thirds of a project. This is because at the completion of a project, the schedule variance (SV), in currency, is forced to zero and the schedule performance index (SPI) is forced to 1, meaning the project schedule was performed as planned—no matter how late actual project delivery is.

These facts have been known since EV was created (for example, see Fleming and Koppleman 1996, figure 9-5, 109). Because the EV system was far superior to previously used guesses and promises, this flaw has been overlooked and users merely cautioned to suspect the SV and SPI at some point (not rigorously defined) in the project's life. For users not actively involved in completing the project, this untidy situation has been a minor annoyance.

For people working on the project and trying to make sense of how they are doing in terms of both cost and schedule, schedule performance information has been a major headache. Trying to explain schedule performance has been so much a problem that an insightful project manager, Walt Lipke, developed a sound alternative (Lipke 2003).

RATIONALE FOR THE DEVELOPMENT OF EARNED SCHEDULE

As explained earlier in Chapter 3, EVMS was modeled after a standard cost system, where variances are denominated in dollars; the time period is usually fixed at one month, quarter, or year; and the focus is on controlling costs compared to the expected standard cost per unit. Because of this cost-per-unit feature, a standard cost system permits flexibility so that quantity (volume) variances reveal the difference between planned volume and units actually produced. Figure 3.1 is repeated here as Figure 16.1.

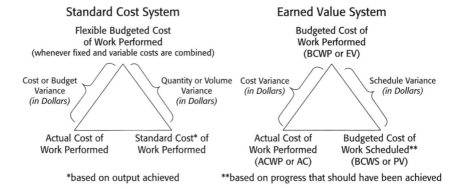

FIGURE 16.1 Periodic Reporting: Standard Cost System versus EVMS

Projects, however, consume varying amounts of time, and the focus is on completion of the project as well as controlling costs. Like the standard cost system, both the CV and SV are denominated in currency (or perhaps labor hours), requiring mental processing to interpret the relationship between the computed schedule variance and its relationship to time; that is, whether the project is early, on time, or late. Unfortunately, the traditional EVMS does not permit flexibility in terms of the quantity of time required to complete the project. Because of this lack of flexibility, as mentioned earlier, the SV at the end of the project is zero and the SPI is 1, regardless of how early or late the completion may be. At some point, typically after about two-thirds of the project has been completed, the SV (in dollars) and the SPI (computed from dollar amounts) become fairly meaningless.

For cost analysis, the basic characteristics of EVMS are not a problem, and the cost metrics (CV and CPI) are meaningful and easily understood. However, toward the last third of a project, for many reported users, especially those working on the project, interpreting SV in dollars (and the resultant SPI) is a major problem.

EARNED SCHEDULE CONCEPTS

Earned schedule (ES) was developed to provide meaningful information throughout the project. At each status (report) date, the earned schedule can be computed graphically by drawing a line from the cumulative EV back (for projects behind schedule) or forward (for projects ahead of schedule) to the project baseline. The point where the line intersects the project baseline, dropped to the horizontal axis, reveals the portion of the baseline that has been "earned." Figure 16.2 uses the same numbers as Figure 4.1: $69,000 planned value (budgeted cost of work scheduled), $65,000 actual costs (actual cost of work performed), and $59,000 EV (budgeted cost of work performed) as of the end of the first quarter. Figure 16.2 shows that even though $69,000 worth of work on the project should have been completed by the end of the first quarter (90 days), only about 60 days of the planned schedule actually were completed. Therefore, at the end of the first quarter of a four-quarter project, work is already 30 days behind.

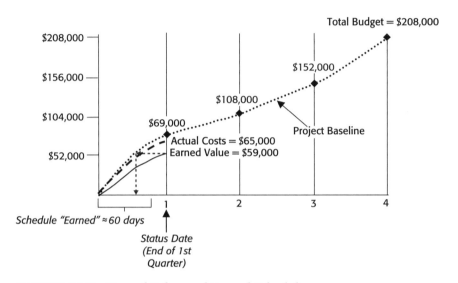

FIGURE 16.2   Earned Value and Earned Schedule

Assuming the late trend continues, the project illustrated in Figure 16.2 could end up four months late. No matter how late the project may be delivered, however, during the last third or so of the project's life, the SV will converge to zero and the SPI will converge to 1, making these metrics meaningless and misleading.

Calculating Earned Schedule

It should be obvious that the graphical approach to computing earned schedule is not terribly precise, and the diagram in Figure 16.2 would not facilitate preparation of derivative metrics such as EAC in time or ETC in time. Even though this graphical method has been known since early in the development of EVMS, few practitioners have adopted it. Starting in 2003, Lipke and others began developing the statistics required to support the development of earned schedule.

When EV is calculated for a reporting period, the earned schedule is the point in the schedule where the calculated EV would be equal to the planned value. ES is expressed as a number of reporting periods, usually months. The number is most often a whole number of months and a fractional part of an additional month. To compute ES, one must have two pieces of data: (1) the greatest number of time increments (usually months) for which EV (BCWP) is greater than or equal to planned value (BCWS) and (2) the *pro rata* portion of EV in excess of the planned value for the time increment found in (1).

Definitions

Because traditional EVMS does not have time metrics, a number of new definitions have been developed to support earned schedule. Table 16.1 shows some basic definitions.[1]

TABLE 16.1   Basic Time-Based Terms

Description	Abbreviation	Definition
Actual time (cumulative)	AT_{cum}	Number of periods since the project began
Earned schedule (cumulative)	ES_{cum}	Number of periods completed plus any portion of the next period completed
Schedule variance in time	SV(t)	Earned schedule minus actual time (number of periods since the project began)
Schedule performance index (time)	SPI(t)	Earned schedule divided by actual time
Planned duration	PD	The time (number of periods) required to complete the project (original projection)

EXAMPLE OF EARNED SCHEDULE COMPUTATIONS

Following Lipke's approach (Lipke 2003), two simple examples—a project completing early and one completing late—illustrate the

---

[1]See Lipke and Henderson (2006) and Lipke et al. (2008).

earned schedule methodology. Detailed data for the two projects are shown in Tables 16.2 and 16.3. Table 16.2 describes a 12-month project that is completed in 11 months (one month early); Table 16.3 describes a 12-month project that requires 14 months to be completed.

The row labels of both tables above the black bar are the familiar standard EV metrics. Below the black bar, the row labels represent the additional information required to compute the ES, the schedule variance in time [SV(t)], and the schedule performance index in time [SPI(t)] (months in these examples).

For example, at the end of the first month (January) in Table 16.2, planned value [BCWS($)][2] is $700 and EV [BCWP($)] is $750. Even though only one month has passed, the ES is 1.091 months. Although the amount of the favorable performance varies from month to month, the project represented in Table 16.2 is always ahead of schedule.

Because, in this example, the project is never more than one month ahead of schedule, to find the ES for any month, add to the current month count a fraction of the future work completed. For March, the cumulative ES[3] would be computed as follows:

$$\text{March ES} = \textit{March Month Count} + \frac{\textit{March BCWP(\$)} - \textit{March BCWS(\$)}}{\textit{April BCWS(\$)} - \textit{March BCWS(\$)}} \text{ or}$$

$$= 3 + \frac{\$2,190 - \$2,100}{\$3,650 - \$2,100} = 3.058.$$

Once the ES is known, the schedule variance in time [SV(t)] is found by subtracting the current month count from the ES. In a related way, the schedule performance index in time [SPI(t)] is found by dividing the ES by the current month count. In Table 16.2,

$$\text{March SV(t)} = 3.058 - 3 = .058, \text{ and SPI(t)} = \frac{3.058}{3} = 1.019.$$

---

[2]Traditional EVMS metrics are now identified with ($) to differentiate the same metrics in time (t).

[3]It also is possible to compute the ES for a single month by subtracting the previous cumulative ES from the current cumulative ES. Monthly ES data then can be plotted over time, if desired.

TABLE 16.2   Early-Finish Project (Cumulative Values)

	Jan	Feb	Mar	Apr	May	Jun	Jul	Aug	Sep	Oct	Nov	Dec
Planned Value	$700	$1,250	$2,100	$3,650	$6,550	$8,700	$12,025	$14,240	$15,990	$17,500	$18,200	$18,500
Earned Value	$750	$1,420	$2,190	$4,600	$7,380	$9,990	$12,380	$14,575	$16,490	$18,100	$18,500	
Actual Cost	$710	$1,325	$2,100	$4,220	$6,630	$6,590	$11,950	$13,290	$15,800	$16,990	$17,700	
CV($)	$40	$95	$90	$380	$750	$3,400	$430	$1,285	$690	$1,110	$800	
CPI($)	1.056	1,072	1,043	1,090	1.113	1.516	1.036	1.097	1.044	1.056	1.045	
SV($)	$50	$170	$90	$950	$830	$1,290	$355	$335	$500	$600	$300	
SPI($)	1.071	1.136	1.043	1.260	1.127	1.148	1.030	1.024	1.031	1.034	1.016	
Month Count	1	2	3	4	5	6	7	8	9	10	11	12
Earned Schedule	1.091	2.200	3.058	4.328	5.386	6.388	7.160	8.191	9.331	10.857	12.000	
SV(t)	0.091	0.200	0.058	0.328	0.386	0.388	0.160	0.191	0.331	0.857	1.000	
SPI(t)	1.091	1.100	1.019	1.082	1.077	1.065	1.023	1.024	1.037	1.086	1.091	

TABLE 16.3   Late-Finish Project (Cumulative Values)

	Year 1												Year 2	
	Jan	Feb	Mar	Apr	May	Jun	Jul	Aug	Sep	Oct	Nov	Dec	Jan	Feb
Planned Value	$700	$1,250	$2,100	$3,650	$6,550	$8,700	$12,025	$14,240	$15,990	$17,500	$18,200	$18,500	$18,500	$18,500
Earned Value	$625	$1,050	$1,500	$2,160	$4,250	$6,600	$7,800	$10,880	$14,600	$15,800	$17,700	$18,100	$18,200	$18,500
Actual Cost	$675	$1,200	$2,100	$3,720	$6,610	$8,750	$12,230	$14,380	$17,820	$18,214	$20,700	$21,350	$22,180	$22,980
CV($)	$(50)	$(150)	$(600)	$(1,560)	$(2,360)	$(2,150)	$(4,430)	$(3,500)	$(3,220)	$(2,414)	$(3,000)	$(3,250)	$(3,980)	$(4,480)
CPI($)	0.93	0.88	0.71	0.58	0.64	0.75	0.64	0.76	0.82	0.87	0.86	0.85	0.82	0.81
SV($)	$(75)	$(200)	$(600)	$(1,490)	$(2,300)	$(2,100)	$(4,225)	$(3,360)	$(1,390)	$(1,700)	$(500)	$(400)	$(300)	$ –
SPI($)	0.893	0.840	0.714	0.592	0.649	0.759	0.649	0.764	0.913	0.903	0.973	0.978	0.984	1.000
Month Count	1	2	3	4	5	6	7	8	9	10	11	12	13	14
Earned Schedule	0.893	1.636	2.294	3.039	4.207	5.023	5.581	6.656	8.206	8.891	10.286	10.857	11.000	12.000
SV(t)	-0.107	-0.364	-0.706	-0.961	-0.793	-0.977	-1.419	-1.344	-0.794	-1.109	-0.714	-1.143	-2.000	-2.000
SPI(t)	0.8929	0.8182	0.7647	0.7597	0.8414	0.8372	0.7973	0.8320	0.9117	0.8891	0.9351	0.9048	0.8462	0.8571

Unfortunately, the happy ahead-of-schedule circumstance shown in Table 16.2 is not the norm for most projects. Table 16.3 reveals a more common situation, in which the project is behind schedule.

Table 16.3 shows a project that starts out behind schedule and never recovers, completing two months after the expected completion date, with a negative cost variance of $4,480 (24 percent overrun). Although the monthly planned values [BCWS($)] are the same as those shown in Table 16.2, the EV [BCWP($)] are different. Once again the traditional metrics are shown above the black bar and the ES metrics below it.

The computation of ES and related metrics for a late project is slightly different from that for an early project. For example, the calculation of cumulative ES in Table 16.3 for August is as follows:

$$\text{August ES} = \textit{June Month Count} + \frac{\textit{August BCWP(\$)} - \textit{June BCWS(\$)}}{\textit{July BCWS(\$)} - \textit{June BCWS(\$)}} \text{ or}$$

$$= 6 + \frac{\$10{,}880 - \$8{,}700}{\$12{,}025 - \$8{,}700} = 6.656.$$

August SV(t) is August ES – August Month Count or $6.656 - 8 = -1.344$, and

August SPI(t) is August ES divided by August Month Count, or $\frac{6.656}{8} = 0.8320$

(clearly indicating less-than-expected performance).

Figure 16.3 shows the typical graphs associated with Table 16.2 (early project), and Figure 16.4 shows the graphs associated with Table 16.3 (late project).

Note that in both situations (early finish and late finish), the schedule metrics in time (black line in all graphs in both figures) always track with actual performance, whereas the schedule metrics in currency (grey line in all graphs in both figures) show the typical "perfect" performance at project completion, regardless of whether the project is early or late.

For comparison purposes, graph d in both Figures 16.3 and 16.4 shows the cost (dashed line) and schedule variances in currency

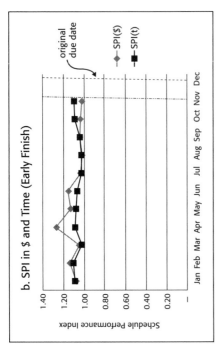

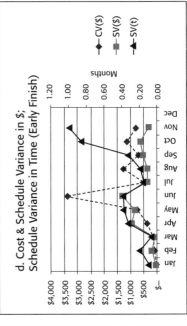

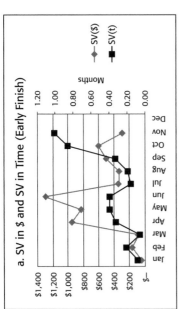

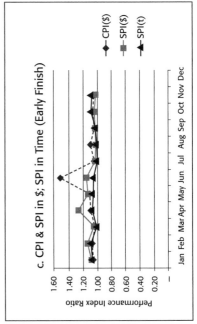

FIGURE 16.3   Graphs for Early-Finish Project

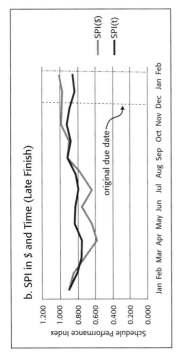

b. SPI in $ and Time (Late Finish)

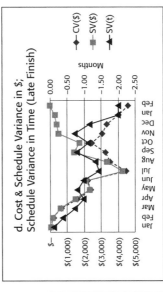

d. Cost & Schedule Variance in $;
Schedule Variance in Time (Late Finish)

a. SV in $ and Time (Late Finish)

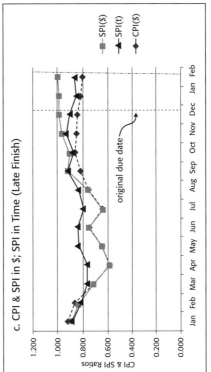

c. CPI & SPI in $; SPI in Time (Late Finish)

FIGURE 16.4 Graphs for Late-Finish Project

and the schedule variance in time. The cost variance in dollars, like the schedule variance in time, tracks with reality. Only the schedule variance in dollars is not informative once the project nears the last third of the project's planned duration.

OTHER EARNED SCHEDULE METRICS

In addition to the basic metrics of ES, SV(t), and SPI(t), several other metrics, comparable to traditional EV metrics, can be developed.

Time-Based Metrics for Forecasting

A customer's independent estimate at completion, IEAC, using time, can be computed using the following formula:

$$IEAC(t) = \frac{Planned\ Duration\ (weeks\ or\ months)}{SPI(t)}\ or$$

$$= \frac{Actual\ Time + (Planned\ Duration - Earned\ Schedule)}{P*}$$

*P(t) is defined in Table 16.4 and in the next section.

In a similar manner, the traditional budgeted cost for work remaining (BCWR) becomes the planned duration for work remaining (PDWR) using ES metrics. Estimate to complete can be easily computed in time and is designated ETC(t). Variance at completion (VAC) is matched with variance at completion in time [VAC(t)]; a supplier's estimate at completion becomes EAC(t); and the to-complete performance index (TCPI) is modified as the to-complete schedule performance index (TCSPI), sometimes shortened to TSPI. Additional time-based terms are shown in Table 16.4.[4]

---

[4]See Lipke and Henderson (2006) and Lipke et al. (2009).

TABLE 16.4   Additional Time-Based Terms

Description	Abbreviation	Definition
Estimated Duration	ED	The projected estimate of the number of periods to complete the project (made after project has begun)
Estimated Duration at Completion	EDAC	Same as the description for Estimated Duration (see above)
To-Complete Schedule Performance Index	TCSPI(t) or TSPI(t)	(Planned Duration minus ES) divided by (Planned Duration minus Actual Time)
Performance Factor (time)	P(t) or PF(t)	Tracks how closely the project plan sequence is being followed
Earned Value (effective)	EV(e)	EV adjusted down for a portion of work completed out of sequence

Performance Factor (time)

Acknowledging that tasks are sometimes initiated out of planned sequence, Lipke developed a metric, termed P or P(t), describing how closely the appropriate task sequence is followed, and that metric can be used to diminish EV for the inevitable rework that arises from working on tasks out of sequence (Lipke 2005). To compute the P-factor for a project, one must have, for each task, (1) task planned value at the relevant planned time, (2) task EV at the actual time, and (3) the "P" number.

Once computed, the P-factor can be used to calculate the effective EV [EV(e)], consisting of the EV from tasks performed in the proper sequence plus the usable fraction of EV from tasks performed out of sequence. Following Lipke (2005), EV(e) is computed as follows:

$$\text{EV(e)} = \left[\frac{1 + P(rework\ percent)}{1 + (rework\ percent)} \right] \times [\text{EV (computed the traditional way)}]$$

where rework percent = estimated rework percentage required for work performed on tasks out of sequence.

For example, if the P-factor is computed as 0.90 and the estimated rework percentage is 60 percent, and EV is computed as $6,600 (from Table 16.3, month of June), the effective EV would be

$$EV(e) = \left[\frac{1+0.90(.6)}{(1+.6)}\right] \times \$6,600 = \$6,352.50.$$

Once found, the effective EV can be used to compute both cost and schedule (in time) variances and estimates at completion[5] as described above and in earlier chapters.

Unfortunately, data requirements for the required calculations described above are extensive, and computation of the P-factor can be onerous. Fortunately, a free spreadsheet can be downloaded from http://www.earnedschedule.com/calculator.shtml,[6] but collecting data for insertion into the spreadsheet may still be a critical issue.

RECONCILING SCHEDULE VARIANCE IN TIME WITH SCHEDULE VARIANCE IN DOLLARS

There is no completely general formula to reconcile SV(t) with SV($). To provide some confirmation that the two schedule variances are not completely independent, it is possible to compute the schedule variance in currency for some months by multiplying the change in planned value [BCWS($)] by the schedule variance in time [SV(t)] in the examples illustrated in Tables 16.2 and 16.3. The reconciling formula for projects that are ahead of schedule is

1. SV($) = Δ BCWS($)*SV(t)
    where
    Δ BCWS($) = $BCWS^{n+1} - BCWS^{n}$ and n = number of periods

    while the formula for late projects is

---

2. $SV(\$) = \Delta BCWS(\$)*SV(t)$
    where
    $\Delta BCWS(\$) = BCWS^{i+1} - BCWS^i$
    and $i = BCWP(\$)^n >= BCWS(\$)^n$.

Formula 1, above, correctly predicts the SV($) from the SV(t) for all months on the early-finish project only because the project is never ahead by more than one month and thus the implied "basis" for the SV($) and that for the SV(t) are the same. The formula would fail during periods when a project is ahead by more than one month.

Likewise, formula 2, above, fails to accurately predict the schedule variance in currency whenever a project is more than one month behind schedule. Also, because the schedule variance in dollars is forced to zero even for very late projects, reconciliation deviations are quite common beginning about halfway through a late project.

Formulas 1 and 2, above, are illustrated in Tables 16.5 (early-finish project) and 16.6 (late-finish project). Formula 1 is capable of reconciling SV(t) to SV($) for every month in Table 16.5 because the project was never more than one month ahead of schedule.

Formula 2 reconciles SV(t) to SV($) only for the first six months in Table 16.6 for the two reasons mentioned earlier. First, the formula fails when the project is more than one month behind schedule because different bases are used in the computation. Second, the SV($) for a late project is forced to zero at the completion of the project, meaning that approximately two-thirds of the way through the project, the currency SV no longer is reliable. Note in Table 16.6, however, that the formula correctly predicted the SV($) in the months of September and November.

One might even claim that about $800 of the total cost variance of $4,780 was due entirely to the project's being two months late. More likely, this would underestimate the true cost of the late finish. In any event, it should be clear that SV(t) is closely related to SV($).

TABLE 16.5   Reconciliation of SV(t) to SV($) for an Early-Finish Project

	Jan	Feb	Mar	Apr	May	Jun	Jul	Aug	Sep	Oct	Nov	Dec
BCSW($)	700	1,250	2,100	3,650	6,550	8,700	12,025	14,240	15,990	17,500	18,200	18,500
SV($)	50	170	90	950	830	1290	355	335	500	600	300	
SV(t)^{cum}	0.091	0.200	0.058	0.328	0.386	0.388	0.160	0.191	0.331	0.857	1.000	
Δ BCWS($)*SV(t)	50	170	90	950	830	1,290	355	335	500	600	300	
Δ BCWS($) = BCWS$_{n+1}$ − BCWS$_n$												

TABLE 16.6   Reconciliation of SV(t) to SV($) for a Late-Finish Project

	Year 1												Year 2	
	Jan	Feb	Mar	Apr	May	Jun	Jul	Aug	Sep	Oct	Nov	Dec	Jan	Feb
BCWS($)	700	1,250	2,100	3,650	6,550	8,700	12,025	14,240	15,990	17,500	18,200	18,500	18,500	18,500
SV($)	(75)	(200)	(600)	(1,490)	(2,300)	(2,100)	(4,224)	(3,360)	(1,390)	(1,700)	(500)	(400)	(300)	—
SV(t)^{cum}	(0.107)	(0.364)	(0.706)	(0.961)	(0.793)	(0.977)	(1.419)	(1.344)	(0.794)	(1.109)	(0.714)	(1.143)	(2.000)	(2.000)
Δ BCWS($)*SV(t)	(75)	(200)	(600)	(1,490)	(2,300)	(2,100)	(3,050)	(4,470)	(1,390)	(1,940)	(500)	(800)	(600)	—
Δ BCWS($) = BCWS$_{i+1}$ − BCWS$_i$; i = BCWP($)$_n$ >= BCWS($)$_n$														

VALIDATION OF USEFULNESS OF EARNED SCHEDULE

As soon as Lipke published his seminal article, project managers began applying the earned schedule methodology retroactively to completed projects.[7] They found that the methodology indicated the correct outcome for late projects (Henderson 2004).

Recently, Lipke and others performed sophisticated simulations and statistical prediction and testing and found that "Earned Schedule offers calculation methods yielding reliable results, which greatly simplify final duration and completion date forecasting." They further state that their results indicate an ". . . overall better prediction for schedule than for cost." (Lipke et al. 2009).

Vanhoucke and Vandevoorde also performed extensive simulations to evaluate the ability of EV metrics, including earned schedule, to forecast project duration. Their results reveal that ". . . the ES method almost always outperforms all other methods, regardless of the stage of completion" (Vanhoucke and Vandevoorde 2007, 1370).

Part VII introduces several emerging practices in conjunction with EVMS, including performance-based earned value and the use of schedule margins, without elaborating on them. Chapter 16 provides more detail about another emerging practice, earned schedule.

Many users have problems with two aspects of earned value: (1) the measurements are denominated in dollars and (2) the metrics become less indicative of project performance as the project proceeds. Because the EV system is superior to the previous performance guesses, most users have overlooked these flaws.

---

[7]For example, see Henderson (2004).

Because of this diminishing validity of EV metrics and because most project team members are more tuned to time schedules than to cost metrics, earned schedule was developed. The earned schedule (ES) is the point in the schedule at which the EV equals the planned value, and it is expressed as the number of reporting periods earned. Using the ES, a schedule variance, a schedule performance index, and a planned duration can be calculated in time measurements. Sample calculations for a project running late and a project running ahead of schedule are shown in accompanying tables.

After development of the ES, the EV itself could be adjusted to an effective EV [EV(e)] by applying a performance factor. The P-factor accounts for the lessened value of tasks that are not started and/or completed according to the planned schedule and thus require rework. The chapter concludes by showing that Earned Schedule and EV are related and referencing the additional benefits of Earned Schedule.

PRACTICE CALCULATIONS AND DISCUSSION QUESTIONS

1. Using the information from Table 16.3 in this chapter, show the computation used to derive the SV(t) and SPI(t) for

   a. December of Year 1 and

   b. January of Year 2.

2. Assume the planned value, actual cost, and EV for the first four months of a project are as follows:

Month	1	2	3	4	5
Planned Value	$90	$250	$380	$500	$875
Earned Value	$75	$240	$360	$550	
Actual Cost	$90	$260	$380	$600	
Earned Schedule					
SV(t)					
SPI(t)					

a. Compute the ES for months 3 and 4.

b. Compute the SV(t) for months 3 and 4.

c. Compute the SPI(t) for months 3 and 4.

3. Would the use of earned schedule concepts be helpful in reporting progress to project team members?

4. Would other project stakeholders likely be interested in Earned Schedule metrics?

5. Does the fact that there is no completely general formula that will reconcile SV(t) to SV($) diminish the value of SV(t)? Why or why not?

CHAPTER 17

Critical Chain
Project Management

Even though the critical path method (CPM) has long dominated the scheduling of projects, it is not required by EVMS. Recently, CPM's scheduling domination has been challenged by a new methodology: critical chain project management (CCPM). This chapter explains the emergence of CCPM and describes how it is used in conjunction with EVMS.

BACKGROUND

As mentioned earlier, the critical path method was developed by mathematicians and engineers in a burst of operations research activity in the late 1950s to assist the U.S. government in developing defense projects. The following paragraph, from one of the first books on the critical path method, introduces it in mathematical terms unfamiliar to most of us:

> Without stretching the theoretical aspects relative to the search for ordinal relations in a graph, this concept, as it will be seen, being nothing else but a set of elements among which oriented relations

exist, we believe it is appropriate to recall a few terms concerned with the theory of graphs and to show how to use the various processes which permit the attainment of ordinal relations. We shall confine ourselves to what is essential for a study of sequencing processes which intervene in the critical path method (Kaufmann and Desbazeille 1969, 1).

Because resources in this government environment were not a problem, and because solving for the optimal critical path with limited resources is an NP-hard problem[1] whose optimization is impossible, there was no attempt to identify a critical path that included leveled resources. In many projects today, perhaps most, resources are not unlimited, and leveling usually results in several possible critical paths. Critical chain was invented as a practical, workable approach to this and several other commonly faced project management problems.

DEVELOPMENT OF CRITICAL CHAIN

Traditional EV metrics are an excellent way of communicating with stakeholders who do not have inside knowledge of how a project is progressing. Cost and schedule variances in dollars are analogous to external financial statements prepared in accordance with generally accepted accounting principles (GAAP). Just as GAAP financial statements report past events, with some delay, EV metrics report past progress, also with some delay. Although we in the United States went through a couple of generations of managers trying to manage companies using external financial statement

---

[1]An *NP-hard problem* is defined as "the complexity class of decision problems that are intrinsically harder than those that can be solved by a nondeterministic Turing machine in polynomial time. When a decision version of a combinatorial optimization problem is proven to belong to the class of NP-complete problems—which includes well-known problems such as satisfiability, traveling salesman, the bin packing problem, etc.—then the optimization version is NP-hard" (*Algorithms and Theory of Computation Handbook,* 1999, pages 19–26.) That is, there is no way to identify an optimal solution that includes both a critical path and leveled resources.

information, most companies now have decided that they need different internal reporting information to make good decisions (Budd and Budd 2007).

People working on a project need current, unambiguous, trend-projecting information to make the best operating decisions. We alluded to this problem in Chapter 3 and illustrated the required tradeoffs between cost and schedule variances in Figure 3.3.[2] Gupta (2008) addresses some additional problems resulting from trying to manage projects using EV metrics.

Drawing on the basic concepts of the theory of constraints, Eli Goldratt introduced the basic critical chain concepts in his 1997 book *Critical Chain*. For example, the constraint of a manufacturing firm may be either an *internal* constraint, such as a piece of equipment or a processing department, or an *external* constraint, such as lack of market demand for the manufacturer's product. In a project environment, the constraint is the time required to complete the project so that project benefits can be realized and resources can be released to work on other projects. Also, although the problem of identifying both the optimal critical path and optimal resource allocations cannot be solved mathematically, it can be solved logically. Several critical chain concepts had been promoted by various persons prior to Goldratt (Millhiser and Szmerekovsky 2008), but he was the first to put the pieces together and also address the human behavior element of worker response to mixed signals.

Critical chain concepts were developed to facilitate the completion of projects in minimum time. Measurements that (1) induce people to take the right actions for the organization and (2) clearly point out to managers when and where they need to intervene are used. In addition, human behavior is considered and addressed.

---

[2]Figure 3.3 is an abbreviated version of a complete current reality diagram prepared from information provided by a defense contractor.

Traditional Project Management Problems

Acquiring *accurate* task times is one of the unachievable goals of both project managers and project offices. Yet the estimates usually given seem to reflect the actual time required to complete the task. For example, most tasks appear to be completed on their estimated due dates or late by a small variance of about 10 percent. An early finish on a task, while it does occur, is rare.

Traditional Project Management Performance Focus

Traditionally, management focus has concentrated on individual project tasks, and resources (people) have been evaluated based on whether their tasks are completed on time. One large organization has evaluated project managers based on the percentage of "bull's eyes"—project tasks completed on time—on their projects. Managers were expected to achieve greater than 80 percent on-time completion. However, since it takes only a few very late task completions (especially tasks on the critical path) to delay a project's completion, most projects still came in late.

The Human Behavior Element

Typically, individual resources estimate the time required to complete a task without knowing exactly how long it will take but knowing that they will be held responsible for delivering on their estimate (promise). Even though a similar task may have been completed in the past, it was accomplished in a different environment with different teammates. Since most resources are not dedicated to a single project but rather have other assignments for which they are responsible (their primary functional assignments, plus work on other projects), the "estimate" (soon to become a promise) must allow for various interruptions and emergencies.

Thus, each task estimate must include significant safety. Evaluations and careers frequently are based on how well people deliver on their promises. For example, rather than give an estimate that has a 50-50 chance of success and a high probability of censure for delivering late, it is far more likely that a savvy resource will provide an estimate that reflects a 90 percent probability of success.

Figure 17.1 illustrates the skewed distributions for four tasks varying in length. If summed and averaged, all the numbers in each of the distributions average the number of weeks represented by the distribution:

- Part a shows an average 10-week task with the 90 percent probability of 18 weeks.
- Part b shows an average 15-week task with the 90 percent probability of 25 weeks.
- Part c shows an average 20-week task with a 90 percent probability of 32 weeks.
- Part d shows an average 30-week task with a 90 percent probability of 48 weeks.

Combined with the fact that project task times are skewed to the right (no task can be completed in less than zero time, but the maximum time can be extremely long), a 90 percent estimate can have considerable safety, as illustrated in Figure 17.2.

It is easy to see that with a skewed distribution, the 90 percent time can be almost three times longer than the 50 percent time. Since reputations depend on delivering on promises, however, the 90 percent probability shown in Figure 17.2 is not unrealistic. Of course, once estimates are submitted, they are quite likely to be reduced by the organization. Knowing that estimates most likely will be cut further supports a longer estimate.

Multitasking, a trait valued by most organizations, where setup and set down time usually goes unnoticed by the organization, magnifies the need for safety. *Setup* time is the time required to understand exactly what is required by the task, or what progress was made earlier (prior to interruption); *set down* time includes whatever activities must be accomplished to leave a trail of the work completed. Setup and set down times include the mental time required to shift from one assignment to another.

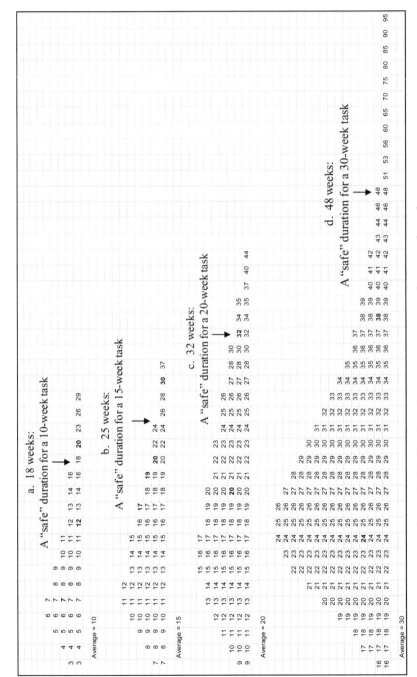

FIGURE 17.1   Discrete Skewed Distributions for 10-, 15-, 20-, and 30-Week Tasks

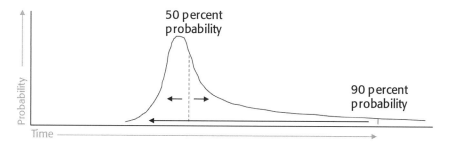

FIGURE 17.2   Time Difference Between a 50 Percent and a 90 Percent Estimate

Workers usually must fight to have their time estimates accepted by management and that encourages two common practices. First, knowing there is some safety in their estimate, they often give precedence to other, more pressing assignments, which uses some of the safety in the original task. If early task safety is absorbed and a problem occurs, it is quite likely that the result will be an impossible-to-hide late finish. *Student syndrome* is the term used to describe this behavior.

The second common reaction is that if things go very well, and the task is completed prior to the due date, the worker will be reluctant to report the early finish. Therefore, the work is "polished" or "enhanced" until just before the due date so acceptance of future estimates will not be jeopardized. The expansion of work to fill the time allowed is known as *Parkinson's Law* (Parkinson 1957).

Further, individuals working on a project typically are responsible for their own work, not for the success of the project. In fact, in matrix organizations, the usual situation is that functional department heads evaluate the performance of people in their area, and they might not even consider project work in the evaluation.

Of course, these human behaviors do not apply to all workers on all projects; but anecdotal evidence and our experience suggest they do apply to a significant number.

Logically extending the single task illustrated in Figure 17.2 to an entire project of tasks results in Figure 17.3. In the figure, estimated *dedicated* time (expected average time) is increased to an expected low-risk estimate (one that has about a 90 percent probability of on-time completion) to arrive at the estimate submitted to management.

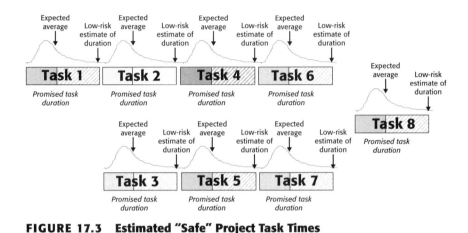

FIGURE 17.3   Estimated "Safe" Project Task Times

Typically, there is a tremendous amount of safety in a project. Unfortunately, it is distributed in each task's duration.

The Critical Chain Solution

Building on the theory of constraints concept that the sum of local optima (each task completing on time, for example) does not equal a global optima (on-time project completion), critical chain redistributes task safety to protect the project. In addition, successful critical chain implementations require that organization policies that encourage student syndrome, Parkinson's Law, and wasteful multitasking[3] be changed. The specific required changes are cov-

---

[3]There is both good and bad multitasking. Wasteful (bad) multitasking occurs when tasks are abandoned simply so that progress can be shown on another task on the same or another project.

ered later. First, we use an example of a simple project, scheduled as typically accomplished and also following critical chain concepts, to illustrate the differences between the two.

A SINGLE PROJECT ENVIRONMENT

A simple project consisting of ten tasks (three paths) serves as an example to illustrate and compare traditional and critical chain scheduling.

Traditional Scheduling

Figure 17.4 is a Gantt chart for a simple project, reflecting traditional scheduling for a resource-leveled project. Dependencies are shown by sequence and arrows; solid portions of each task represent dedicated times, and cross-hatched portions represent the safety imbedded in each task.

FIGURE 17.4   Gantt Chart for a Simple Ten-Task Project

Each square of cross-hatched area following a named resource, and its expected duration represents four weeks of safety. The first Blue resource on the far left in Figure 17.4, for example, has a dedicated time of 15 weeks and safety of ten weeks, computed from the 15-week discrete and skewed distribution shown in Figure 17.1, part b.

The first Black resource following the first Blue (from the left) has a dedicated time of 30 weeks and safety of 18 weeks, computed from the discrete and skewed distribution in part d of Figure 17.1. Safety for each of the other tasks was chosen in a similar manner from their respective distributions in Figure 17.1.

We assume that management likely responds to the initial project duration estimate with a statement that the project must be completed in no more than 145 weeks and requests that all resources compress their estimates. The reluctantly amended times are shown in Figure 17.5.

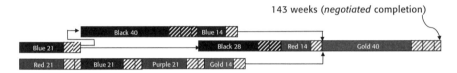

FIGURE 17.5   Negotiated Project Task Times and Completion Date

A Simulated Result from Traditional Scheduling

For purposes of this simulation, we performed random drawings from the various distributions for tasks of each length (shown in bold in Figure 17.1). These random drawings are the simulated actual times in Table 17.1. Table 17.1 also shows the original dedicated time and the negotiated time. Because resources have fought for the time they have been allowed, however, it is unlikely that they will report an early finish, even if it should occur. Therefore, the reported time in Table 17.1 is either the negotiated time or the actual time.

TABLE 17.1   Traditional Task Times (weeks): Original, Negotiated, Actual, and Reported

	Original Dedicated Time	Negotiated Time	Actual Time	Reported Time		Original Dedicated Time	Negotiated Time	Actual Time	Reported Time
Blue 15	21	30	30		Red 15	21	19	21
Black 30	40	24	40		Blue 15	21	17	21
Purple 15	21	20	21		Black 20	28	32	32
Blue 10	14	7	14		Gold 10	14	20	20
Red 10	14	12	14		Gold 30	40	38	40

Using the reported times in Table 17.1, the traditionally scheduled project would be completed in 156 weeks and would require 253 resource weeks of work, as shown in Figure 17.6.

FIGURE 17.6   Reported Completion Dates for Project

Because the original estimate was 171 weeks, and the revised negotiated delivery date was 143 weeks, 156 weeks isn't bad—less than a 9.1 percent overrun. This same example, using the same dedicated and actual times, will now be scheduled using critical chain methodology and assumptions.

Critical Chain Scheduling

The procedure to establish a critical chain schedule involves the following steps:

1. Remove some of each task's safety, and schedule the project backwards from project completion to the start of the project. Eliminate resource contention by staggering resources required on different paths at the same time.
2. Determine the *critical chain* (the longest chain of task- and resource-dependent events).
3. Establish an appropriate project buffer that uses some of the safety that was removed from task safety.
4. Establish feeding buffers for paths joining the critical chain, again eliminating any newly discovered resource contention.
5. Communicate start dates to tasks with no preceding tasks, and establish resource buffers to communicate when critical chain work is required.

6. If project duration is too long, determine what additional re-sources are needed for what period of time to decrease project duration.

Step 1: Schedule Dedicated Task Times

The first step in scheduling a critical chain project involves us-ing dedicated task times, with approximately 50 percent of the original safety removed from individual task times. Tasks are then back-scheduled from the last project task. Resource contention is resolved by starting from the end of the project and working back to the beginning. When scheduling manually, a general rule is to schedule shorter tasks nearer the end of the project, when you must make a choice. The resulting schedule will be a "workable" one, not necessarily an "optimal" one.

Figure 17.7 illustrates this first step. Note that tasks are scheduled to begin as late as possible to minimize resource contention within the project.

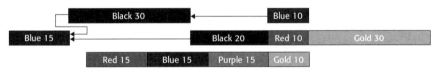

FIGURE 17.7   First Step in a Manual Critical Chain Schedule

Step 2: Determine the Critical Chain

Next, identify the longest chain of resource and task dependen-cies. In Figure 17.7, the longest (critical) chain is Blue 15, Black 30, Black 20, Red 10, and Gold 30, totaling 105 weeks. Since there is only about a 50-50 chance of each task finishing within the dedicated task times, however, a project buffer must be established to protect project completion.

Step 3: Establish an Appropriately Sized Project Buffer

While individual tasks have skewed distributions, the *project distribution* (the sum of all independent task distributions), due to the central limit theorem, can be assumed to be normally distributed. Thus, two standard deviations will cover about 90 percent of the distribution.[4] However, because the dedicated times are rough estimates, for our purposes there is no need to be statistically precise in computing buffer size.

A workable rule of thumb is to compute the project buffer size at approximately 50 percent of the length of the critical chain. Using this rule and a critical chain length of 105 weeks, the project buffer should be about 52 weeks. As we will see after the next step, though, this amount will be increased to add additional protection for a feeding buffer.

Step 4: Establish Feeding Buffers

Non-critical paths feeding into a critical path or critical chain frequently can become critical and delay the project. Therefore, feeding buffers should be placed at the end of each feeding path, prior to the point where it joins the critical chain. Feeding path sizes are determined using the same rule as that for project buffers: 50 percent of the length of the dedicated task times on the feeding chain. Figure 17.8 shows the placement of the feeding buffers for the example project.

Note that the lower feeding path in Figures 17.8 and 17.9 (Red 15, Blue 15, Purple 15, and Gold 10) requires about 28 weeks (one-half of the total dedicated path of 55 weeks) of feeding buffer. However, moving the path back a full 28 weeks would require the feeding path to commence its work before work is begun on the critical chain. Rather than have the unnatural effect of a feeding path beginning work before critical chain work, the black bar through two weeks of

---

[4]See Leach (2005), pages 135–137, for the statistical background.

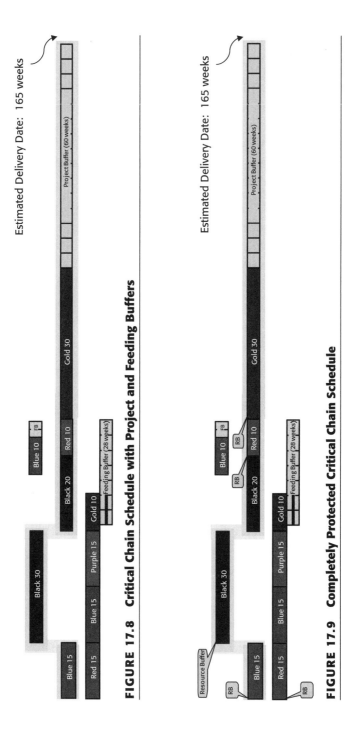

FIGURE 17.8   Critical Chain Schedule with Project and Feeding Buffers

FIGURE 17.9   Completely Protected Critical Chain Schedule

the lower feeding buffer means that eight weeks of the feeding buffer time have already elapsed when the project begins. To insulate this feeding path shortage, we will add eight weeks to the project buffer, resulting in 60 weeks of protection.

The estimated duration of the critical chain schedule is 165 weeks, 22 weeks longer than the revised traditional schedule. This does not mean that the critical chain schedule will force the project to finish later. On the contrary, we will soon show that the critical chain methodology results in both a shorter actual duration and fewer resource weeks.

Step 5: Develop a Communication Plan

Tasks with no predecessor tasks must be "told" when they should begin work (i.e., they must be triggered). (More on the topic of triggering path starts is provided when we discuss the multiproject environment.) In addition, resources assigned tasks on the critical chain must be ready to begin their work as soon as the preceding task is completed. To eliminate unnecessary multitasking, a general work policy is that once a task is begun, it is completed before a new task is started and queued tasks are completed FIFO (first in, first out).

An exception to this general work policy occurs when a resource is needed for work on the critical chain. The project manager agrees with each resource about the amount of advance notice the resource needs to be prepared to begin work on a critical chain task. Typically, one or two weeks is sufficient notice, and the notice is termed a *resource buffer*. Resource buffers are merely communication tools; they do not add time to a project. Figure 17.9 illustrates the complete project plan with all buffers.

Resource buffers are required to start every path and for each new resource whose task is upcoming on the critical chain. Note that in Figure 17.9, no resource buffer notification is required for the Black 20 task because the Black resource was already working on the critical chain.

Step 6: Determine How the Project Duration Can Be Shortened

If the program evaluation and review technique (PERT) is used, or if resources are not leveled in a traditional (critical path) schedule, it can be difficult to determine what additional resources may be required, for what period of time, in order to shorten project duration. A critical chain schedule points out not only when an additional resource will shorten a project's duration, but also the period for which it is needed. It is clear that if the duration of 165 weeks needs to be shortened, an additional Black resource could be acquired to begin work as soon as the Blue 15 task is complete, resulting in shortening the estimated duration by as much as 20 weeks.

Critical Chain Results

We will use the same actual (randomly determined) results as those for the traditional project simulation shown in Table 17.1. Because of the critical chain emphasis on changed behavioral traits, there will be some differences in reporting. The critical chain simulation results are shown in Table 17.2.

TABLE 17.2   Critical Chain Task Times (weeks): Original, Negotiated, Actual, and Reported

	Original Dedicated Time	Negotiated Time	Actual Time	Reported Time		Original Dedicated Time	Negotiated Time	Actual Time	Reported Time
Blue 15	15	30	**30**		Red 15	15	19	**19**
Black 30	30	24	**24**		Blue 15	15	17	**17**
Purple 15	15	20	**20**		Black 20	20	32	**32**
Blue 10	10	7	**7**		Gold 10	10	20	**20**
Red 10	10	12	**12**		Gold 30	30	38	**38**

The critical chain project will be completed in 136 weeks, as shown in Figure 17.10.

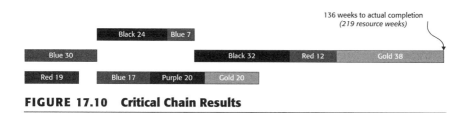

FIGURE 17.10   Critical Chain Results

The critical chain project finished 20 (156 – 136) weeks faster than the critical path project, and it used 34 (253 – 219) weeks less resource time. These results are not unusual.

Because each project is unique, it is extremely difficult to compare real projects using empirical studies. Simulation results using identical projects to compare critical path projects with critical chain projects have shown that critical chain schedules are completed in 30 to 40 percent less time (depending on the length of the project) than those using critical path (Cooper and Budd 2007). We have also seen similar results in tests with actual projects that had closely related properties.

Using Buffer Management to Control Projects

In the example project demonstrated above, no management intervention was permitted. The purpose of all critical chain buffers is to serve as an advance warning system so project managers can anticipate problems and address them before they become critical. Because the use of some, or perhaps all, of the buffer time is expected, however, managers should intervene only when the last third of any buffer (abnormal variation) is penetrated.

Deming called excessive intervention in operations "meddling." "The consequences of 'meddling' can result in chaos and lack of focus as lower-level managers scramble for explanations, perhaps neglecting other responsibilities" (Budd and Budd 2007, p. A-1307). Two-thirds of the buffer is expected to be consumed. Because "normal" variation can quickly turn into "abnormal" variation, the project manager should establish an action plan that can be implemented quickly should the time in the middle third of the buffer be required to absorb task variation. Figure 17.11 demonstrates the three parts of each buffer.

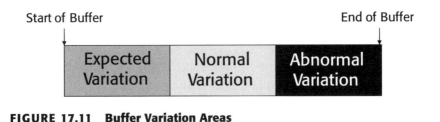

FIGURE 17.11   Buffer Variation Areas

For the example project discussed in this chapter, 60 weeks in the project buffer initially would be divided into three portions: 20 weeks of expected task variation, 20 weeks of normal variation (where action plans such as overtime, outsourcing, acquisition of additional resources, etc., would be devised but not implemented), and 20 weeks of abnormal variation (where previously developed action plans are put in place to prevent further deterioration of the buffer and to regain a portion of the lost buffer protection).

It is important to note that the size of the project buffer, relative to the remaining critical chain, should reflect the same ratio as that originally developed. For the example project, this ratio is $60/105 \approx 0.57$. If half of the critical chain has been completed, meaning about 52 weeks of task time remains on the critical chain, the remaining buffer should contain about 34 weeks of protection.

Feeding buffers are managed in the same way as project buffers. In setting priorities, other things being equal, focus usually should be given first to the project buffer, then to the feeding buffer. The basic idea is to protect the delivery date of the project, not the delivery of feeding paths.

To get up-to-date information on every active task that has been started but not completed, an assistant to the project manager should inquire, once or twice weekly, "How much more time do you require to complete the task?" There is no need to ask for a due date or percent of the work that has been completed.

If the projected duration is longer than the originally estimated dedicated time, the assistant marks as "consumed" an equivalent portion of the buffer. The project manager then uses this information to determine the buffer stage (expected, normal, or abnormal) and can take appropriate action.

MULTIPROJECT ENVIRONMENTS

Multiproject environments are much more complex and difficult to handle than single project environments. Software is necessary to prepare schedules in both critical path and critical chain methodologies.

From our experience working with companies, it is extremely difficult to get organizations to prioritize projects (everyone believes his or her project is number one), and it is impossible to level resources across all projects. While it is beyond the scope of this chapter to address multiprojects in detail, critical chain does offer a way to bring order to the typical chaos.

In a multiproject environment, individual projects are scheduled as was shown in the previous section, but their initiation into the system is controlled by a *sequencing resource*. The chosen sequencing resource should be a resource used on most projects in the system, typically involving task integration. This chosen resource is leveled across all projects according to project priority. Assuming the Black resource is selected as the sequencing resource, Figure 17.12 shows how inserting a sequencing buffer in succeeding projects staggers each project's entry into the system. In Figure 17.12, partial schedules are shown for three different projects, with the critical chain in each project identified by small white circles. The sequencing resource is located on the critical chain in Figure 17.12, but this is not always so.

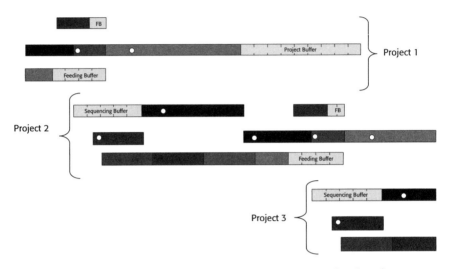

FIGURE 17.12   Sequencing Project Entry into an Organizational System

To protect the sequencing resource from total exhaustion, the size of the sequencing buffer typically is larger than those calculated for the project and feeding paths.

Rather than giving projects a hard-and-fast start date, resource buffers are used to alert the next highest priority project that sequencing resource work on the current project is being completed and work on the next project (the Blue resource in Project 2) will begin shortly. In this way, as one project is completed, another can enter the system, avoiding clogging the system with work.

USE OF CRITICAL CHAIN WITH EVMS

Critical chain concepts may be used with any of the partial EV implementations discussed in Chapter 15. Buffer management can be used for reporting to the project manager and project team members; EV reporting can be used for project owners.

When a full Department of Defense-type EVMS is required, the recent expansion of the Defense Contract Management Agency's (DCMA) role in project schedule assessment will dictate close communication with the DCMA auditors. We suggest two possibilities for gaining most of the benefits of critical chain while still meeting the full intent of EVMS.

Critical Chain in Lower Levels of the Performance Measurement Baseline

The U.S. government requires detailed reporting down to the control account (CA) level. As explained earlier, CAs are established at the intersection of the work breakdown structure (WBS) and the organizational breakdown structure (OBS). This intersection typically occurs at about the third or fourth level (task or subtask level[5]) of a WBS, when the identified work can be uniquely assigned to a functional area responsible for controlling and reporting at the CA level. Below the CA level, there may be numerous work packages and planning packages.

When the work is scheduled, the CA can be established as a summary-level task. As the summary level is subdivided, each group of tasks below the CA summary level can be scheduled as a mini critical chain "project" using all the critical chain concepts with feeding and resource buffers. A "project" buffer can be added at the end of each group of CA subtasks. The group of tasks then could have the same duration as if scheduled with more traditional methods but with significantly more control and performance reliability. The planned value, EV, and actual costs would still be calculated and reported at the CA level.

One defense contractor turned work packages into projects, and the projects were aggregated into individual CAs. To be conservative, EV was reported only when tasks on a "project" work package were completely finished. In this way, along with following the behav-

---

[5]As defined by Lewis (2000), 91.

iors indicated by critical chain methodology,[6] most of the benefits of critical chain project management were achieved (Holt 2007). Another defense contractor, compelled to follow EVMS, received benefit from merely following critical chain behaviors and not even establishing buffers.

Two Project Plans

Although not in strict adherence to EVMS requirements and validation, we know of a contractor who was allowed to schedule a project with two different project plans. One was a critical chain project schedule, which was used to actually manage the project. The other was a more traditional EVMS project schedule, used for reporting. There was no complaint from the auditors and reviewers as long as there were timely and accurate EVMS reports. The contractor reports significant cost savings and improved project performance.

We expect that as government agencies recognize the benefits of critical chain project management, there will be more flexibility in the formal criteria. Critical chain project management is becoming more widespread and accepted. The latest edition (2008) of the Project Management Institute's *A Guide to the Project Management Body of Knowledge* (*PMBOK® Guide*) gives critical chain roughly the same treatment as critical path.[7]

---

[6]Such as leaving a task only when it is completed, unless the resource is needed for a more critical task, turning work over as soon as it is complete, and receiving no praise for finishing earlier than their dedicated estimate and no criticism if work took longer than the estimated dedicated time.
[7]There are four index listings for each methodology, but the space devoted to critical path is slightly larger than that devoted to critical chain.

The critical path method was developed in the late 1950s, and its initial utilizations did not attempt to level resources. Just as there are differences between external financial reporting and the internal information required for effective organizational management, there can be differences in external project reporting and information required for effective project management. Critical chain concepts were developed to facilitate the completion of projects in minimum time. Critical chain addresses problems with human behavior and provides management guidelines.

One of the problems with traditional project scheduling and management is that it is overly focused on the completion of individual tasks. Nor is there a process to address the dysfunctional human traits manifested in the student syndrome, Parkinson's Law, and inappropriate multitasking. A logical extension of these problems to an entire project is demonstrated, followed by the suggested critical chain approach.

A traditional project schedule and simulated project results are illustrated. The same single project, but scheduled and managed with critical chain concepts, and its simulated result follows. The six steps of critical chain methodology are:

1. Remove some of each task's safety, and schedule the project backwards from project completion back to the start of the project. Eliminate resource contention by staggering resources required on different paths at the same time.

2. Determine the critical chain (the longest chain of task- and resource-dependent events).

3. Establish an appropriate project buffer that uses some of the safety that was removed from task safety.

4. Establish feeding buffers for paths joining the critical chain, again eliminating any newly discovered resource contention.

5. Communicate start dates to tasks with no preceding tasks, and establish resource buffers to communicate when critical chain work is required.

6. If project duration is too long, determine what additional resources are needed for what period of time to decrease project duration.

In critical chain, safety buffer allocation, consumption, and management are used to control project management.

There is also a discussion of the multiproject environment. The biggest problem in that environment is that there are usually too many projects running at one time, which causes an extended completion time for all of them. Projects must be prioritized and their initiation carefully sequenced.

The last point in the chapter discusses how critical chain methodology can be used in an EVMS environment. Critical chain concepts are becoming more common, and as government entities recognize the benefits, we expect some accommodation in the requirements of the EVMS.

PRACTICE CALCULATIONS

Use Figure 17.13 and the information given below to answer the questions shown below.

- Figure 17.13 represents the scheduling for work packages for one control account.
- Five different resources are used to complete the six tasks.
- The scheduled time to completion (leveled and unleveled) is 52 days.
- Only one resource of each type is available to work on this project; Task 2 and Task 5 must be completed by the same resource.
- Assume that focused (dedicated) times are 50 percent of the estimates given.
- Costs for Task 1 and Task 4 include material costs of $5,000 and $8,000, respectively.

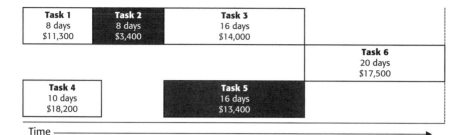

FIGURE 17.13   Traditional Project Gantt Chart, Leveled

Calculate the following values (assuming that all tasks incur all costs uniformly over time, except for materials that are added at the start of Task 1 and Task 4):

1. What is the budget for this control account?

2. Identify the (traditional) critical path of Figure 17.13.

3. If each task in Figure 17.13 has a 90 percent probability of completion within the estimated time, what is the probability that the project will finish in 52 days?

4. Assuming critical chain scheduling is used, fill in the estimated focused times for the following task lengths:

    a. 8 days _____

    b. 10 days _____

    c. 16 days _____

    d. 20 days _____

5. How many critical chain buffers would be required?

6. Where would the critical chain buffer(s) be positioned?

7. In about how many days would a critical chain schedule indicate that delivery of the project could be promised?

8. What is the likelihood of a critical chain project's delivering the project by the estimated promise date?

The 32 EVMS Criteria

In the *Defense Contract Management Agency Guidebook* (Defense Contract Management Agency 2009), the 32 EVMS criteria are grouped into five areas:

1. Organization
2. Planning and Budgeting
3. Accounting Considerations
4. Analysis and Management Reports
5. Revisions and Data Maintenance.

Organization

1. Define the authorized work elements for the program. A work breakdown structure (WBS), tailored for effective internal management control, is commonly used in this process.
2. Identify the program organizational structure, including the major subcontractors responsible for accomplishing the authorized work, and define the organizational elements in which work will be planned and controlled.

3. Provide for the integration of the company's planning, scheduling, budgeting, work authorization, and cost accumulation processes with each other, and as appropriate, the program work breakdown structure and the program organizational structure.
4. Identify the company organization or function responsible for controlling overhead (indirect costs).
5. Provide for integration of the program work breakdown structure and the program organizational structure in a manner that permits cost and schedule performance measurement by elements of either or both structures as needed.

Planning and Budgeting

6. Schedule the authorized work in a manner that describes the sequence of work and identifies significant task interdependencies required to meet the requirements of the program.
7. Identify physical products, milestones, technical performance goals, or other indicators that will be used to measure progress.
8. Establish and maintain a time-phased budget baseline at the control account level against which program performance can be measured. Budget for far-term efforts may be held in higher-level accounts until an appropriate time for allocation at the control account level. Initial budgets established for performance measurement will be based on either internal management goals or the external customer-negotiated target cost including estimates for authorized but undefinitized work. On government contracts, if an over-target baseline is used for performance measurement reporting purposes, prior notification shall be provided to the customer.
9. Establish budgets for authorized work with identification of significant cost elements (labor, material, etc.) as needed for internal management and for control of subcontractors.
10. To the extent it is practical to identify the authorized work in discrete work packages, establish budgets for this work in terms of dollars, hours, or other measurable units. Where the

entire control account is not subdivided into work packages, identify the far-term effort in larger planning packages for budget and scheduling purposes.

11. Provide that the sum of all work package budgets plus planning package budgets within a control account equals the control account budget.

12. Identify and control level-of-effort activity by time-phased budgets established for this purpose. Only that effort that is unmeasurable or for which measurement is impractical may be classified as level of effort.

13. Establish overhead budgets for each significant organizational component of the company for expenses that will become indirect costs. Reflect in the program budgets, at the appropriate level, the amounts in overhead pools that are planned to be allocated to the program as indirect costs.

14. Identify management reserves and undistributed budget.

15. Provide that the program target cost goal is reconciled with the sum of all internal program budgets and management reserves.

Accounting Considerations

16. Record direct costs in a manner consistent with the budgets in a formal system controlled by the general books of account.

17. When a work breakdown structure is used, summarize direct costs from control accounts into the work breakdown structure without allocation of a single control account to two or more work breakdown structure elements.

18. Summarize direct costs from the control accounts into the contractor's organizational elements without allocation of a single control account to two or more organizational elements.

19. Record all indirect costs that will be allocated to the contract.

20. Identify unit costs, equivalent units costs, or lot costs when needed.

21. For EVMS, the material accounting system will provide for:
    a) Accurate cost accumulation and assignment of costs to control accounts in a manner consistent with the budgets, using recognized, acceptable costing techniques.

b) Cost performance measurement at the point in time most suitable for the category of material involved, but no earlier than the time of progress payments or actual receipt of material.

c) Full accountability of all material purchased for the program, including the residual inventory.

Analysis and Management Reports

22. At least on a monthly basis, generate the following information at the control account and other levels as necessary for management control using actual cost data from, or reconcilable with, the accounting system:
   a) Comparison of the amount of planned budget and the amount of budget earned for work accomplished. This comparison provides the schedule variance.
   b) Comparison of the amount of the budget earned and the actual (applied where appropriate) direct costs for the same work. This comparison provides the cost variance.

23. Identify, at least monthly, the significant differences between both planned and actual schedule performance and planned and actual cost performance, and provide the reasons for the variances in the detail needed by program management.

24. Identify budgeted and applied (or actual) indirect costs at the level and frequency needed by management for effective control, along with the reasons for any significant variances.

25. Summarize the data elements and associated variances through the program organization and/or work breakdown structure to support management needs and any customer reporting specified in the contract.

26. Implement managerial actions taken as the result of earned value information.

27. Develop revised estimates of cost at completion based on performance to date, commitment values for material, and estimates of future conditions. Compare this information with the performance measurement baseline to identify vari-

ances at completion important to company management and any applicable customer reporting requirements, including statements of funding requirements.

Revisions and Data Maintenance

28. Incorporate authorized changes in a timely manner, recording the effects of such changes in budgets and schedules. In the directed effort prior to negotiation of a change, base such revisions on the amount estimated and budgeted to the program organizations.
29. Reconcile current budgets to prior budgets in terms of changes to the authorized work and internal replanning in the detail needed by management for effective control.
30. Control retroactive changes to records pertaining to work performed that would change previously reported amounts for actual costs, earned value, or budgets. Adjustments should be made only for correction of errors, routine accounting adjustments, effects of customer- or management-directed changes, or to improve the baseline integrity and accuracy of performance measurement data.
31. Prevent revisions to the program budget except for authorized changes.
32. Document changes to the performance measurement baseline.

(Defense Contract Management Agency 2009).

On August 3, 2002, NASA issued some modifications to the criteria in Directive NPD 9501.3A. The most significant change was the addition of another criterion at the end of the section on analysis and management reports. That criterion reads, "Maintain, manage, and safeguard all records/reports, when appropriate, according to the guidance provided in NPG 1441.1, NASA Records Retention Schedules, and dispose of the records according to these schedules" (National Aeronautics and Space Administration 2002, 1).

Discussion Responses and Exercise Solutions

CHAPTER 3

Exercise Solutions

1. TV = $289,000 = ($40,000 + $30,000 + $28,000 + $17,000 + $22,000 + $24,000 + $38,000 + $90,000)

2. PV = $178,540 = ($40,000 + $30,000 + $28,000 + $17,000 + $21,120 + $23,040 + $19,380)

BCWP or EV
$129,800

Cost Variance
$(7,700)
0.944

Schedule Variance
$(48,740)
0.727

ACWP or AC
$137,500

BCWS or PV
$178,540

3. AC = $137,500

4. EV = $129,800 = ($40,000 + $30,000 + $28,000 + $17,000 + $11,000 + $0 + $3,800)

5. CV = ($7,700) unfavorable = ($129,800 − $137,500)
   CPI = .944; project over budget = ($129,800 / $137,500)

6. SV = ($48,740) unfavorable = ($129,800 – $178,540); SPI = .727; project behind schedule = ($129,800 / $178,540)

7. "Optimistic" EAC = $306,144 = ($137,500 + $168,644). "Pessimistic" EAC = $369,473 = ($137,500 + $231,973).

CHAPTER 10

Exercise 1 Solution

a) BAC = $289,000 = ($40,000 + $22,000 + $30,000 + $24,000 +$28,000 +$17,000 + $38,000 + $90,000).

b) BCWS (PV) = $226,000 = [$40,000 + $22,000 + $30,000 + $24,000 +$28,000 +$17,000 + $38,000 + (.3 X $90,000)]

c) EV = $244,000 = [$40,000 + $22,000 + $30,000 + $24,000 +$28,000 +$17,000 + $38,000 + (.5 X $90,000)]

d) AC = $240,000

e) Cost variance = $4,000 favorable = $244,000 – $240,000;

$$\text{CPI} = 1.02 = \frac{\$244,000}{\$240,000}$$

f) Schedule variance = $18,000 favorable = $244,000 – $226,000;

$$\text{SPI} = 1.08 = \frac{\$244,000}{\$226,000}$$

g) $$\text{ETC} = \$44,118 = \frac{\$289,000 - \$244,000}{1.02};$$

EAC = $284,118 = $44,118 + $240,000

h. $$\text{TCI} = 0.92 = \frac{\$289,000 - \$244,000}{\$289,000 - \$240,000}$$

Exercise 2 Solution

All variances in Exercise 1 are favorable. As of the end of the third quarter, the planned value of work that should have been completed is $226,000. However, the project team has completed work with an earned value of $244,000, generating a favorable schedule variance of $18,000 and an SPI of 1.08, indicating that the project is ahead of schedule. Whereas the earned value is $244,000, actual costs are only $240,000, resulting in a $4,000 favorable variance and a CPI of 1.02; both indicate very good performance.

At this point, the estimate to complete is $44,188, meaning that the estimated total cost at completion is $284,118. This compares favorably with the original budget at completion of $289,000. From this point to the end of the project, the team needs to exert only 92 percent of the effort expended thus far to complete the project on budget.

Because the schedule variance also is favorable, the estimate to complete, estimate at completion, and to-complete index would become more favorable only if the SPI were included in these measures. The project team has done an outstanding job!

CHAPTER 11

Discussion Points

1. a. Risk assessment

   b. Risk disposition

   c. Risk monitoring

2. a. Problems will occur; it's not just a possibility.

   b. Risk management is crucial for project success.

   c. Risk management must be considered an integral part of the project plan.

3. a. A statement about the potential event, including cause

   b. A rating of its probability of occurrence

   c. The severity of the consequence of the occurrence

4. Possibilities include fantasy questions, brainstorming, surveys, checklists, interviews, lessons learned from previous projects, and the examination and evaluation of each work breakdown structure element.

5. There are several possibilities, but answers should include ratings for probability and the three project constraints—schedule, cost, and performance.

6. Avoidance, transference, mitigation, acceptance

7. It provides periodic comparisons of actual accomplishments with the plan, which will provide evidence of risk events and the effectiveness of risk handling.

8. a. Replanning is appropriate when the project objectives have been changed, a major resource has changed, budgetary restrictions occur, and/or significant changes have occurred in the assumptions of the original plan.

   b. Replanning is not appropriate just to eliminate variances.

9. Change request form, budget revision records, work authorization records, change control documents, notification lists, and logs

10. Only for correction of errors, routine accounting adjustments, effects of customer- or management-directed changes, or to improve the baseline integrity and accuracy of performance measurement data

CHAPTER 13

Our suggested responses to the discussion questions:

1. b

2. d

3. Reasons might include lack of a compelling reason for implementation, lack of senior management support, lack of educational resources, parochial attitudes within the organization, and fear of change.

4. Two steps might be making a point of how close existing procedures match EVMS and using political strength, if the CEO has a positive influence.

5. Practically none, but the project manager will need serious assistance from the accounting department, and EVMS-tuned software will help.

6. The two most serious are the inclination toward unproductive tinkering and the cost of gathering additional information.

CHAPTER 16

Exercise Solutions

1. a. SV(t) for December = Earned Schedule for December minus the Month Count of 12

$$= 10.857 - 12 = -1.143$$

SPI(t) for December = Earned Schedule, December, divided by the Month Count of 12

$$= 10.857 \div 12 = 0.90475$$

b. SV(t) for January = Earned Schedule for January minus the Month Count of 13

$$= 11 - 13 = -2.0$$

SPI(t) for January = Earned Schedule, January, divided by the Month Count of 13

$$= 11 \div 13 = 0.8462$$

2. a., b., and c. (see below):

TABLE B.16.1

Month	1	2	3	4	5
Planned Value	$90	$250	$380	$500	$875
Earned Value	$75	$240	$360	$550	
Actual Cost	$90	$260	$380	$600	
Earned Schedule	0.8333	1.9375	2.8462	4.0667	
SV(t)	−0.1667	−0.0625	−0.1538	0.0667	
SPI(t)	0.8333	0.9688	0.9487	1.0167	

CHAPTER 17

1. Total budget for this control (cost) account = $77,800.

2. In Figure B.17.1a the critical path appears to be the upper path (Tasks 1, 2, 3, and 7). However, as is clear from Figure B.17.1b, all tasks in this project are critical.

3. The probability of the project's completing on time is about 59 percent. Even if all tasks except Tasks 3 and 5 finish on time, a delay in either Task 3 or Task 5 will cause the project to be late.

4. Safe (traditional) and focused (critical chain) task times:

Safe time	Focused time
a. 8 days	4 days
b. 10 days	5 days
c. 16 days	8 days
d. 20 days	10 days

5. Normally, a feeding buffer or buffers and one project buffer would be required for a critical chain schedule.

6. Because of the close duration of the upper and lower paths, the computer solution to this project has one feeding buffer (for the one noncritical task, Task 4) and two project buffers (at the end of Task 3 and Task 6).

7. As shown in Figure B.17.2, critical chain schedule indicates that delivery could be promised in 55 days.

8. Critical chain proponents claim that their projects come in by the promised date 95 percent of the time. (The other 5 percent are late by a very small amount of time.)

a. Unleveled Critical Chain Project

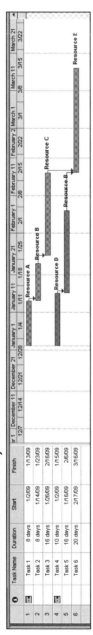

b. Leveled Critical Chain Project

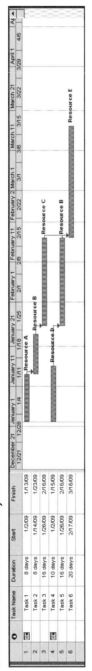

FIGURE B.17.1   Gantt Charts – Chapter 17 Practice Question

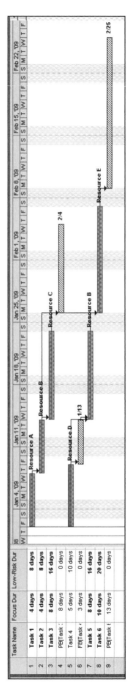

FIGURE B.17.2   Critical Chain Gantt Chart (only one task not critical)

Glossary

Some of the following terms are adaptations of terms from the military acquisition website at http://www.acq.osd.mil/pm/faqs/glossary.htm. Similar definitions can be found at an Australian website, http://www.defence.gov.au/dmo/esd/evm/DefAust5655.pdf. A very extensive list of project management terms appears in the Wideman Comparative Glossary of Project Management Terms at http://www.maxwideman.com/pmglossary/index.htm.

Acquisition Program: A directed, funded government effort that provides a new, improved, or continuing material, weapon, or information system or service capability in response to an approved need.

Activity: A self-contained effort or task that occurs over a period of time and consumes resources.

Activity-Based Costing (ABC): An accounting technique that computes the cost of resource consumption for each product in order to determine its profitability.

Actual Cost (AC): See **Actual Cost of Work Performed.** An incurred cost, as distinguished from a forecasted, estimated, or budgeted cost.

Actual Cost of Work Performed (ACWP): Costs actually incurred and recorded in accomplishing the work performed within a project status time period.

Administrative Contracting Officer (ACO): The person in the government contract administration office responsible for ensuring that the functions described in DFARS 242.302 are completed by a contractor in accordance with the terms and conditions of the contract.

Advance Agreement (AA): An agreement between the contractor and the contract administration office concerning the application of an approved integrated management system for a contracted project.

Algorithmic Method: Creating an estimate by using mathematical formulas. The formulas may be derived from research and/or historical data and use known cost driver attributes. Parametric cost estimating is considered an algorithmic method.

Allocated Budget: Also referred to as **Total Allocated Budget (TAB).**

Analogy Method: Creating a cost estimate by deriving cost factors from a similar project that has been completed and for which the cost and schedule are known.

Applied Direct Costs (ADC): Direct costs incurred during the status time period without regard to the date of commitment or payment. These costs are associated with the consumption of labor, material, and other direct resources.

Apportioned Effort: Effort that is not readily divisible into work packages but is proportionately related to another discrete effort that is measured.

Arrow Diagramming Method: A project network design to depict task sequence or precedence relationships of project activities. The design uses nodes (events) connected by arrows to show the flow of activity. The activities may be shown on the node (AON) or on the arrow (AOA).

Audit: The systematic examination of records and documents to determine the adequacy and effectiveness of budgeting, accounting, financial, and related policies and procedures. The audit determines compliance with applicable statutes, regulations, and prescribed policies and procedures and determines the reliability, accuracy, and completeness of records and reports.

Audit Trail: Information allowing record and report data to be tracked back to the original source for verification.

Authorization to Proceed (ATP): Official authority, usually from the procuring activity, for the contractor to begin work.

Authorized Unpriced Work (AUW): Includes work that is outside the scope of the contract but is planned and/or performed by the contractor in advance of a formal contract amendment.

Authorized Work: All effort performed by the contractor, conforming with the contract and within the contract price.

Bar Chart: A presentation of data using horizontal or vertical bars to represent values of the data. For projects, the horizontal bars on a time scale represent project tasks, their duration, and sometimes their relationships.

Baseline: See **Performance Measurement Baseline (PMB)**. Also sometimes used as an abbreviated reference to an **Integrated Baseline Review (IBR)**.

Basis of Estimate: Documentation describing the primary methods, ground rules, models, assumptions, and data sources used to estimate the project cost.

Bill of Material (BOM): A list of material items required to complete the production of a single unit.

Bottom-Up Method: A method of cost estimating characterized by a thorough, detailed analysis of all tasks, components, and assemblies and rolling the results up to summarize an estimate of the entire project. This method may be referred to as "detailed" or "grassroots" estimating.

Budget at Completion (BAC)—Total Value: The initial planned and authorized budget for the entire project. The total of all budgets for the contract. Management reserve is not included. See also **Performance Measurement Baseline** and **Total Allocated Budget**.

Budgeted Cost of Work Performed (BCWP)—Earned Value: The sum of the budget amounts (not actual amounts) for completed work packages and completed portions of work packages, plus the applicable portion of the budgets for level of effort and apportioned effort.

Budgeted Cost of Work Scheduled (BCWS)—Planned Value: The sum of the budgets for all work packages (or portions thereof), planning packages, etc., scheduled to be accomplished, plus the amount of level of effort and apportioned effort scheduled to be accomplished within a given time period.

Calibration: A process of adjusting a commercial parametric model by a specific organization to its own cost experience and business culture.

Contingency Costs: An amount to be included in a project budget that represents costs that might result from incomplete design, unforeseen and unpredictable conditions, or uncertainties in the defined project scope.

Contract Administration Office (CAO): The organization assigned responsibility for ensuring that the contractor complies with the terms and conditions of the contract.

Contract Budget Base (CBB): The negotiated contract cost plus the estimated cost of authorized unpriced work. The CBB is equal to the **Total Allocated Budget** unless an over-target baseline has been implemented.

Contract Data Requirements List (CDRL): A list of all data elements that the contractor is obligated to submit to the government. Each task on a statement of work (SOW) is associated with a CDRL. The CDRL identifies a document or other data, along with specific information about that document (e.g., schedule, number and frequency of revisions, distribution). A data item description specifies the content and format of the document.

Contract Performance Report (CPR): (Previously called the **Cost Performance Report.**) A project report required in some government contracts, prepared by the contractor and containing information derived from the internal management system to provide a status of progress on the contract.

Contract Target Cost: The total of all cost accounts plus undistributed budget and management reserve.

Contract Work Breakdown Structure (CWBS): The complete hierarchal graph of the activities or intermediate deliverables necessary to complete a contract (including the Department of Defense–approved work breakdown structure for reporting purposes and its discretionary extension to the lower levels by the contractor). The CWBS includes all the elements for the hardware, software, data, or services that are the responsibility of the contractor.

Control Account (CA): A management control point where actual costs can be accumulated and compared with earned value. A control account (or *cost account*) is usually defined as the intersection of the program's work breakdown structure (WBS) and organizational breakdown structure (OBS). In effect, each cost account defines the value of a portion of work to be performed (and who will perform it).

Control Account Manager (CAM): A member of a functional organization responsible for cost account performance and the management of resources to accomplish the control account effort.

Correlation: A statistical technique used to determine the degree to which variables are related or associated. Correlation does not prove or disprove a cause-and-effect relationship.

Cost Account: See **Control Account.**

Cost Analysis: The accumulation and analysis of actual costs, statistical data, and other information on current and completed contracts or programs. Cost analysis also includes comparisons and analyses of these data, as well as cost extrapolations of data for future projections of cost. In Department of Defense procurement organizations, cost analysis is the review and evaluation of a contractor's cost or pricing data and the judgmental factors applied in projecting from the data to the estimated costs. Cost analysis is performed to establish an opinion on the degree to which the contractor's proposed costs represent what the performance of the contract should cost, assuming reasonable economy and efficiency.

Cost/Benefit Ratio: The ratio of a project's total cost to its total return.

Cost Drivers: The characteristics of a system or item that have a major effect on the system's or item's cost.

Cost-Estimating Relationship (CER): A mathematical expression of varying degrees of complexity that expresses cost as a function of one or more cost-driving variables. See **Parametric Cost Estimating**.

Cost Performance Index (CPI): The cost efficiency factor representing the relationship between the actual costs expended and the value of the physical work performed. The CPI is calculated as BCWP/ACWP, or earned value divided by actual cost.

Cost Performance Report: See **Contract Performance Report**.

Cost or Pricing Data: All facts that, as of the date of the price agreement, prudent buyers and sellers would reasonably expect to affect price negotiations significantly. Cost or pricing data require certification in accordance with Federal Acquisition Regulation (FAR) 15.406-2. Cost or pricing data are factual, not judgmental, and verifiable. Cost or pricing data are all facts that can be reasonably expected to contribute to the soundness of estimates of future costs and to the validity of determinations of costs already incurred.

Cost/Schedule Control Systems Criteria (C/SCSC): In 1967, 35 defined standards were established for private contractor management control systems to ensure that government cost-reimbursable and incentive-type contracts were managed properly. These 35 criteria have been reduced to 32, and the standards are now known as the Earned Value Management System (EVMS).

Cost/Schedule Status Report (C/SSR): (Required use was rescinded in 2005.) A performance measurement report established to capture information on smaller government contracts when the cost performance report was not required.

Cost Variance (CV): A metric for cost performance on a contractor project:

$$\text{Cost Variance} = \text{Earned Value} - \text{Actual Cost}$$
$$\text{or } CV = BCWP - ACWP.$$

A positive value indicates a favorable position, and a negative value indicates an unfavorable position.

Critical Chain: A project scheduling system that identifies the longest path of resource-dependent activities. It attempts to provide a realistic project network by addressing the adverse effects of human behavior and using a buffering technique to protect the estimated project completion date.

Critical Path: The longest path of interdependent activities through a project network. See **Network Schedule**.

Critical Ratio Index: See **Schedule Cost Index**.

Data Item Description (DID): A description of a document on a contract data requirements list (CDRL) that specifies the document's content and format. Government agencies maintain standard sets of DIDs.

Defense Acquisition Executive (DAE): The person responsible for supervising the Defense Acquisition System. The DAE takes precedence on all acquisition matters after the secretary and the deputy secretary.

Defense Acquisition System: The management process by which the Department of Defense provides effective, affordable, and timely systems to the users.

Defense Contract Audit Agency (DCAA): The organization tasked with monitoring a contractor's design and implementation of an acceptable accounting system.

Defense Contract Management Agency (DCMA) (formerly Defense Contract Management Command): An independent combat support agency within the Department of Defense that serves as the department's contract manager, responsible for ensuring that federal acquisition programs, supplies, and services are delivered on time and within cost and meet performance requirements. The DCMA usually participates in government contract quality assurance (GCQA).

Defense Federal Acquisition Regulation Supplement (DFARS): Department of Defense (DoD) regulations governing DoD acquisitions. A supplement to the Federal Acquisition Regulation (FAR).

Delphi Technique: A technique for applying the informed judgment of a group of experts without direct confrontation between the members of the group and using feedback from multiple rounds of investigation for the solution of problems.

Deterministic Model: A model that predicts an inevitable consequence based on the sufficiency of antecedent events.

Direct Costs: Costs, such as labor and materials, that can be directly related to a specific item of work.

Discrete Efforts: Tasks that have a specific measurable end product or end result. They are ideal for EVMS because their measurement is based on objective indicators of accomplishment, such as project milestones.

Earned Value (EV): See **Budgeted Cost of Work Performed.** The value of completed work in terms of the planned (not actual) cost of that work.

Earned Value Management System (EVMS): A management system that integrates project scope, schedule, and cost and establishes a baseline plan for the accomplishment of the project deliverables. The system uses earned value to measure performance progress objectively.

Earned Value Management System Criteria: The set of 32 guidelines, established by DoD 5000.2R, that defines the parameters within which the contractor's integrated cost/schedule management system must fit.

Equivalent Units: The quantity of units produced during a single period by assuming that a particular flow of units (e.g., first-in first-out, average) and partially completed units may be netted together to find the number of equivalent full units. This equivalent number is similar to that of full-time equivalent (FTE) employees.

Estimate at Completion (EAC): The value, usually expressed in dollars, that represents the projected final cost of the project (or task):

EAC = Actual Cost (ACWP) + Estimate to Complete.

Estimate to Complete (ETC): The value, usually expressed in dollars, that represents the cost of the work required to complete the project (or task). One way to calculate ETC is to subtract the Earned Value (Budgeted Cost of Work Performed, or BCWP) from the Budget at Completion (BAC) and divide by the Schedule Cost Index. The effect is to modify the remaining budget by current performance.

EVMS Certification: A process to determine that the proposed EVMS fully complies with the ANSI 748-A-1998 Standard. The process involves a lengthy evaluation of the management system to ensure that the characteristics expected in a good EVMS relative to the 32 ANSI criteria are present and supported with typical documents.

Executive Agent (EA): "The Head of a DoD Component to whom the Secretary of Defense or the Deputy Secretary of Defense has assigned specific responsibilities, functions, and authorities to provide defined levels of support for operational missions, or administrative or other designated activities that involve two or more of the DoD Components" (Department of Defense 2003, 3.1).

Expert Judgment Method: Method that uses the experience and understanding of experts to develop cost estimates for a project.

Federal Acquisition Regulation (FAR): Regulations governing all federal acquisitions.

Fixed Costs: Costs that do not vary with the volume of business, such as facility/equipment depreciation and property taxes.

Fixed-Price Contract: A contract for which the total cost is all-inclusive and not dependent on contractor expenses or other variables.

Focal Point: The principal point of contact with a government agency for the coordination and exchange of information related to acquisition contracts. Focal points provide EVMS policy and guidance. A table of Department of Defense focal points is available from the Defense Contract Management Agency (DCMA).

Forward Pricing Rate Agreement (FPRA): A written agreement negotiated between a potential contractor and the federal government to make certain rates available during a specified period to price contracts. Such rates represent reasonable projections of specific costs that are not easily estimated.

Frontloading: Unnecessarily performing work out of sequence to obtain credit in a period earlier than the one in which it was scheduled for completion. The practice can cause distortions in EVMS measurements for both periods.

Full-Time Equivalents (FTE): A measurement of staffing units usually expressed as the number of persons employed full-time per month.

Functional Organization: An organization in which the staff is arranged in a hierarchal structure by functional specialty (e.g., accounting, manufacturing, marketing).

General and Administrative (G&A): A grouping of indirect costs that are distributed to all units within a business entity, such as corporate headquarters expenses.

Government Contract Quality Assurance (GCQA): A review that determines whether contractual requirements have been met prior to the acceptance of supplies and services.

Indirect Costs: Costs that are not directly identified with a single work element, such as those for overhead and general and administrative (G&A) costs. These costs may be variable or fixed and are allocated to individual work elements by a selected arbitrary process.

Initial Compliance Review: A federal government review done at a contractor's facility to assess the contractor's application of EVMS principles.

Integrated Baseline Review (IBR): A joint review of the contractor's performance measurement baseline by the federal government and contractor to determine whether the baseline captures the entire technical scope of work consistent with contractual schedules and whether the baseline has adequate resources assigned.

Integrated Management System (IMS): A management system and related subsystems that establish the relationship between the cost, schedule, and technical aspects of the project. An IMS should be designed to measure progress, accumulate actual costs, analyze deviations from plans, forecast completion of contract events, and make contract changes to the project in a timely manner.

Integrated Master Schedule (IMS): See **Integrated Management System.** Details of the military IMS are provided by the Defense Acquisition University (Defense Acquisition University 2005c).

Integrated Product Team (IPT): Representatives from all appropriate functional disciplines working together to build successful processes and make sound and timely decisions. The IPT participants are empowered, to the maximum extent possible, to make commitments for the areas they represent.

Integrated Surveillance Team (IST): A selected group of individuals from participating agencies involved in the surveillance of the contractor's EVMS implementation.

Internal Replanning: Actions performed by the contractor to change the plans for the remaining effort, but within the recognized contract value and schedule.

Level of Effort (LOE): Work that cannot be effectively associated with a definable end product, such as the project manager's support activities. The earned value for LOE is measured only by the passage of time, not by any specific accomplishment.

Life Cycle: The total life span of a system, commencing with concept formulation and extending through operation and eventual retirement of the system.

Line of Balance: A tool for managing repetitive processes. One aspect of this philosophy is to plot activities and their planned durations across a graph as the "line." When actual completion times are plotted against this line, activities can be seen in terms of whether or not they are "in balance" and whether future task completions are behind schedule.

Linear Responsibility Chart (LRC): A graphical illustration of which elements of the work breakdown structure (WBS) are performed or managed by the elements of the organizational breakdown structure (OBS) and to what degree.

Management Council: A team of senior representatives involved with business activities at a particular contractor facility, typically including representatives from the contractor, major customers, the Defense Contract Management Agency (DCMA), and the Defense Contract Audit Agency (DCAA). The council serves as a forum to discuss, coordinate, and resolve issues of common concern affecting the efficiency and effectiveness of contractor operations and to facilitate the coordination of business and manufacturing process reengineering initiatives.

Management Reserve (MR): An amount of the **total allocated budget** withheld for management control purposes rather than designated for the accomplishment of a specific task or set of tasks. It is not a part of the **performance measurement baseline (PMB).**

Matrix Organization: An organization structured so that project managers share management responsibility with functional managers. A weak matrix style puts almost all of the management authority with the functional manager.

Memorandum of Agreement (MOA): An agreement between a government program manager and a contract administration office (CAO) establishing the scope of responsibilities for contract audit services.

Milestone: A specific and definable event set at a particular point in the project network. It may mark the start or finish of an interim step or project phase.

Milestone Decision Authority (MDA): The designated person with overall responsibility for a program. The MDA has the authority to approve entry of an acquisition program into the next phase of the acquisition process and is accountable for cost, schedule, and performance reporting to a higher authority, including congressional reporting.

Negotiated Contract Cost: The estimated cost negotiated in a cost-plus-fixed-fee contract or the negotiated target cost in either a fixed-price incentive contract or a cost-plus-incentive-fee contract.

Network Schedule: A project schedule format in which activities and milestones are represented along with the interdependencies between activities to show the logical flow of the project. Network schedules are the basis for critical path analysis, a method for identifying and assessing schedule priorities and impacts.

Normalize: To adjust data for effects such as inflation, anomalies, seasonal patterns, technology changes, accounting system changes, and reorganizations.

Order-of-Magnitude Estimates: General cost estimates that are calculated by using only very basic criteria and are not considered highly accurate. They may be "first-time" estimates to determine project feasibility and further study or final estimates for smaller contracts that do not require a firm cost.

Organizational Breakdown Structure (OBS): A hierarchical graph indicating the functional relationships in an organization, which is used as the framework for assigning work responsibilities. The OBS is broken down progressively to the lowest levels of management.

Original Budget: The budget established on or near the contract effective date based on the negotiated contract cost. See also **Budget at Completion**.

Overhead: Costs incurred in an operation that cannot be directly related to the individual products or services being produced. See **Indirect Costs**.

Overrun: Costs incurred in excess of the contract's target cost for an incentive-type contract or the estimated costs for a fixed-fee contract.

Over-Target Baseline (OTB): A project baseline that results from increasing the budgets for remaining work without a related increase in the contract value. The process of implementing the OTB is called reprogramming, and it results in a **total allocated budget** in excess of the contract budget base.

Parametric Cost Estimating: A cost-estimating methodology using statistical relationships between historical costs and other program variables. This technique employs one or more cost-estimating relationships (CERs) for measuring costs based on the deliverable's technical, physical, or other characteristics.

Performance-Based Earned Value (PBEV): A variation of traditional earned value project management (EVMS) in which technical requirements are included as tasks on the project schedule. Progress toward meeting these requirements is apportioned earned value "credit." Risk, such as estimated rework, is also formally incorporated into the project schedule.

Performance Measurement Baseline (PMB): The time-phased budget plan against which project performance is measured. It is formed by the budgets assigned to scheduled cost accounts, summary-level planning packages, and applicable indirect budgets. The PMB equals the Total Allocated Budget minus Management Reserve.

Planned Value (PV): See **Budgeted Cost of Work Scheduled**.

Planning Package: A logical aggregation of work within a cost account, normally a far-term effort, that can be identified and budgeted in early baseline planning but is not yet defined in work packages.

Plant Visit: A short-duration, summary-level review of the contractor's EVMS procedures to verify that they provide timely and reliable data.

Post-Acceptance Review: A government review performed on a specific element of the contractor's EVMS that has displayed a lack of discipline in application or no longer meets the intent of the EVMS guidelines.

Procuring Activity: A military subordinate command to which the procuring contracting officer (PCO) is assigned. The procuring activity is the organization that executes a project or acquisition contract. It may include the program office, related functional support offices, and procurement offices.

Program Evaluation and Review Technique (PERT): A management technique designed for the planning and control of complex projects. PERT is used by constructing a network model of the project's integrated activities and periodically evaluating the time and cost implications as the work progresses. The technique requires three estimates of the expected time to complete each activity.

Program Manager: The government's designated person with responsibility for and authority to accomplish program objectives for development, production, and sustainment of the end user's operational needs. The program manager is accountable for credible cost, schedule, and performance reporting to the milestone decision authority (MDA).

Program Work Breakdown Structure (PWBS): The work breakdown structure (WBS) that covers the acquisition of a specific defense material master item, is related to contractual effort, and includes all applicable elements consisting of at least the first three levels. These levels are then extended by the program manager and/or contractor to create the contract work breakdown structure.

Project-Oriented Organization: An organization that assigns staff primarily by projects and not by functional specialties. The project manager has full management authority for people assigned to the project.

Reimbursable Cost Contract: A contract on which the total cost is the sum of the contractor's expenses plus a percentage or fixed amount for contractor profits.

Replanning: The redistribution of the budget for future work. Replanning must be able to trace relationships to previous baselines, and attention to funding requirements needs to be considered in any replanning effort.

Reprogramming: The process of implementing an over-target baseline, which entails restructuring the effort remaining in the contract and results in a new budget allocation that exceeds the contract budget base.

Request for Proposals (RFP): A document that sets out the parameters of the expected deliverables of a proposed project and solicits responses from potential suppliers.

Responsibility Assignment Matrix (RAM): A graphical depiction of the relationship between the work breakdown structure (WBS) elements and the organizational units (OBS) that are assigned responsibility for ensuring their accomplishment.

Schedule Cost Index (SCI): (Often called the **Critical Ratio Index.**) The product of multiplying the Schedule Performance Index and the Cost Performance Index. The SCI is used in forecasting project completion. See also **Estimate to Complete**.

Schedule Performance Index (SPI): A factor representing schedule efficiency. The SPI is calculated as the earned value divided by the planned value:

$$SPI = BCWP / BCWS.$$

Schedule Variance (SV): A metric that indicates the project's schedule performance. SV is calculated as the earned value minus the planned value:

$$SV = BCWP - BCWS.$$

A positive value is favorable; a negative value is unfavorable.

Should-Cost Estimate: An estimate of a contract price that reflects reasonably achievable contractor economy and efficiency. It is usually developed by a team of procurement, contract administration, cost analysis, audit, and engineering representatives. Its purpose is to identify uneconomical or inefficient practices in a contractor's management and operations by quantifying the findings in terms of their impact on cost, and to develop a reasonable price objective for negotiation.

Significant Variances: Differences between planned and actual performance that require further review, analysis, or action. Appropriate thresholds should be established at a magnitude of variances that will provide reasonable analysis.

Software Development Life Cycle: Stages and processes through which software passes during its useful life. The cycle includes requirements definition, analysis, design, coding, testing, and maintenance.

Stakeholder (Project): A person who will be affected by a project or who has influence over some aspect of the project. The term does not usually apply to the project team members.

Statement of Objectives (SOO): A document identifying the high-level product-oriented goals of a proposed project. The SOO is usually part of a request for proposals (RFP).

Statement of Work (SOW): A document that identifies the specific tasks the contractor will perform during the contract period. The SOW could include tasks such as system engineering, design, and build. For security, the SOW includes the contractor tasks necessary to achieve specific levels of assurance, including studies and analyses, configuration management, security test and evaluation support, delivery, and maintenance of the system. These work statements also specify the development of the required documentation to be provided under the contract data requirements list (CDRL).

Stochastic System: Events proceeding in a probabilistic fashion. Outcomes cannot be predicted with certainty, but probabilities are known.

Summary Effort Control Package (SECP): An aggregation of work for far-term effort that cannot yet be defined in enough detail for the control account level but can be assigned to higher-level work breakdown structure (WBS) elements and is therefore not "undistributed budget."

Summary-Level Planning Package (SLLP): See **Summary Effort Control Package**.

Third-Party Certification: Approval of an EVMS, to a standard recognized by the Department of Defense as equivalent to the EVMS criteria, by an independent organization accredited by the standards authority and recognized by DoD.

Top-Down Method: An estimating technique that calculates the overall cost and effort of a proposed project on the basis of the global properties of a past project.

Total Allocated Budget (TAB): The sum of all budgets allocated to the contract. The TAB consists of the Performance Measurement Baseline and all Management Reserve. The TAB will reconcile directly to the contract budget base.

Total Value (TV)—Budget at Completion: The original planned cost of the total project.

Undistributed Budget (UB): A budget applicable to contract effort that has not yet been identified to contract work breakdown structure (CWBS) elements at or below the lowest level of reporting.

Unit Price Contract: A type of contract in which the total price of the contract will be equal to the number of units produced, multiplied by a fixed-and-agreed cost per unit. This type of contract is considered a fixed-price contract, as opposed to a cost-priced contract.

Validation₁: In parametric estimating, a process used to determine whether the cost-estimating relationship or model selected for a particular estimate is a reliable predictor of cost for the system being estimated. For a complete validation process, the model users must also demonstrate that they have adequate experience and training and that their processes, policies, and procedures are established, documented, and enforced.

Validation₂: A formal recognition of certification by an independent party that a contractor's EVMS meets the guidelines in ANSI/EIA-748.

Variable Cost: A cost that varies in parallel with the volume or rate of production of goods or the performance of services.

Variance at Completion (VAC): The difference between the total budget assigned to a contract or contract element and the estimate at completion:

$$VAC = BAC - EAC.$$

VAC represents the amount of expected overrun or underrun.

Variance Threshold: The amount of variance that determines whether a variance is significant enough to warrant a variance analysis. Thresholds should be set at a level that will provide for a reasonable analysis and discernment of potential contract performance problems without unnecessarily burdening resources.

Variances: Those differences between planned and actual performance, both cumulative and at completion, that require further review, analysis, or action. See **Significant Variances** and **Variance Threshold.**

Visit Coordinator: The person responsible for all aspects of a plant visit, including planning, on-site activities, and visit follow-up and closure. The program manager may choose to be the visit coordinator or may delegate the responsibility.

What-if Analysis: The process of evaluating alternative strategies.

Work Breakdown Structure (WBS): A product-oriented family tree division of hardware, software, services, and other work tasks that organizes, defines, and graphically displays the product to be developed and relates the elements of the work to be accomplished to each other and the end product. The WBS is developed into layers of more detail, with the number of layers depending on the complexity of the project and on the purpose of the WBS. See **Contract Work Breakdown Structure** and **Program Work Breakdown Structure.**

Work Package (WP): A set of detailed jobs or material items identified by the contractor for accomplishing the work required to complete the contract. A WP represents units of work at levels where work is performed and has the following characteristics:

1. It is clearly distinguishable from all other work packages.
2. It is assigned to a single organizational element.
3. It has scheduled start and completion dates (and interim milestones if applicable).
4. It has a budget or assigned value expressed in terms of dollars, man-hours, or other measurable units.
5. Its duration is limited to a relatively short span of time or has milestones to enable the objective determination of earned value. It may be level of effort.
6. Its schedule is integrated with other related organizational schedules.

Work-Package Budget: Resources that are formally assigned by the contractor to accomplish a work package, expressed in dollars, hours, standards, or other measurable units.

Bibliography

American Institute of Certified Public Accountants. October 17, 2008. "Content and Skill Specifications for the Uniform CPA Examination." Approved by the Board of Examiners, AICPA. New York. Accessed 2/2/09. Available online at http://www.cpa-exam.org/download/CPA_Exam_CSOs-SSOs_2008.pdf.

Archibald, Russell D. 1987. "The History of Modern Project Management: Key Milestones in the Early PERT/CPM/PDM Days." *Project Management Journal* 18, no. 4: 29.

Arrow, Kenneth J. 1971. *Essays in the Theory of Risk Bearing*. Chicago: Markham Publishing.

Austin, Robert D. 1996. *Measuring and Managing Performance in Organizations*. New York: Dorset House Publishing.

Batten, Joe. 2003. *Expectations and Possibilities: How to Create Your Path to Discovery and Achievement*. Eugene, OR: Wipf and Stock Publishers.

Bembers, Ivan, et al. 2003. *Over Target Baseline and Over Target Schedule Handbook*. In Defense Acquisition University. Washington, DC. Accessed 5/4/04. Available online at http://acc.dau.mil/simplify/ev.php?ID=17993_201&ID2=DO_TOPIC.

Billet, David. January 15, 2009. "Everything changes: Multitasking, home offices, BlackBerrys and anxiety." *Wall Street Journal* book review of *Elsewhere, USA* by Dalton Conley. New York: Dow Jones.

Boehm, Barry W. 1988. "A Spiral Model of Software Development and Enhancement." *Computer* 21, no. 5: 61–72.

Budd, Charlene S. 2003. "Planning a Project: Six Steps to Success." *Today's CPA* (January–February): 20–23.

Budd, Charlene S., and Charles I. Budd. 2007. *Internal Reporting and Improvement Initiatives*. BNA Accounting Policy & Practice Portfolios. Arlington, VA: Tax Management, Inc.

Christensen, David S. 1998. "The Costs and Benefits of the Earned Value Management Process." *Acquisition Review Quarterly* (Fall): 373–386.

Christensen, David, and Carl Templin. 2000. "An Analysis of Management Reserve Budget on Defense Acquisition Contracts." *Acquisition Review Quarterly* (Summer): 191–208.

Cleland, David I., and Lewis R. Ireland. 2002. *Project Management: Strategic Design and Implementation*, 4th ed. New York: McGraw-Hill.

Cooper, Marjorie, and Charlene Budd. 2007. "Tying the Pieces Together: A Normative Framework for Integrating Sales and Project Operations." *Industrial Marketing Management* (special issue on projects), 36: 173–182.

Crawford, J.K. 2006. *Project Management Maturity Model*. 2nd ed. Boca Raton, FL: Auerback Publications.

Dayal, Sham. 2008. *Earned Value Management Using Microsoft Office Project*. Fort Lauderdale, FL: J. Ross Publishing.

Defense Acquisition University. 2005a. *Defense Acquisition Guidebook*. In Defense Acquisition University. Fort Belvoir, VA. Available online at http://akss.dau.mil/dag.

Defense Acquisition University. 2005b. *Risk Management*. In Defense Acquisition University. Fort Belvoir, VA. Available online at https://acc.dau.mil/simplify/ev.php?ID=1203_201&ID2=DO_COMMUNITY.

Defense Acquisition University. 2005c. IMS DID DI-MGMT-81650. March 30, 2005. *DoD Policy & Guidance*, ACC EVM CoP. Available online at http://acc.dau.mil/CommunityBrowser.aspx?id=19545&lang=en-US.

Defense Acquisition University. 2006. *Earned Value Implementation Guide*. October 2006. Available online at https://acc.dau.mil/CommunityBrowser.aspx?id=19557.

Defense Contract Management Agency. 2005. *EVMS Reviews*. In Defense Contract Management Agency. Available online at http://guidebook.dcma.mil/39/instructions.htm.

Defense Contract Management Agency. 2008. *EVMS System-Level Surveillance*. In Defense Contract Management Agency. Available online at http://guidebook.dcma.mil/79/instructions.htm.

Defense Contract Management Agency. 2009. *Earned Value Management Systems Criteria*. In Defense Contract Management Agency. Available online at http://guidebook.dcma.mil/79/criteria.htm.

Deming, W. Edwards. 1993. "The New Economics for Industry, Government, Education." Cambridge, MA: Massachusetts Institute of Technology, Center for Advanced Engineering Study.

Department of Defense. 2003. DoD Directive 5101.1, *DoD Executive Agent*. In U.S. Department of Defense. Washington, DC. Available online at http://www.dtic.mil/whs/directives/corres/html/51011.htm.

Department of Defense, Acquisition, Technology & Logistics. 2004. *Earned Value Management*. In Office of the Under Secretary of Defense. Washington, DC. Accessed 4/2004. Available online at http://www.acq.osd.mil/pm/.

Department of Defense. 2005a. MIL-HDBK-881A. In Department of Defense. Washington, DC. Accessed 2/4/09. Available online at http://www.acq.osd.mil/pm/currentpolicy/wbs/MIL_HDBK-881A/MILHDBK881A/WebHelp3/MILHDBK881A.htm.

Department of Defense. 2005b. *Integrated Master Schedule*. DID DI-MGMT-81650. DoD Policy & Guidance, ACC EVM CoP. Available online at http://www.acq.osd.mil/pm/currentpolicy/cpr_cfsr/IMS%20Final%203-30-05.pdf.

Department of Defense. 2006a. *Earned Value Management Implementation Guide*. In Department of Defense (ACQ). Washington, DC. Accessed 2/3/09. Available online at http://www.acq.osd.mil/pm/currentpolicy/currentpolicy.html.

Department of Defense. 2006b. *Risk Management Guide for DoD Acquisition*, 6th ed. In Department of Defense (ACQ). Washington, DC. Accessed 2/16/09. Available online at http://www.dau.mil/pubs/gdbks/risk_management.asp.

Department of Defense. 2008a. *Defense Federal Acquisition Regulation Supplement* subpart 234.2. In Department of Defense. Washington, DC. Available online at http://www.acq.osd.mil/dpap/dars/dfars/pdf/r20090115/234_2.pdf.

Department of Defense. 2008b. Department of Defense Instruction Number 5000.02. In Department of Defense. Washington, DC. Accessed 2/6/2009. Available online at http://www.dtic.mil/whs/directives/corres/pdf/500002p.pdf.

Department of Defense. 2008c. *Material Management and Accounting System*. In Department of Defense. Washington, DC. Accessed 2/2/09. Available online at http://www.acq.osd.mil/dpap/dars/dfars/html/current/252242.htm#252.242-7004.

Department of Energy. 1997. Directive DOE G 430.1-1. In U.S. Department of Energy. Washington, DC. Accessed 2/10/09. Available online at http://www.directives.doe.gov/pdfs/doe/doetext/neword/430/g4301-1toc.html.

Department of Energy. December 2004. "Indirect Cost Rate Administration." *Acquisition Guide*, chapter 42.1. In U.S. Department of Energy. Washington, DC. Accessed 2/11/09. Available online at http://www.management.energy.gov/documents/AcqGuide42pt1.pdf.

Department of Energy. 2006. "Program and Project Management for the Acquisition of Capital Assets." Order 413.3A. U.S. Department of Energy. Washington, DC. Accessed 2/16/09. Available online at http://www.directives.doe.gov/pdfs/doe/doetext/neword/413/o4133ac1.html.

Department of Energy. 2008a. *Information Technology Project Guide*. G 413.3-14. U.S. Department of Energy. Washington, DC. Accessed 2/16/09. Available online at http://www.directives.doe.gov/pdfs/doe/doetext/neword/413/g4133-14.pdf.

Department of Energy. 2008b. *Risk Management Guide*. DOE G 413.3-7. U.S. Department of Energy. Washington, DC. Accessed 2/15/08. Available online at http://www.directives.doe.gov/pdfs/doe/doetext/neword/413/g4133-7.pdf.

Department of the Navy. 1997. MIL-DTL-81927C (AS). In Department of Defense. Washington, DC. Accessed 2/4/04. Available online at http://assist.daps.dla.mil/quicksearch/basic_profile.cfm?ident_number=32849.

Department of the Navy. 2001. MIL-HDBK-3001 (AS). In Department of Defense. Washington, DC. Accessed 2/4/09. Available online at http://www.everyspec.com/MIL-HDBK/MIL-HDBK+(3000+-+8999)/MIL-HDBK-3001_(AS)-_Guide_to_the_General_Style_and_Format_of_U--S--_Navy_Work_Package_Technical_Manuals_2773.

Electronic Industries Alliance. 2002. *Earned Value Management Systems*. Arlington, VA: Electronic Industries Alliance.

Federal Aviation Administration. 2003. *Documentation Guidance for FAA Cost Estimates*. In U.S. Federal Aviation Administration. Washington, DC. Accessed 2/10/2009. Available online at http://fast.faa.gov/investment/cboe.htm.

Flamholtz, E.G. 1979. "Toward a Psycho-Technical Paradigm of Organizational Measurement." *Decision Sciences* 10, no. 1: 71–84.

Flannes, Steven W., and Ginger Levin. 2001. *People Skills for Project Managers*. Vienna, VA: Management Concepts.

Fleming, Quentin W., and Joel M. Koppelman. 1996. *Earned Value Project Management*. 1st ed. Newtown Square, PA: Project Management Institute.

Fleming, Quentin W., and Joel M. Koppelman. 2000. *Earned Value Project Management*. 2nd ed. Newtown Square, PA: Project Management Institute.

GEIA Standards & Technology Department. 2007. *GEIA Standard for the Earned Value Management Systems*. Arlington, VA: Government Electronics and Information Technology Association.

Glickman, Rosalene. 2002. *Optimal Thinking*. New York: John Wiley & Sons.

Goldratt, Eliyahu M. 1997. *Critical Chain*. Great Barrington, MA: North River Press.

Goldratt, Eliyahu M., and Jeff Cox. 1992. *The Goal: A Process of Ongoing Improvement*. 2nd rev. ed. Great Barrington, MA: North River Press.

Government Printing Office. 2008. *Federal Register.* In National Archives and Records Administration. Washington, DC. Available at http://www.gpoaccess.gov/fr/retrieve.html.

Gupta, Sanjeev. May/June 2008. "Earned Value Management Clogs Profits." *Industrial Management* 50, No. 3: 12–16.

Henderson, Kym. 2004. "Further Developments in Earned Schedule." *The Measurance News* (Spring): 15–23.

Hillson, D. 2009. *Risk Doctor.* In Risk Doctor and Partners. Hampshire, UK. Accessed 2/15/09. Available online at http://www.risk-doctor.com/publications-papers_general.asp.

Holt, Steven. 2007. "TOC Case Study: The Application of Critical Chain Project Management to the Design of Large Commercial Aircraft at Boeing Commercial Airplanes." Presentation at TOCICO 2007 Conference in Las Vegas, NV. DVD available online at http://www.tocico.org\i4a\pages\index.cfm?pageid=3660.

Hughes, Thomas P. 1998. *Rescuing Prometheus.* New York: Pantheon.

Humphreys, Gary C. 2002. *Project Management Using Earned Value.* Orange, CA: Humphreys & Associates.

Institute of Electrical and Electronic Engineers, Inc., and Electronic Industries Alliance. 1996. IEEE/EIA 12207.0-1996. New York: Institute of Electrical and Electronic Engineers, Inc.

International Organization for Standardization. 2008. "Quality Management Systems." In *The International Organization for Standardization.* Geneva, Switzerland. Accessed 2/3/09. Available online at http://www.iso.ch/iso/iso_catalogue/catalogue_tc/catalogue_detail.htm?csnumber=46486.

Kaufmann, A., and G. Desbazeille. 1969. *Critical Path Method: Application of the PERT Method and Its Variants to Production and Study Programs.* New York: Gordon & Breach Science Publishers, Inc.

Kerzner, Harold. 2005. *Project Management: A Systems Approach to Planning, Scheduling, and Controlling.* 8th ed. New York: John Wiley & Sons.

Klingel, A.R. 1966. "Bias in PERT Completion Times: Calculations for a Real Network." *Management Science* 13, no.4: 476–489.

Leach, Lawrence P. 2005. *Critical Chain Project Management.* 2nd ed. Norwood, MA: Artech House, Inc.

Lencioni, Patrick M. 2002. *The Five Dysfunctions of a Team.* New York: John Wiley & Sons.

Lewis, James P. 2000. *The Project Manager's Desk Reference.* Boston: McGraw-Hill.

Lipke, Walt. 2003. "Schedule is Different." *The Measurable News* (March): 10–15.

Lipke, Walt. 2005. "Connecting Earned Value to the Schedule." *The Measurable News* (Winter): 6–16.

Lipke, Walt, and Kym Henderson. 2006. "Earned Schedule: An Emerging Enhancement to Earned Value Management." *CrossTalk* (November): 26–30. Available online at http://www.stsc.hill.af.mil/crosstalk/2006/11/0611LipkeHenderson.pdf.

Lipke, Walt, Ofer Zwikael, Kym Henderson, and Frank Anbari. 2009. "Prediction of Project Outcome: The Application of Statistical Methods to Earned Value Management and Earned Schedule Performance Indexes." *International Journal of Project Management* 27, no. 4: 400–407.

Locke, Edwin A., Gary P. Latham, Ken J. Smith, and Robert E. Wood. 1990. *A Theory of Goal Setting and Task Performance.* Upper Saddle River, NJ: Prentice Hall.

Management Technologies. 2004. "The Earned Value Management Maturity Model." In *Management Technologies.* Brea, CA. Accessed 9/21/04. Available online at http://www.mgmt-technologies.com/evmtech.html.

Meredith, Jack R., and Samuel J. Mantel, Jr. 2003. *Project Management: A Managerial Approach.* 5th ed. New York: John Wiley & Sons.

Millhiser, William P., and Joseph G. Szmerekovsky. October 2008. "Teaching Critical Chain Project Management: An Academic Debate, Open Research Questions, Numerical Examples and Counterarguments." Working paper. Accessed 1/12/09. Available online at http://blsciblogs.baruch.cuny.edu/millhiser/files/2008/10/teaching-ccpm-millhiser-and-szmerekovsky-2008.pdf.

National Aeronautics and Space Administration. 2002. *NPD 9501.3A. Earned Value Management*. In NASA Online Directives Information System Library. Washington, DC. Accessed 7/4/04. Available online at http://www.ksc.nasa.gov/procurement/kics/docs/ npd95013a.pdf.

National Aeronautics and Space Administration. 2008a. *Cost Estimating Handbook*. Washington, DC. Accessed 2/10/09. Available online at http://www.nasa.gov/pdf/263676main_2008-NASA-Cost-Handbook-FINAL_v6.pdf.

National Aeronautics and Space Administration. 2008b. NPR 7120.7. NASA Online Directives Information System (NODIS) Library. Washington, DC. Accessed 12/16/08. Available online at http://nodis3 .gsfc.nasa.gov/main_lib.html.

National Aeronautics and Space Administration. 2009. *NASA Schedule Management Handbook*. Washington, DC. Accessed 07/03/09. Available online at http://evm.nasa.gov/docs/Handbooks/NASA%20 SMH%20DRAFT_%20rev%202016a_Apr03.

National Defense Industrial Association. 2006. *Earned Value Management Systems Intent Guide*. Arlington, VA. Available online at http://management.energy.gov/documents/NDIA_PMSC_EVMS_ IntentGuide_Nov_2006.pdf.

Neave, Henry. 1990. *The Deming Dimension*. Knoxville: SPC Press.

Newbold, Robert C. 2008. *The Billion Dollar Solution: Secrets of ProChain Project Management*. Lake Ridge, VA: ProChain Press.

Office of Management and Budget. 2008. Circular A–11, Part 7. In the White House. Washington, DC. Available online at http://www .whitehouse.gov/omb/circulars/a11/current_year/s300.pdf.

Palisade. 2009. @Risk for Project. 2009. Ithaca, NY: Palisade Corporation. Accessed 2/9/09. Available online at http://www.palisade.com/ riskproject/default.asp.

Peterson, Rein. 1965. "Critical Path Scheduling." *Business Quarterly* 30, no. 2: 70.

Parkinson, C.N. 1957. *Parkinson's Law*. Boston: Houghton Mifflin.

Pritsker, A.A.B., and W.W. Happ. 1966. "GERT: Graphical Evaluation and Review Technique. Part 1: Fundamentals." *Journal of Industrial Engineering* 17, no. 5: 267–274.

Project Management Institute. 2008a. *A Guide to the Project Management Body of Knowledge (PMBOK® Guide)*. 4th ed. Newtown Square, PA: Project Management Institute.

Project Management Institute. 2008b. *Organizational Project Management Maturity Model (OPM3^R)*. 2nd ed. Newtown Square, PA: Project Management Institute.

Rouse, Margaret. 2004. *Gantt Chart*. In TechTarget. Needham, MA. Accessed 2/5/09. Available online at http://whatis.techtarget.com/definition/0,,sid9_gci331397,00.html.

Sarbanes, Paul S., and Michael G. Oxley. 2002. *Sarbanes-Oxley Act of 2002, H.R. 3763*. Washington, DC.

Schulte, Ruthanne. 2004. "Use Earned Value to Comply with Sarbanes-Oxley." White paper. Projects@Work. Accessed 2/3/09. Available at http://www.projectsatwork.com/article.cfm?ID=217708.

Schulte, Ruthanne. June 22, 2006. "Is Poor Project Management a Crime?" Presentation at 50th annual meeting of the Association for the Advancement of Cost Engineering (AACEI). Las Vegas, NV.

SETI@home. 2005. "Ksetiwatch." In *The Planetary Society*. Berkeley, CA. Accessed 2/6/09. Available online at http://ksetiwatch.sourceforge.net/index.php3.

Software Engineering Institute. November 2007. *CMMI®-ACQ* (Capability Maturity Model Integration for Acquisition). In Carnegie Mellon University. Cited 2/1/09. Available online at http://www.sei.cmu.edu/pub/documents/07.reports/07tr017.pdf.

Software Engineering Institute. 2009. *Risk Management Overview*. In Carnegie Mellon University. Pittsburgh. Accessed 2/1/09. Available online at http://www.sei.cmu.edu/risk/overview.html.

Solomon, Paul J. and Ralph R. Young. 2007. *Performance-Based Earned Value*. Hoboken, NJ. John Wiley & Sons, Inc.

Standish Group International. 1995. *Chaos: Charting the Seas of Information Technology*. West Yarmouth, MA: Standish Group International.

Standish Group International. 2004. *CHAOS Chronicles*. West Yarmouth, MA: Standish Group International.

Steinberg, Richard M., Miles E.A. Everson, Frank J. Martens, and Lucy E. Nottingham. 2004. *Enterprise Risk Management—Integrated Framework.* Jersey City: American Institute of Certified Public Accountants.

Stevenson, James P. 1993. *The Pentagon Paradox: The Development of the F-18 Hornet.* Annapolis: Naval Institute Press.

Stratton, Ray W. 2006. *The Earned Value Management Maturity Model®.* Vienna, VA: Management Concepts.

U.S. Securities and Exchange Commission. 2003. *Management's Reports on Internal Control over Financial Reporting and Certification of Disclosure in Exchange Act Periodic Reports.* In U.S. Securities and Exchange Commission. Washington, DC. Accessed 7/03. Available online at http://www.sec.gov/rules/final/33-8238.htm.

U.S. Securities and Exchange Commission. 2008. *Internal Control over Financial Reporting in Exchange Act Periodic Reports of Non-Accelerated Filers.* In U.S. Securities and Exchange Commission. Washington, DC. Accessed 2/1/09. Available online at http://www.sec.gov/rules/final/2008/33-8934.pdf.

Vanhoucke, M., and S. Vandevoorde. 2007. "A Simulation and Evaluation of Earned Value Metrics to Forecast the Project Duration." *Journal of the Operational Research Society* 58: 1361–1374.

Westney, R.E. 2001. "Risk Management: Maximizing the Probability of Success." In *Project Management for Business Professionals*, ed. Joan Knutson. New York: John Wiley & Sons.

Wideman, R.M. 2004. *The Role of the Project Life Cycle (Life Span) in Project Management.* In R. Max Wideman. Vancouver, BC. Accessed 2/15/09. Available online at http://www.maxwideman.com/papers/plc-models/intro.htm.

Index

A

AA. *See* advance agreement
AC. *See* actual cost
accounting and finance team, 257
accounting software, 180
ACO. *See* administrative contracting
  officer
activity-based costing method, 174–
  176
activity on arrow, 128
activity on node, 128
actual cost (AC), 188
actual cost of work performed
  (ACWP), 39
actual time, 307
actual value, 39
ACWP. *See* actual cost of work
  performed
administrative contracting officer
  (ACO), 278
advance agreement (AA), 278

agency definitions, 277–278
American Institute of Certified Public
  Accountants, 13
American National Standards Institute
  Guidelines for EVMS (ANSI/EIA-
  748-1998), 6, 54
archiving project documents, 246–247
Association of Project Management,
  15
AT&L. *See* Under Secretary of Defense
  for Acquisition, Technology and
  Logistics

B

BAC. *See* budget at completion
bar charts, 125–126
basic project characteristic, 4
BCWR. *See* budgeted cost for work
  remaining
BCWS. *See* budgeted cost of work
  scheduled

benefits, of using EVMS, 60–61
brainstorming, risk identification
    technique, 218–219
budget
    basic project characteristic, 4
    basis of cost estimate, 152–153
    control account plan, 144
    cost data, 152
    cost estimation package, 153
    EVMS Criterion 9, 140–142
    EVMS Criterion 10, 142–144
    EVMS Criterion 11, 145
    EVMS Criterion 12, 145–146
    EVMS Criterion 13, 147–148
    EVMS Criterion 14, 148–150
    EVMS Criterion 15, 150–151
    importance of, 139–140
    level of effort, 146–147
    organizational breakdown structure,
        144
    planning package, 144
    price cost estimation, 151
    project controls, 152
    special packages, 144–145
    work package, 144
budget at completion (BAC), 38, 197
budgeted cost for work remaining
    (BCWR), 314
budgeted cost of work scheduled
    (BCWS), 38
buffer management, 339–341

C

C/SCSC. *See* Cost/Schedule Control
    System Criteria
CA. *See* control account
CAO. *See* contract administration
    office
CAP. *See* control account plan
Capability Maturity Model Integration
    for Acquisition Software (CMMI-
    ACQ), 28

cause-effect diagram, 45–46
CCPM. *See* critical chain project
    management
Certified Public Accountant (CPA), 13
CFSR. *See* contract funds status report
challenges, of using EVMS
    dysfunctional behavior, 68
    measuring progress, 67
    missing information, 65–67
change
    authorized, 228
    control board, 228–230
    directed effort, 231
    documenting, 230–231
    evaluating risk, 220–221
    EVMS Criterion 28, 227–228
    EVMS Criterion 29, 232
    EVMS Criterion 30, 232–233
    EVMS Criterion 31, 233
    EVMS Criterion 32, 233–234
    identifying risk, 218–220
    importance of, 213
    necessity of, 226–227
    risk, 215–216
    risk assessment, 217–218
    risk disposition, 222–223
    risk management, 216–217, 224
    risk management tools, 225–226
    risk monitoring, 223–224
    uncertainty, 213–214
change request form (CRF), 230–231
checklist, risk identification technique,
    219
closeout phase, 23
closing event, 245
CMMI-ACQ. *See* Capability Maturity
    Model Integration for Acquisition
    Software
CMO. *See* contract management office
Committee of Sponsoring
    Organizations of the Treadway
    Commission (COSO), 214

common cause variation, 45
constraints, 217
contract administration office (CAO), 278
contract funds status report (CFSR), 206–208
contract management office (CMO), 278
contract performance report (CPR), 109, 204–205, 271
contract types, 108
contract work breakdown structure (CWBS), 78–79
control account (CA), 56, 88–90, 133
control account plan (CAP), 105–107, 144
COSO. *See* Committee of Sponsoring Organizations of the Treadway Commission
cost account. *See* control account
Cost Accounting Standards Board Disclosure Statement, 162
cost performance index (CPI), 40, 45–47, 197
Cost Pool Drivers, 169–170
Cost Pools, 169
Cost/Schedule Control System Criteria (C/SCSC), 6, 59
cost variance (CV), 39–40, 189, 192–193
CPA. *See* Certified Public Accountant
CPI. *See* cost performance index
CPM. *See* critical path method
CPR. *See* contract performance report
crashing, 117
CRF. *See* change request form
critical chain method, 5
critical chain project management (CCPM)
  background, 323–324
  buffer management, 339–341
  critical chain scheduling, 333–339
  critical chain solution, 330–331
  development, 324–325
  importance of, 117–118
  multiproject environments, 341–342
  traditional scheduling, 331–333
  using critical chain with EVMS, 342–345
critical chain scheduling, 333–339
critical path, 63–65
critical path method (CPM), 5, 124, 130–131
critical ratio, 42
customer relations management (CRM), 10
CV. *See* cost variance
CWBS. *See* contract work breakdown structure

D

DAG. *See* Defense Acquisition Guidebook
DAU. *See* Defense Acquisition University
DAU EVM Gold Card, 269–270
DCMA. *See* Defense Contract Management Agency
DCMA 14-Point Assessment Metrics, 282–283
DCMC. *See* Defense Contract Management Command
decision metrics, 48–49
Defense Acquisition Guidebook (DAG), 268, 271–272
Defense Acquisition University (DAU), 268
Defense Contract Management Agency (DCMA), 272, 277–278
Defense Contract Management Command (DCMC), 277
Defense Federal Acquisition Regulation Supplements (DFARS), 269–271

deliverables, 5, 9, 17–18, 78, 243
Department of Defense (DoD), 19, 166, 205, 268–269
Department of Defense supplement to Federal Acquisition Regulation (DFARS), 57–58
Department of Energy (DOE), 164
DFARS. *See* Defense Federal Acquisition Regulation Supplements
direct allocation method, 171–172
direct costs, 194
directed effort, 231
DoD. *See* Department of Defense
DOE. *See* Department of Energy

E

EAC. *See* estimate at completion
earned schedule (ES)
    actual time, 307
    calculating, 306–307
    computation examples, 307–314
    concepts, 305–306
    definition, 307
    overview, 303–304
    performance factor, 315–316
    planned duration, 307
    rationale for development, 304–305
    reconciling variances, 316–318
    schedule performance index, 307
    schedule variance in time, 307
    time-based metrics, 314–315
    validation of usefulness, 319
earned value (EV), 39, 55, 188, 197
earned value management (EVM), 54–55
Earned Value Management Implementation Guide (EVMIG), 271–273
Earned Value Management Maturity Model (EVM³), 29

earned value management support office (EVMSO), 277
earned value management system (EVMS)
    concepts, 54–55
    evolution of, 53–54
    importance of, 6
    purpose, 3
    reasons to use, 57–59
earned value metrics
    calculating ratios, 40–44
    cost performance index, 40
    cost variance, 39–40
    critical ratio, 42
    earned schedule, 40
    earned value, 39
    estimate at completion, 40, 42–44
    estimate to complete, 40, 42–44
    importance of, 37
    planned value, 38
    schedule performance index, 40
    schedule variance, 40
    to-complete performance index, 42–44
    total value, 38
ED. *See* estimated duration
EDAC. *See* estimated duration at completion
EDI. *See* electronic data interchange
education and training, 257–260
efficiency variance, 192
electronic data interchange (EDI), 204
Electronic Industry Alliance (EIA), 18, 54
enterprise resource management (ERM), 180
equivalent unit costs, 177
ES. *See* earned schedule
estimate at completion (EAC), 40, 195, 314
estimate to complete (ETC), 40, 197

estimated duration at completion (EDAC), 315
estimated duration (ED), 315
estimates of future conditions, 203
estimating methods
  analogy method, 156
  bottom-up method, 154
  expert opinion method, 156
  importance of, 153–154
  parametric method, 155
  rolling wave method, 154–155
estimating task times, 114–115
ETC. *See* estimate to complete
EV. *See* earned value
EVM. *See* earned value management
EVM³. *See* Earned Value Management Maturity Model
EVM Implementation Policy, 275
EVM Implementation Roadmap, 274
EVMIG. *See* Earned Value Management Implementation Guide
EVMS. *See* Earned Value Management System; earned value management system
EVMS criteria
  accounting considerations, 69–70
  analysis and management reports, 70
  Criterion 1, 75
  Criterion 2, 99
  Criterion 3, 102–103
  Criterion 4, 107–108
  Criterion 5, 109–110
  Criterion 6, 121
  Criterion 7, 131–132
  Criterion 8, 132–133
  Criterion 9, 140–142
  Criterion 10, 142–144
  Criterion 11, 145
  Criterion 12, 145–146
  Criterion 13, 147–148
  Criterion 14, 148–150
  Criterion 15, 150–151
  Criterion 16, 163
  Criterion 17, 166
  Criterion 18, 166–167
  Criterion 19, 167–169
  Criterion 20, 176–177
  Criterion 21, 178–180
  Criterion 22, 188–191
  Criterion 23, 191
  Criterion 24, 194–195
  Criterion 25, 195–196
  Criterion 26, 196
  Criterion 27, 197
  Criterion 28, 227–228
  Criterion 29, 232
  Criterion 30, 232–233
  Criterion 31, 233
  Criterion 32, 233–234
  organization, 69
  overview, 68
  planning and budget, 69
  revisions and data maintenance, 70
EVMS Guidance Roadmap, 274
EVMS metrics triangle, 189
EVMSO. *See* earned value management support office
example project, 10–11
execution phase, 23

F
failure, 5
Federal Acquisition Regulation (FAR), 269
fixed costs, 176
full kit concept, 38
functional style, 96–97

G
GEIA. *See* Government Electronics and Information Technology Association

generally accepted accounting
   procedures (GAAP), 163
GERT. *See* graphical evaluation and
   review technique
government components, 277
government contracts
   agency definitions, 277–278
   Defense Acquisition Guidebook,
      271–272
   Defense Federal Acquisition
      Regulation Supplements, 269–271
   DoD Instruction 5000.02, 273
   DoD websites, 268–269
   Earned Value Management
      Implementation Guide, 272–273
   EVM Implementation Policy, 275
   EVMS Guidance Roadmap, 274
   Federal Acquisition Regulation, 269
   initial compliance review, 279
   integrated baseline review, 279–280
   overview, 267–268
   Regulatory Contract Reporting
      Requirements, 276
   surveillance, 280–284
Government Electronics and
   Information Technology
   Association (GEIA), 55–56
graphical evaluation and review
   technique (GERT), 130

I

IBR. *See* integrated baseline review
IEC. *See* International Engineering
   Consortium
IEEE. *See* Institute of Electrical and
   Electronics Engineers
IMP. *See* integrated master plan
implementation
   accounting and finance team, 257
   approaches to, 261–262

cost, 263–264
details, 255
education and training, 257–260
organizational support, 256
plan, 255
reasons, 254–255
resource managers, 256
software assistance, 262–263
IMS. *See* integrated master schedule
indirect costs, 107–108, 167–169
information technology (IT), 10
informational measurements, 48
initial compliance review, 279
initiation phase, 23
Innovation Empowerment Model, 260
Institute of Electrical and Electronics
   Engineers (IEEE), 18
integrated baseline review (IBR), 271,
   279–280
integrated master plan (IMP), 205
integrated master schedule (IMS),
   205–206, 271–272
integrated product and process
   development (IPPD), 205
integrated product teams (IPT), 205
internal control environment, 6
International Engineering
   Consortium (IEC), 18
International Organization for
   Standardization (ISO), 18
International Project Management
   Association, 15
IPPD. *See* integrated product and
   process development
IPT. *See* integrated product teams
ISO. *See* International Organization
   for Standardization
ISO 9001. *See* Quality Management
   Systems
IT. *See* information technology

L

lessons learned, 219, 244
letter of acceptance (LOA), 278
level of effort (LOE), 146–147
life span, 18
linear responsibility chart (LRC), 103–105
LOA. *See* letter of acceptance
LOE. *See* level of effort
LRC. *See* linear responsibility chart

M

matrix style, 97–98
measurements, 24, 49–50
metrics, 56–57
missing information, 65–67
motivational measurements, 48
multiplication rule, 119
multiproject environments, 341–342

N

National Defense Industrial Association (NDIA), 284
nonrecurring costs, 168

O

OBS. *See* organizational breakdown structure
Office of Management and Budget (OMB), 271
OPM3. *See* Organizational Project Management Maturity Model
organization
    configurations, 95–96
    control account plan, 105–107
    EVMS Criterion 2, 99
    EVMS Criterion 3, 102–103
    EVMS Criterion 4, 107–108
    EVMS Criterion 5, 109–110
    functional style, 96–97
    importance of, 95

linear responsibility chart, 103–105
    matrix style, 97–98
    organizational breakdown structure, 99–102
    project-oriented style, 98–99
    project staffing, 100–101
organizational breakdown structure (OBS), 99–102, 144
Organizational Project Management Maturity Model (OPM3), 28
over-target baseline, 135–136
overhead costs, 107–108

P

partial implementation
    following basic EVMS principles, 291–294
    high-level control accounts, 290–291
    informal EVM implementation, 289–290
    overview, 287–288
    project control, 288–289
    simplest application, 295
PDCA Cycle. *See* Plan, Do, Check, and Act Cycle
PDWR. *See* planned duration for work remaining
performance-based earned value, 299–300
performance factor, 315–316
performance measurement baseline (PMB), 133, 227, 271
performance reporting, 203–204
performance to date, 197–200
personal interview, risk identification technique, 219
PERT. *See* program evaluation and review technique
PIER. *See* post-implementation evaluation report

Plan, Do, Check, and Act (PDCA)
  Cycle, 20
planned duration, 307
planned duration for work remaining
  (PDWR), 314
planned value (PV), 38, 188
planning package (PP), 90, 144
planning phase, 23
PM. *See* program manager
PMB. *See* performance measurement
  baseline
PMO. *See* program management
  office; project management office
PMSC. *See* Program Management
  Systems Committee
post-implementation evaluation
  report (PIER), 242–243
PP. *See* planning package
price variance, 192
program evaluation and review
  technique (PERT), 128–130
program management office (PMO),
  278
Program Management Systems
  Committee (PMSC), 284
program manager (PM), 54
program work breakdown structure
  (PWBS), 78–79
project, definition, 14–15
project charter
  components, 16
  essential elements, 17
  purpose, 15–16
  statement of work, 18
project control, 7
project life cycle, 18–19
Project Management Institute, 13, 15
project management maturity, 8–9,
  27–29
Project Management Maturity Model,
  28

project management office (PMO),
  25–27, 96–97
project manager, 29–30
project maturity model, 8–9
project-oriented style, 98–99
project plan
  constructing WBS, 79–81
  contract work breakdown structure,
    78–79
  control accounts, 88–90
  defining the project, 81–83
  overview, 75–76
  program work breakdown structure,
    78–79
  WBS charts, 84–86
  WBS definitions and standards,
    77–78
  WBS dictionary, 87–88
  WBS levels, 86–87
  WBS mechanics, 83
  work breakdown structure, 76
  work packages, 90–93
project reporting, 61–63
project staffing, 100–101
project team, 30–32
project termination
  archiving project documents,
    246–247
  closing event, 245
  completion, 239
  deliverables, 243
  importance of, 238–239
  lessons learned, 244
  project review, 239–242
  releasing resources, 246
  reporting, 242–243
Public Company Accounting
  Oversight Board, 7
PV. *See* planned value
PWBS. *See* program work breakdown
  structure

Q

Quality Management Systems (ISO
    9001), 28–29
quantity variance, 192

R

ratios, calculating, 40–44
reciprocal allocation method, 173–174
recurring costs, 168
Regulatory Contract Reporting
    Requirements, 276
releasing resources, 246
replanning activity, 226–227
reporting variances
    contract funds status report, 206–
        208
    contract performance report,
        204–205
    cost variance, 192–193
    estimates of future conditions, 203
    EVMS Criterion 22, 188–191
    EVMS Criterion 23, 191
    EVMS Criterion 24, 194–195
    EVMS Criterion 25, 195–196
    EVMS Criterion 26, 196
    EVMS Criterion 27, 197
    explaining variances, 193
    importance of, 187–188
    integrated master schedule, 205–
        206
    interpreting variances, 200
    performance reporting, 203–204
    performance to date, 197–200
    schedule variance, 192
    technical performance, 200–202
    updated values for materials,
        202–203
resource managers, 256
risk
    assessment, 217–218
    changes, 215–216

disposition, 222–223
evaluating, 220–221
identifying, 218–220
internal controls, 4
management, 216–217, 224
management tools, 225–226
monitoring, 223–224
risk/benefit decision grid, 26–27

S

Sarbanes-Oxley Act of 2002 (SOX), 6–7,
    59, 254
schedule
    activity on arrow, 128
    activity on node, 128
    bar charts, 125–126
    basic project characteristic, 4
    challenges, 114
    controls and reporting, 135
    crashing, 117
    critical chain project management,
        117–118
    critical path method, 130–131
    dysfunctional behaviors, 115–116
    estimating task times, 114–115
    EVMS Criterion 6, 121
    EVMS Criterion 7, 131–132
    EVMS Criterion 8, 132–133
    graphical evaluation and review
        technique, 130
    importance of, 113
    lists, 125
    networks, 126–127
    over-target baseline, 135–136
    overcoming problems, 117
    program evaluation and review
        technique, 128–130
    sequence of work, 121–123
    statistics and probability, 118–121
    summary-level planning packages,
        134

target baseline, 133–134
task dependencies, 123–124
uncertainty, 114
unnecessary fixes, 118
schedule margin, 300–301
schedule performance index (SPI), 40,
   45–47, 197, 303, 307
schedule variance in time, 307
schedule variance (SV), 40, 189, 192,
   303
scope, 4
Security and Exchange Commission
   (SEC), 7
sequence of work, 121–123
slack, 131
SLPP. *See* summary-level planning
   package
software assistance, 262–263
SOW. *See* statement of work
SOX. *See* Sarbanes-Oxley Act of 2002
special cause variation, 45
SPI. *See* schedule performance index
spiral development model, 21–22
standard cost system *versus* EVMS,
   304
standard surveillance plan (SSP), 280
statement of work (SOW), 18, 91–93
statistics and probability, 118–121
step-down allocation method, 172–
   173
subjective project reporting, 61–63
summary-level planning package
   (SLPP), 90, 134
surveillance, 280–284
surveys, risk identification technique,
   219
SV. *See* schedule variance

T

target baseline, 133–134
task dependencies, 123–124

TCPI. *See* to-complete performance
   index
TCSPI. *See* to-complete schedule
   performance index
technical performance, 200–202
time-based metrics, 314–315
to-complete performance index
   (TCPI), 42–44, 314
to-complete schedule performance
   index (TCSPI), 314
total budget, 38
total cost, 38
total value (TV), 38, 197
tracking performance
   accounting, 162–163
   accounting software, 180
   activity-based costing method,
      174–176
   cost allocation methods, 170–171
   Cost Pool Drivers, 169–170
   Cost Pools, 169
   direct allocation method, 171–172
   direct costs, 163–165
   EVMS Criterion 16, 163
   EVMS Criterion 17, 166
   EVMS Criterion 18, 166–167
   EVMS Criterion 19, 167–169
   EVMS Criterion 20, 176–177
   EVMS Criterion 21, 178–180
   importance of, 161–162
   reciprocal allocation method,
      173–174
   special circumstances, 165–166
   step-down allocation method,
      172–173
TV. *See* total value

U

uncertainty, schedule, 114
Under Secretary of Defense for
   Acquisition, Technology and
   Logistics (AT&L), 268

unit costs, 176
updated values for materials, 202–203

V

VAC. *See* variance at completion
variable costs, 176
variance. *See* reporting variances
variance at completion (VAC), 314

W

waterfall model, 20–21
websites, DoD, 268–269
work breakdown structure (WBS)
 charts, 84–86
 constructing, 79–81
 contract, 78–79
 control accounts, 88–90
 defining the project, 81–83
 definitions and standards, 77–78
 dictionary, 87–88
 element examination, risk
  identification technique, 219
 importance of, 76
 levels, 86–87
 mechanics, 83
 program, 78–79
work package (WP), 23, 90–93, 144
work unity, 23